THE GOOD
SAMARITANS
MEMOIR OF A BIOGRAPHER

ANTHONY J. JORDAN

Anthony J. Jordan

Acknowledgements

I would like to thank Pat O'Keeffe, Edward Moran, Brendan Hester, Michael McEvilly, staff of the Gilbert Library, Bill Cotter, Phil Bates, Patricia Hastings-Hardy, David Rowe, Aidan Sweeney, Patrick Lynch, Donnchadha O'Corráin, Theresa Downes, Gerry Carroll, Maggie Hayden, Aidan Sweeney, Ciaran Benson, Tony Greene, Michael Mullin, Jarlath Duffy, Francis Carroll. David Lowe, Seán Donnelly, David Bolger, and Paul Kiely, of the Central Remedial Clinic for assistance rendered.

Also to thank Brendan Keane of Sandymount
for reading the manuscript.

Copyright Anthony J. Jordan 2008

ISBN 9780952444756

EDITOR EN PART

JUDITH JORDAN

Graphic Design, Layout, and Print Reproduction, David Lowe,
in association with the Central Remedial Clinic DTP Training Unit,
Contarf, Dublin 3, Ireland. Telephone: (01) 805 7400.

Published by

Westport Books,

Dublin 4.

westportbooks@yahoo.co.uk

Dedication

For Mary, Antonia, Judith, Fiona and Murphy.
and
The Jordans of Aughamore, Ballyhaunis, Cummer,
Manchester, Tooreen, and Solihull.
and
The good Samaritans throughout the story.

CONTENTS

THE GOOD SAMARITANS

CHAPTER 1

THE SAMARITANS

ARCHBISHOP OPPOSES THE SAMARITANS

For those who call and those who listen

The Irish have a penchant for bitter divisions. Brendan Behan said that the first item on the agenda for any new Irish organisation was a split. Fr. John O'Donoghue explained it rather more elegantly, by saying that the absence of a discursive tradition in Ireland has had a paralysing effect on the articulation and unfolding of questions. When an issue surfaces, the two sides of the question often become quickly polarised and it's further discussion locked in the repetitive symmetry of tribal combat[1]. Voluntary Organisations are notorious for engaging in civil wars. In the early 1970s, to my great surprise and embarrassment, I found myself leading the recently founded Dublin Samaritans to the edge of such a precipice.

The Reverend Chad Varah founded the Samaritans in London in 1953 as an organization which would befriend the suicidal and despairing. His book *The Samaritans in the 70s* (London: Constable, 1973), gives its background and philosophy. Trained volunteers answer telephones twenty-four hours a day and people are welcome to call in in-person. It is run as a charity offering a non-professional, confidential and anonymous service to anyone in distress. Samaritans will listen as long as they are needed and the service is free. They offer little advice, believing that their callers will be helped to make their own decisions by talking to someone who cares. In Dublin, a Church of Ireland minister named Billy Wynne had begun an individual ministry to despairing and suicidal people during the 1960s. Inspired by contact with Chad Varah, he set about organizing the Samaritans in Dublin. This was not without its pitfalls as Wynne strove to placate the powerful Catholic Archbishop of Dublin, John Charles McQuaid. The latter was not used to any major initiative being taken within his archdiocese without his approval, if not his permission. Wynne acted to gain Catholic approval by liaising with a leading Catholic priest and Professor of Psychology at University College Dublin, Rev. EF O'Doherty. Wynne felt that the latter would keep Dr. McQuaid informed, and hopefully on side. Wynne and others decided to call a private meeting of interested parties for 2 July 1969 and circulated a printed notice on 25 June.

He sent a copy to McQuaid, with a covering letter. The text of this notice may have appeared discourteous to the Archbishop. It read in part:

"As is known I have been acting as Samaritan contact for about ten years, during which time a need for a branch has been realised; a number of people have offered to help; meetings for the interested have been held and in keeping with Samaritan policy of including the major denomination, approaches have been made, so far without any clear indication of a response officially. At this meeting we hope to have present Archbishop Simms and clerical representatives of the churches in addition to many laypersons. It is hoped to have representatives from the Belfast branch of Samaritans, which includes on the staff, some clergy of the Roman Catholic Church". His cover letter to Dr. McQuaid, Rev. Wynne was most conciliatory, hoping that McQuaid might send a representative or an observer to the meeting. He added that, *"unfortunately Professor O'Doherty was unable to attend the meeting and expressed the view that, "in all likelihood he has told your Grace about the meeting".*

Unfortunately, McQuaid did not receive Wynne's letter until after the meeting. In his subsequent reply he told Wynne that O'Doherty had not informed him about the Samaritans. Wynne was taken aback to hear this and replied saying that he had met O'Doherty *"on several occasions, discussing the matters and he has been most helpful".* Wynne added, *"that as there were likely to be further meetings, it would be proper and courteous that your Grace be informed fully on the matter. To that end I would be willing to call upon Your Grace, bringing with me a responsible person well qualified to speak about the subject"*[2]. Professor O'Doherty, holidaying on the Azores at the time, was contacted by Archbishop's House and replied post haste to Archbishop McQuaid on 22 July. He confirmed that he had met Wynne, *"about two years ago, as far as I can recall, discussing the Samaritans".* O'Doherty gave a very accurate account of the Samaritans' work to his Archbishop, but clearly reading the mind of his superior, distanced himself from the need for such an idea for Dublin. He added, *"as priests were on call on permanent duty in all city churches, such a service did not seem to me to be as necessary in Dublin as perhaps it is in other cities. Please may I offer my apologies for not having informed Your Grace of above matters".*

VINCENT GROGAN SC

The Rev. Wynne had organized a meeting for 18th September to formally launch the Samaritans in Dublin. He hoped to have Mr. Vincent Grogan, a leading Catholic layman and member of the Order of Knights of St. Columbanus, act as Chairman. The order of the Knights of St. Columbanus was an organization of Catholic laymen, founded in 1915 as a response to the papal encyclical *Rerum Novarum*. In the ordinary course of events it would be a very wise move for the Rev. Wynne to have a former Chief Knight on board.

Vincent Grogan, though, had long since ceased to be in Archbishop McQuaid's good books. In one incident as far back as 1967, Grogan had agreed on a panel of the *Late Late Show,* that the Archbishop's ban on Catholic students attending Trinity College was outmoded and indefensible. Associating Grogan with the new organization was adding salt to the ecumenical wounds being experienced by Dr. McQuaid. One could presume that Rev. Billy Wynne was well aware of that fractious relationship. One of the most disagreeable experiences of Dr. McQuaid's later archbishopric was the Second Vatican Council, 1965-8. It was convened by Pope John XXIII to modernize church teaching, discipline and organization. Its decrees were most disagreeable to conservatives like Dr. McQuaid and he announced that there would be no major changes. One of the most contentious issues at that time was artificial contraception. Pope Paul VI had set up a Commission to advise him on the issue. The Pope subsequently pronounced against artificial contraception in an encyclical, *Humanae Vitae.* This delighted and relieved conservative Catholics. In Ireland a conference to consider the encyclical was held at Bargy Castle, Co. Wexford, and was attended by theologians, doctors, academics and journalists.

The ensuing report found apparent inadequacies and inconsistencies in *Humanae Vitae* between the recommendation on the use of the 'safe period' and condemnation of artificial contraception. It said that, "contraceptive methods often fostered conjugal love and helped towards the attainment of maturity in married relationships"[2a.] The task of transmitting the report to the hierarchy fell to the former Supreme Knight of St. Columbanus, Vincent Grogan. The replies from the bishops varied. Dr. McQuaid wrote in a vitriolic manner to Vincent Grogan; *"I thank you for your manifesto. I feel sure you would prefer to go to your judgment with the knowledge that you had done all in your power, to secure full assent to the teaching of the Vicar of Christ"*[3].

Professor O'Doherty accepted an invitation to attend the Samaritans meeting on 18th September from the Rev. Wynne. O'Doherty wrote to Dr. McQuaid informing him of the meeting, adding, "I think he intends to ask your Grace to nominate a representative to attend". O'Doherty did not receive a reply. Rev. Wynne was very pleased to have a group of Belfast Samaritans in attendance, including the local Catholic Deputy Director, Fr. Kevin McMullan.

In a letter to Fr. McMullan, Rev. Wynne wrote *"Let's hope that this time, there will be an attendance and proposal coming from your church to investigate starting a 'Samaritan's branch in Dublin".* Rev. Wynne did not know that this letter was immediately copied to Dr. McQuaid. Fr. McMullan wrote to McQuaid, *"At the suggestion of my Bishop, I am seeking your approval before I agree to attend the meeting as requested".* Professor O'Doherty was in a quandary about his attendance, as he had received no reply from Dr. McQuaid. O'Doherty also had received an invitation for the Archbishop.

On the morning of the 18th September he phoned the Archbishop's House to seek, "His Grace's direction regarding his attendance at a public meeting of the Samaritans in Dublin". He was advised;

To please return Archbishop's letter of invitation.
To please deny that the Archbishop has blocked this work for five years, as reported in Belfast.
That Fr. McMullan will be attending this meeting
and That Dr. O'Doherty is not to attend this meeting and is to keep a certain distance from the movement at this time[4]

Fr. Kevin McMullan told me, in an interview in February 2008, that he thought that he had initially been invited by his bishop to become involved with the Belfast Samaritans. He noted that priests had little freedom of action in those days. He recalled that Dr. McQuaid, while giving him permission to attend said meeting, had reiterated that he was not to act as chair.

At the meeting in the Royal Hibernian Hotel on 18th September 1969, the Rev. Billy Wynne and Vincent Grogan founded the Dublin Branch of the Samaritans, the 110th branch to that date. The meeting elected a steering committee consisting of Rev. Wynne, Vincent Grogan SC, Rev. John Brennan SJ (Rector Milltown Park), Rev John Chapman (National Council on Alcoholism), Rev. James Hagan (Adelaide Road Presbyterian Church), Canon Maurice Handy (Marriage Guidance Council), Miss Patricia Hastings-Hardy, Miss Ann Connolly, Dr. James Quinn and Mr. Gerald Fitzgerald[4a]. Miss Patricia Hastings-Hardy, was secretary to Dr. Otto Simms, Church of Ireland, Archbishop of Dublin.

Dr. McQuaid had been out-manoevered by forces within and without his own church. Archbishop McQuaid remains a target for ongoing criticism. One of the best critiques of him comes from an unusual source, that of two Trinity College Professors. It says; *"He is a man of great energy, ability and (as far as personal contact was concerned) suavity and charm"*. The most prominent of his aims was to make the Catholic Church the unchallenged arbiter of all questions in which it could reasonably claim to have an interest. Protestants and infidels were entitled to their civil rights and to the direction of their private institutions, but they need not expect any share in the direction of public education, welfare, medicine or even famine relief. Ireland was to be in as full a sense as possible a Catholic country. This attitude was not enunciated with any arrogance, or even very explicitly, but it was implemented by continuous hints, directives and pressures, and more than one mixed committee for charitable work had to be dissolved and reconstituted on sectarian lines. McQuaid was able to carry out his policy all the more effectively because he was obviously a devout, and indeed a holy man, and was not primarily in pursuit of personal power"[4b.] Despite the posturing of John Charles McQuaid, the Dublin Samaritans began in a welter of publicity and goodwill. Initially volunteers were mainly from middle and upper class Catholic and Protestant backgrounds.

A debate on *The Late Late Show* and a public meeting at the RDS helped to publicise the new organisation. At a service in St. Patrick's Cathedral Dublin in 1995 to mark the 25th anniversary of the founding of the Dublin Samaritans, Canon Billy Wynne said, "People wanted to help but they'd lose interest when there wasn't enough for them to do. The turning point came when I was a guest on the *Late Late Show* in 1969, and from there the idea took off. I had great encouragement from the late Archbishop George Simms and then from others such as Fr. Jack Brennan S.J., and Vincent Grogan. With their help, we gained support for the establishment of a branch of the Samaritans in Ireland. This eventually happened in 1970". The inaugural public meeting on 4th March 1970 took place before 600 people, to a welter of publicity, in the library of the Royal Dublin Society and was addressed by Dr. Richard Fox, honorary consultant psychiatrist to the Samaritans in Britain, the Rev. William Wynne and Professor Ivor Browne.[5]. The first Center was opened on 1st March 1970 at 39 Kildare St. The building itself was scheduled for demolition and was given to the Samaritans rent-free in the interim. The one-room centre was open to the public and equipped with a single telephone line. By November of 1970 it had become a twenty-four hour service[6]. In 1971 the centre moved to an upstairs flat in 85 Harcourt St. The first director, Desmond Kilroy, a bank official, resigned prematurely as director of the Samaritans due to a bank strike during 1971[6a]. The first annual meeting was held at the Royal Dublin Society in April 1971. The Minister for Health, Erskine Childers, addressed the gathering; *"The pressures of modern living are severe, and are growing all the time. The simple fact that the Samaritans exist is valuable in itself. Their compassion and common sense and selflessness are the best brands of medicine, the most practical kind of therapy"*[7]. The first Annual Report was given in April 1972 by Rev. John F Brennan SJ. He stated that the Dublin branch had dealt with 1,048 cases covering sexual, financial, gambling and unemployment issues. Of the 1,048 cases 12% had attempted suicide at some stage of their lives, or had serious suicidal tendencies. Fr. Brennan reported that the branch had over 200 volunteers. The latter were split into groups; each group was led by a companion and held regular meetings. Fr. Brennan went on to say, *"A wonderful team-spirit has evolved. This development within the organisation owes much to Olive Cotter. She was appointed from amongst the volunteers to be our full-time Executive Director, and, true to the spirit of the Samaritans, she has given of herself far beyond the 'call of duty"*.

I was a teacher at the Central Remedial Clinic School in Dublin in 1972. One afternoon I was called to the Principal's office to take a personal telephone call. After the call, I told the Principal that a person living nearby urgently required my assistance and I asked to be excused. She agreed but commented, *"that sounded like the person should really be calling the Samaritans"*. Mrs Maureen Byrne was a colleague and a friend. As I was leaving her office I said quietly, *"in fact, in this instance, I am the Samaritans"*. I had joined the Samaritans during their first year of operations in Dublin.

We then operated a 'Flying Squad', described by Fr. Brennan as being "formed from volunteers with cars who are prepared to travel to where they are needed, when, for example, a client is unable to come to us, or is in some exceptional need. Volunteers are also ready to 'befriend' a particular client over a period of time, by accompanying him or her to various social functions". These calls were rare enough and were filtered through a Branch hierarchy before Volunteers were actually contacted to go on the road. It was a useful service and assisted many individuals for several years, before it was discontinued.

THE SAMARITAN ORGANISATION

When the Samaritan organisation had developed so rapidly in the United Kingdom, it became necessary to develop a constitution and become a charitable company limited by guarantee. Its Council of Management consists of one representative of each Branch, elected by the respective Branch Committees. Its most important task is to appoint a director[8]. The Council is serviced by an Executive Committee consisting of regional representatives who appoint 'visitors', to report on the work of the Branches. The Branch Director has the onerous task of managing the work of the Branch and making final decisions. Directors are appointed or reappointed each year, though this is not automatic. Chad Varah writes, "The Director of a Branch may appear to be a dictator, the needs of the clients dictate that decisions should be made swiftly and loyally executed without dithering"[9]. Each Branch has a Central Committee with a Chairman. The only publicly known persons within a Branch are the Chairman and Director. The first publicly known names of Dublin Samaritans were Directors Desmond Kilroy and Fr. Brennan and the Chairman Vincent Grogan. In January 2006 the Samaritans underwent a restructuring which streamlined authority. This created a Board of Trustees consisting of 10-15 members who are Directors of the Company. One Council of Representatives from the 202 Branches and 13 Regional Representatives advises the Board. The Board meets at least six times a year, the Council twice a year. An Audit and Risk Committee meet 4 times a year and report to the Board on its activities. The organisation has a chief executive officer. Each of the 202 Branches has its own constitution or governing document. The new position of 'Director Ireland' was created in 2007 with the aim of identifying and delivering particular requirements on the island of Ireland. A Christian name, followed by a number, e.g. Olive 7, generally only identifies the individual volunteers and their seniority within the organization.

EXECUTIVE DIRECTOR "RESIGNS"

The third Annual Report in April 1973, found the Dublin branch based at 66 South William St. It had six interview rooms and greatly improved facilities. The number of contacts had increased to 3,614, with 270 volunteers. The Committee announced, with regret, the resignations of Fr. Brennan and Vincent Grogan. Olive Cotter had become Executive Director. The latter position led to the major convulsion, which I referred to at the outset. Within a few months her role led to a split and I, rather unwittingly, forced the matter to its conclusion.

Olive Cotter was a strong personality who, I believed, managed the Branch firmly but fairly. As a salaried executive Director she was on site during office hours. This was new, particularly for the volunteers who did duty during office hours. My usual duty was on either a Friday or a Saturday afternoon, so I came in contact with Olive infrequently. Like many volunteers my interest was purely to be available to callers and not to get involved in the myriad of groups and sub-committees. This aspect of the Organisation undoubtedly was attractive to some Volunteers, who gave unstintingly of their time as Companions. I was unaware there was major unease with the way Olive was performing her duties and was surprised to find that only three months after above AGM, serious management differences had arisen. During duty on 17th July, I read a statement on the notice board. It was dated 13th July, and said:

"The Central Committee wishes to announce with great regret that Olive 7 is no longer Executive Director. As a result a new situation has been created which requires a modified organisation. Details of this will be worked out by the Chairman and Deputy Directors and will be discussed with the Companions as soon as possible. Olive's tremendous contribution to the Branch and her kindness and warmth to those who needed her help will mean that her presence here will be missed."

David 520, as Chairman signed it and assumed the role of the Acting Director. He appointed Deputy Directors to assist with specific aspects of the operation. David's number indicated that he was a relative newcomer as my number was Anthony 307. I had originally been surprised when an Executive Director was appointed. I was familiar with quite a few Voluntary organisations and knew how difficult they were to manage and was also fully aware that the relationship between paid and unpaid staff could be difficult. The latter is especially relevant where a purely voluntary body decides to employ someone in full-time paid position for the very first time. It can be a period of adjustment and can lead to great misunderstanding between the executive, professional staff, volunteers and the Board. The notice in the Centre gave little indication of what had taken place and, while praiseworthy of Olive's contribution to the work, did not indicate her view of the new situation. As I was not so directly involved on an organizational level, I found it difficult to discover the true story. I did find out that Olive was distraught by what had transpired. I did a few more duties during July and was on holidays for most of August, still none the wiser to the situation.

DISMISSAL OF EXECUTIVE DIRECTOR

My next duty was on Saturday 31st August. There was consternation in the Centre as that day's *Irish Times* carried an article by Paul Murray about the *'dismissal'* of Olive as Director, headlined, THE SAMARITANS. It read:

"The dismissal of the executive director of the Dublin branch of the Samaritans raises some questions – as does the sacking of any employee. The questions, however, are not on the reasons for dismissal, which seem to ensue from the personality frictions, which beset any organisation, but on the relationship between paid employees of benevolent organisations and the voluntary unpaid committees, which run them.

Disputes in organisations, particularly of the calibre of The Samaritans, which last year made first contact with over 3,800 people and received over 12,800 calls either at its centre or by phone, tend to shock. As James Hemmings, an educational psychologist, stated in New Society last year, "hatchet work in the halls of humanity shakes our faith in mankind at a fundamental level". Mrs Olive Cotter who was dismissed at the end of July according to the acting director of the branch, Mr. David Rowe, had been running the day-to-day affairs of the branch, but her work has been taken over by seven deputy directors of the branch (there were four before Mrs Cotter's dismissal). The spokesman for the Samaritan company in Britain says that paid posts of executive Directors are unusual – only one branch has such an office. All the others utilise the deputy directors, who are of course, unpaid volunteers, to run daily affairs.

However it might seem to an outsider that it would be more efficient for the various statutory and voluntary bodies which must liase with the Samaritans to deal with one person, but the other system works well in Britain, says the Slough based general-secretary of the organisation...

Some might say it is wrong to air the internal differences of the Samaritans. There is a naturally justified reluctance on all sides to discuss personnel changes in the organisation, but £2,500 to meet the cost of premises has been granted by the Eastern Health Board this year (the size of the grant being proof of the value being placed on the organisation) and the Board, at least, as well as social workers and volunteers, have an interest in the branch's efficiency.

Mr. Rowe, however, whose appointment as acting director will be considered by the Council of Management of the Samaritans Company on September 14th at York, says that the principles of the branch have not changed since Mrs Cotter's departure. There has merely been an alteration in the internal structure of the branch. Unpaid volunteers instead of an employee now have day-to-day control... Mrs Cotter's dynamism will be missed, but any members who have shown any disquiet about her removal can take heart from Mr Hemming's article on the ambiguities of altruism.

Mr. Hemmings said that the altruistic institutions are particularly explosive (such a word does not apply in this instance) because they have principles and are humane. Altruists are not made in heaven. The altruist is a mixture, not a pure type Indeed, the altruistic life can be just as rewarding in terms of self-satisfaction as the hedonistic life. A point which should encourage some more people to phone 775566 to ascertain whether they will be accepted as volunteers"

I was shocked and annoyed when I read the article. I felt that it was disloyal to Olive Cotter and to what we were all about. Given the kind of organisation it was and the disengaged member I was, it was not easy to discover what had really happened, behind the scenes. You had to be wary whom you spoke to about it all. It was clear there was obviously a powerful element that felt Olive had to go, and go quickly. It was unclear though whether there was any pro-Olive element, or an element even that was unhappy with her removal. The term 'dismissal' seemed abusive to me. The publication of the article also ensured there was no way back for Olive and whoever leaked the story was well aware of that. I had long suspected that it might have been a volunteer close to a senior figure in the *Irish Times,* but in my research I have been happily reassured that was not the case. I decided that I would await the next Branch meeting, scheduled for the 24th September, and would take the opportunity to ask whether other Volunteers wished to make their feelings known.

About one hundred Volunteers were present at the meeting. As it progressed, nobody mentioned the matter that was on everyone's mind. Eventually I put a question to the Chairman, seeking information on the reasons behind the sacking of Olive. He replied that the Central Committee had dealt with the matter in a constitutional way and it should be left at that. I persisted, saying that what I wanted was information about such a drastic step. I made the point that what concerned me was the possibility that the Samaritans had not acted in a Samaritan way to one of our own. The Chairman said that the only way the matter could be debated internally was by the calling of an Extraordinary General Meeting on the production of twenty-six signatures. He then put his ruling to the meeting; thirty-nine Volunteers supported him, twenty-two voted against. During my next duty on 7th October, I put up a notice calling for an EGM to discuss the dismissal of Olive Cotter and signed it myself. Two weeks later there were nineteen signatures on my notice, almost enough to force the EGM. One week later a volunteer phoned me to say that her signature had taken the notice to the required number. There was always a great sense of protectiveness internally, towards the organisation, which I felt was a good thing. It also meant though that it could be relatively easy for those at the centre to manipulate events to suit their own ends. I was not enjoying the position I had put myself in but I have always believed, however, that structure within an organisation is essential for the protection of the organisation and those within it, and should be used accordingly. I knew that a daughter of Olive's was a volunteer, and that I knew her slightly, but had no contact with her.

In early November I received a phone call from the husband of Olive Cotter, who, to my surprise, was also a Samaritan volunteer. He offered to brief me on the events which had taken place during that previous summer. It appeared to have been a tempestuous and difficult time for all involved. The officer board appeared to hope that the matter had become a fait accompli until, as Bill Cotter wrote in his chronology, *"the next event was the Branch meeting at which you called for an E.G.M., to my surprise. I didn't know who you were and couldn't identify you at the time, to thank you for your spirited words that evening"*[10].

It appeared that earlier that year a sub-committee, to which Olive was appointed but was asked by the convenor not to attend, was set up to consider the advisability of continuing with an executive director. A series of meetings was held, followed by a meeting of the Central Committee. Olive was also asked not to attend this latter meeting. Subsequent to this, the Chairman accompanied by another member, visited Olive and asked for her resignation, ostensibly for family reasons. Olive was told that her inability to coordinate with others was the main problem. She refused to resign and was then prohibited from returning to the Centre, even to collect her personal belongings.

The next day Bill Cotter phoned the Chairman to reiterate Olive's refusal to resign. He informed him that Olive intended to request a visit from Samaritan Headquarters in Slough. Bill also informed him that Olive felt that no disturbance should be caused to the Volunteers at the moment. That very same day, 13th July, the notice that Olive was no longer Executive Director appeared on the notice board in the Centre. Olive wrote to the head office but nothing came of it. It appeared likely that the chairman travelled to England to appraise and satisfy the head office that the Dublin Branch was acting correctly. He told Olive that her request to resume duty as a Volunteer would be considered at some later time.

The notice had caused concern among some Volunteers. Some Companion groups considered calling for a general meeting to discuss the matter. The chairman was made aware of this and wrote to one Companion on 13 August as Acting Director, saying:

"Your group I think are contemplating putting up a notice calling for a General Meeting. Before they actually do so, I would be very grateful for an opportunity of meeting them together with perhaps one or two of the Deputy Directors".

Bill Cotter then said that a meeting of Companions was held where some disquiet among Volunteers was reported. The meeting was told that Olive had to go as 'she ruled with her heart instead of her head'. The Companions were asked to dissuade any tendency among Volunteers to call for an EGM, as that would cause further disruption.

Olive had sent the following letter to that Companion meeting:

"18 August 1973

I know that some Volunteers contemplated calling for an Extraordinary General Meeting arising from recent happenings at Committee level in the Dublin Branch of the Samaritans, but there are difficulties concerning this and I would like to put these constructive considerations before them. While mistakes can be made, the existing committee consists of very hardworking volunteers for the most part, putting a great deal of their time into it, and they would not easily be replaced.

1. *Many of the most suitable volunteers in the Branch are unable or unwilling to serve on committees, as they desire , for various reasons, to serve only as volunteers directly helping clients.*

2. *The uneasiness that exists now could lead to serious disruption in the work of the Branch if too much attention were given to my dismissal.*

I would ask, therefore, that we all be constructive about this and that we give the new Director a chance to improve the efficiency of the Dublin Branch in its primary function of caring for people in need.

While I have felt very upset, I am indeed grateful for all the expressions of goodwill given to me by so many volunteers and would like to thank them and hope to be working alongside them in the near future".[11]

Three days later two Companion groups met. The meeting heard that among the reasons for Olive's dismissal was her tendency to establish a little kingdom of her own in the Centre. The meeting was told that the authorities in England were in full agreement with the decision. It was at this point that the *Irish Times* was given the story and decided to publish. That paper sought an interview with Olive, who informed the Samaritan Committee secretary of her decision to refuse that request. According to Bill Cotter some volunteers resigned at this time. Owing to the nature of the organisation where only first names were known and most volunteers only knew a small number of the total membership, it is always difficult to keep track of comings and goings. That article would have been the first time many volunteers would have realised that a major upheaval had occurred within the organisation. Bill described the *Irish Times* article as, 'The Dublin Samaritans first unfavourable press'.

At a meeting of Companions and the Committee, a proposal was made that a joint statement by the Committee and Olive would be helpful to restore confidence. This idea was not accepted. In early September Bill Cotter exchanged distressing letters with the Centre on the matter, defending himself and his wife. I had continued to do duty during all this period. I do not know whether I would have been deterred from my action had I been privy to any of the above. I felt that it was important I adhere to an independent stance on the matter. My position was to seek to have information made available to the volunteers as a body.

On one occasion while on duty in the Centre, I encountered a few of the Deputy Directors and found, to my pleasant surprise, that they were very friendly towards me. On 12th November I wrote formally to the secretary of the Central Committee seeking an EGM to consider holding an inquiry into the dismissal of the Director. I indicated that I had received the required mandate from the volunteers. The meeting was scheduled for Friday 14th December. There were about one hundred and fifty volunteers in attendance. It was a tense affair. David Rowe outlined the course of action the Committee felt obliged to take. He did not elaborate on their reasons. I indicated that, as a volunteer, I was concerned that, whatever had actually happened, I was fearful a major injustice may have been done to our Executive Director. I said that if we could not treat our own people in a fair and just and understanding way, what right had we to set ourselves up in society as carers, as Samaritans? I called for an internal inquiry into the matter. There were many speakers. It was an emotional night for many, particularly those who spoke with some hostility towards Olive and her style of management. Eventually the matter was put to a vote. The call for an inquiry was defeated by forty-six votes to thirty-nine. Many volunteers abstained.

Over the next few days I was surprised to get phone calls from some senior volunteers, whom I knew had voted against an inquiry, congratulating me on my stand and on my restraint at the meeting. In particular I would mention Joan Carr, who was later to become a Director. I continued to maintain a non-aligned stance and accepted the democratic verdict. It was an unfortunate experience for all concerned. I accept entirely that David Rowe acted throughout with the utmost propriety, as did Olive Cotter. In retrospect, I believed that it might have been a mistake to appoint an executive Director to the Dublin Samaritans. Such an appointment closed the possibility for those volunteers who aspired to filling the position of Director as it became available on a rotational basis. It has been demonstrated over time that such a system, with a new Director and Deputy-Directors, taking office every three years, works moderately well. The Samaritans have to be grateful to David Rowe for initiating this procedure. As the *Irish Times* article said, though, there are arguments for an executive appointment. A three-year term is quite short for someone who wished to make any kind of major changes. There is also an argument that 'temporary' Branch Directors, scattered around the UK and Ireland, are easily 'handled' by full time executive staff in head office. The appointment probably also had the immediate effect of lessening the roles of some volunteers who had been used to exercising greater influence. Many voluntary organizations now find it essential to be represented by a permanent, recognizable figure.

Agreeing to waive her right to sit on the sub-committee and to attend the subsequent crucial Central Committee meeting were mistakes by the Executive Director.

CHAD VARAH

The Reverend Chad Varah

Such manoeuvrings were not unknown to the central Samaritan organisation and its founder Chad Varah. In his autobiography *"Before I Die"* (Constable, London) Chad Varah recounts several instances of 'political intrigue' within the Samaritans. In 1967 he writes of being, "persuaded to resign as chairman of the Samaritans Inc., although I had been re-elected by twenty votes to four.... If I had known that I was not only going to be replaced as Chairman but also be excluded from the Executive committee, I probably would have heeded the advice of a wise City gent who had been distressed by the way in which the founder of the Abbey Field Society, had been ousted by that Society"[12]. Some years later, in 1974, Chad Varah managed to get permission to put proposals to the Council of Management of the Samaritans concerning 'Befrienders International'. He began his address, *"Chairman, fellow Samaritans, today is the twenty first anniversary of the founding of our movement." "Oh is it today?"*, asked the Chairman in a tone of astonishment. It was my own, our, twenty first birthday; the Chairman neither knew … and nobody had briefed him"[13]. In recent times Chad Varah went so far as to say of the organisation, *"It's no longer what I founded. I founded an organisation to offer help to suicidal or equally desperate people. The last elected chairman re-branded the organisation. It was no longer to be an emergency service, it was to be emotional support"*[14]. Chad Varah died in November 2007 aged ninety-seven. The Rev. Billy Wynne was wise enough to realise that he was essentially an individualist who would always want to pursue his own path, unencumbered by any organisation, and he did not resist being squeezed out of any formal role in the Dublin Samaritans. While he was the inspiration and motivator behind the Dublin Samaritans, he did not take any formal role in the running of the organisation, but remained available for advice. Thus the Dublin Samaritans has continued successfully to provide a listening service to the public.

When I interviewed David Rowe about these matters in June 2007, his memory was initially hazy. As I prompted him on the events his recall improved. He felt that despite the trauma of the occasion for everyone involved, the correct move was made by the organisation at the time. He was clear that the grounds for the Companions and himself coming to the conclusion that they did were justified. He then had instituted the creation of enough Deputy Directors to take responsibility for running the organisation for one day a week. He would not have been able to devote the necessary time to his new position otherwise. He echoed my own view that it was all so long ago that it's recounting now should not damage the Dublin Samaritans. He made the interesting observation that while many volunteers leave the organisation on an ongoing basis, they bring with them a wealth experience of listening to people in distress, which remains of value to society.

He noted that An Garda Síochána was none too happy that the organisation treated their callers with total confidentiality and would never divulge any information. He was delighted to hear of the story with which I end this chapter below.

In 1998, a Volunteer named Gerry, told me of her recent experience at a church gate collection for the Samaritans in south county Dublin. An elderly lady, whom she did not know, took a five- pound note out of her bag and put it into the collection box. The lady told Gerry that she used to be in the Samaritans many years previously. When asked for her name, the lady identified herself as Olive Cotter.

DUBLIN SAMARITANS

LIST OF DIRECTORS, NUMBER OF VOLUNTEERS AND CONTACTS[15]

Year	Director	Volunteers	Contacts
1970	Desmond Kilroy	200	1,048
1971	John F. Brennan	220	7,188
1972	(exec) Olive Cotter	270	12,884
1973	David Rowe	315	19,000
1974	" "	330	23,000
1975	" "	300	26,000
1976	Joan Carr	320	30,000
1977	" "	320	34,000
1978	" "	320	33,000
1979	Kevin O'Higgins	320	28,000
1980	" "	350	28,000
1981	" "	350	28,312
1982	Phil Bates	350	42,000
1983	" "	350	42,235
1984	" "	350	54,060
1985	Val Watson	350	58,900
1986	" "	350	57,305
1987	" "	350	69,402
1988	Des Moore	360	73,200
1989	" "	360	72,535
1990	" "	360	61,490
1991	Jean Lynch	360	70,000
1992	" "	296	74,197
1993	" "	309	79,400
1994-1997	Mary Bryans	340	83,060
1997-2000	Joe Gallagher	300	80,000
2001-2002	Liam Regan	300	80,000
2002-2005	Aidan Carr	325	72,444
2005-2006	Phil Huston	325	70,547
2007-	Maggie Hayden	353	87,385

CHAPTER 2

"WHERE'S YOUR BABY MRS?"

For the little angels and their parents

I sat in the bedside chair, quietly observing the busy life of the hospital ward. One hand rested beneath the bedclothes, clasping my wife's hand, as she, too, though gravely wounded, watched the nurses do their work. We did not utter words; there was no need and the effort caused her too much discomfort. We were united in our pain, shattered in our grief and utterly vulnerable. At the end of each bed hung a wire basket, where the mothers could observe their newborn babies and where each baby could be gently rocked. A coloured ribbon was tied to each basket, green for a boy, white for a girl and red to indicate danger. It was feeding time and the nurses were entering the ward to remove the babies individually, returning them soon again. Mary's bed would soon be on their path. A stocky nurse came and peered into our basket. Then, in a voice which carried round the small ward, she asked, "Where's your baby, Mrs?" I was transfixed to the chair and rendered speechless, as the ward went deadly quiet. Then I heard Mary, my wife, with great difficulty, utter, " My baby is dead, Nurse".

It was the worst outcome in the worst possible circumstances. She had gone full term, endured a caesarean operation and now had nothing to show for it. Though our baby had lived for two days, Mary never saw her, alive or dead, and remained full of doubt. Nine months earlier, she had begun to get morning sickness and told me she believed she was pregnant. Our local doctor soon confirmed this. He referred her to a consultant, who had a private practice at a prominent Dublin address and also at the Rotunda Hospital. Though we were not well off, we did not intend to take any chances with the pregnancy. Five months later I wrote my first letter to our baby.

15 April 1970

"Dear Baby,
This morning I felt you kick furiously, for the first time. Today is my birthday. Your mother and I anxiously await yours, our first born to be.

Daddy".

During that academic year, I was engaged in full-time study for a Diploma in Special Education at St. Patrick's, Drumcondra, in Dublin. Part of the course dealt with the causes of children's disabilities and of their long-term results. I was very well versed in the dangers accruing to childbirth. As the course ended, I hoped that we would be lucky and that all would be well with our own experience.

Two months later I wrote a second letter:

10 July

"Dear Baby,

Today you were a fortnight late in coming. It is over nine months since you began to be. Today also happened to be an appointment day for your mother with the doctor in the hospital. "Everything is fine, he said, the baby will come in its own good time. What's a week or two extra after waiting all these months?" The heat is really great at the moment and your mother is almost immobile.

Come soon. Father".

Within a few days I wrote again:

"Dear Baby,

Last night and this morning were hectic times, for your mother especially, and also for me. It was a great surprise but a mighty relief when you began to make a push for the outer world. We had all the preparations long since made and it only remained to rouse our good neighbour, Pat MacSweeney, in the early hours. She had agreed to give us a lift into the hospital. I felt sad leaving your mother there. It seemed a betrayal of sorts. But the nurse insisted and I was advised to return home and get some sleep. I slept until ten o'clock. I've just now had my breakfast and dashed up to the local hotel to phone the hospital. The lady who took the call checked Mary's name and said, " There's no news yet on her. She has not delivered so far". I must admit I was a bit shaken by that news. I was sure that you would have arrived by then. I didn't intend going into the hospital, until there had been positive developments, but Pat MacSweeney suggested that I should go in. " I've been thinking about my own time in hospital and I believe you should go in. No matter what condition she's in, she'll be glad to see you. You may be able to help her. She might need you". So I'm off, hopefully to see you as well.

Love, Daddy".

That same night I wrote again:

21 July

"Dear Darling Girl, Antonia Marie,

This day must have been the worst of my life, so far, though I do know that it could have been worse. When I reached the hospital, there were a lot of people milling about reception. There was some confusion and I heard someone say that no visitors were being allowed in. I decided to bypass reception and seek out your mother myself. I made my way upstairs and wandered about for a few minutes, going into wards and seeing lots of strange women in bed. Eventually I met a nurse who knew something about your mother. "Are you the husband?" she asked. "Yes, I am" I replied. "Where's Sister", the nurse shouted to another nurse. Sister was in a nearby room. She was a middle-aged lady with greying hair and a kindly face. "Mr. Jordan?" she asked. "Yes" I said. "Have you seen anyone else? Has Dr. X been in touch with you?" "No" I replied to both questions, becoming perplexed. "Well Mr. Jordan, I'm afraid there's been some trouble with the baby. There was no telephone number. The doctor had to do an emergency operation to try to save the baby, or else the two of them might have gone. Anyway your wife is awake now. You'd better see her. The baby is in an oxygen tent and is doing as well as can be expected".

Words, words, words, they would not stop coming to assail me, there, on the bare hospital floor. The corridor seemed to close in on me. Others had been listening too, though I couldn't see them. Only her, the Sister, as she went on, speaking her piece, fulfilling her duty. The world within my own being was being crushed, as the long suppressed fears became nightmare reality. How often had I put such thoughts out of my mind as horrid phantasm? How often during the last year did I say - this could happen to us - I wanted to grasp all those words spoken by the Sister and choke them, annihilate them. But all my thoughts, all my wishes couldn't get me away from the reality that faced me. Though my legs were like lumps of jelly, scarcely able to support me, I heard myself calmly ask, "Where is she?". "Just through here" the Sister said, indicating a nearby door. "Nurse, will you take Mr. Jordan in to see his wife; she has awakened again?" the Sister asked a nurse who was standing beside me, but whom I had not noticed previously. "Yes, I will Sister. Mrs Jordan has just awakened now. Will you come with me please?"

I followed her as she opened the door to reveal a room containing about seven beds. Several women looked at me. The nurse led me to a corner of the room and she bent over a bed asking, "are you awake Mrs Jordan, your husband is here to see you". She turned to me saying, "she is still a bit groggy but she is awake". The nurse left and I stood looking down on the distracted face of my wife, and your mother, Antonia. Her eyes were open and she recognised me, but did not speak. The message on her face was clear to me; - it has happened, what we were afraid of has happened-

I sat on the chair beside the bed and slid a hand beneath the bedclothes to seek and hold her hand. I didn't know what to say; I didn't want to ask her what had happened, and I couldn't say I was sorry. Her lips moved; she was trying to speak. Her wounded eyes cried out for the mercy she had been denied. Then she spoke and I bent close to listen; "They didn't believe I was so bad. They laughed at me. The baby is dead, I think. They won't give me a direct answer. The pain is terrible". I clenched her hand and hoped my eyes were telling her what my tongue could not utter. "Hurt me, hurt me, let me take the burden off you", ran through my mind, but I knew they were futile wishes. It was Mary who lay there on the bed, not I. She was the tortured one with the brutalised body. She was the one who had to be cured. That was what had to be done. Her torment had to be eased. "They told me that the baby is alive" I said, "I'll ask to see it before I leave and I can tell you". We spoke no more words but looked at each other, keeping our hands clasped tightly. In a little while a nurse came to the bed and said, "I've got to give you an injection now Mrs Jordan".

The nurse began to close the curtains around the bed making for some privacy. I decided that while that was going on, I would ask the nurse if I might see the baby. "I'll go and ask Sister" she replied. Returning in a few moments, she beckoned me to follow her. I gave Mary's hand an extra squeeze as I left. On the corridor the Sister, who was waiting for me, asked how did I find her. "Poorly" I said wondering what she expected me to say. Just a few paces along the corridor lay the nursery. The Sister rang an outside bell and in a moment, an orderly opened the door from within. "Would you ask one of the nurses to come?" Sister asked. A young dark-haired nurse arrived and was told who I was. Sister departed and the door closed. To my left, through a glass partition, I saw a room that must have contained thirty babies, each in its own cot. We passed that room and went along a short corridor. The nurse said, "I can only show her to you through the doorway, I'm afraid". Then it is a girl, I said, the first time I had thought about your gender. "Yes, a little girl", the nurse confirmed. We reached the doorway and the nurse entered the room. She put a mask around her mouth and nose and entered another smaller room where I could see four babies, each within a glass case on a trolley. Tubes and wires led into the cases. She opened the top of one of them and turned the baby on her side to face me.

That was how I saw you, my dearest little one. "Jesus, God help her the poor innocent thing. How beautiful, how perfectly formed she is; with her little crop of black hair. Why did it have to happen to you, poor little creature, my extension, our flesh and blood"? The tears rushed to my eyes as I tried to think. But the nurse was already turning you over on your back; your agitated breathing, fighting for life, continued. I didn't cry but I should have sobbed. I remained outwardly calm. The nurse came out and I asked, "How is she?" She didn't hesitate as she replied gently. "Not good, I'm afraid. If you wait a minute, I'll ask the doctor to have a word with you". A female doctor arrived and said that they were doing all they could for the baby. She said that internal bleeding had affected you and that you did not breathe for some time after you were born. Then with the help of oxygen you did. "But she is breathing now herself, with some help. She is critically ill and has no more than a fifty-fifty chance. Four days should decide on the baby's survival". The doctor then left and the nurse returned. I took one last look through the door and loved fiercely the baby, you, who was mine, ours. "Live, please, live for life", I uttered silently as we left. When the nurse ushered me through the outer doorway, I paused for a moment to exert control of myself. I walked to a small window and put my head outside to breathe some fresh air. Beneath me I could see into a kitchen where women worked near large cookers. I heard footsteps behind me on the corridor, but no one interrupted me. When I felt that I could control myself, I walked towards the ward Mary was in. The nurse who had given her the injection was just emerging. She told me, "She'll be asleep in a little while". "How long will she be out for?" I asked. "Oh anything for up to five hours and then we may give her some more. It's to relieve the pain, you know". "There's little point in me staying then?" I asked. "No, none" she replied, "apart from just seeing her now, before she dozes off". Within the ward the other women were sitting up, reading. All eyes followed me but no one spoke. Mary was as before; only now she knew that sleep was near, and pain would be at an end for a time. I did not feel like remaining. I too wished to be away anywhere. "I saw the baby and she's a lovely girl, just like you. I'm not going to wait any longer. I'll let you sleep. There's no point in coming in again for visiting at eight o'clock, as you'll be asleep".

Outside I met the Sister. "Did you see the doctor in the nursery?" she asked, adding, "I'm sure she told you everything. They did their best". I agreed with her. Then I thought of baptism. "Has the baby been baptised Sister?" I asked. "I'm sure she has. That's standard procedure in a case like this. But I don't know if the priest has officiated yet or not. Would you like me to double check?" "No, no, it's alright if she has been baptised" I said. "Are there any names you would like used if the priest is here tonight?" she said. "Antonia Marie" I replied. She wrote them down on a piece of paper and we parted, she to her work and me to - I knew not what. I walked out of that hospital, my world crumbling in on me. What was to have been the best day became the worst. I have had to leave your wounded mother alone and near demented. I still don't know the full story of what happened to her, but I can guess that it was awful. She seems made for tragedy. And you; how have I left you? Alive at least, but with some hope. I am alone in all this and that makes it harder. We three are alone separately, each in our bitter bed.

Goodnight, my two dearest, goodnight".

The next morning I made my weary way to the hospital on the number thirty-two bus. I wrote again that same noon.

Wednesday 12.00hrs

"Dear Antonia,

When I got to the hospital this morning I went straight to the nursery to see if you were still there. Within the hospital, you had to ring the doorbell and wait to be admitted. The same nurse as yesterday let me in. "She's much the same as yesterday" she said, forestalling my tortured question. At the glass door, she handed me over to another nurse saying, "I'll tell the doctor you're here. He will be looking at your baby in a moment". This time the door remained open and the nurse wheeled the glass container across the room and close to me. You were as yesterday, still breathing heavily and quickly, almost as if afraid you might miss one breath and it might be your last. I longed to open the glass cover and lift you out and hold you in my arms. After all, you were mine, ours; you did not belong here, you belonged at home, in the beautiful cot your mother had worked so hard on. Would you ever snuggle into the baby clothes that waited for you? Would you ever take my finger in your tiny hand and grasp it tightly, smiling playfully up at me? Would you ever do any of the thousands of things a normal baby would do, for I knew that a loss of oxygen at birth could have dire consequences for a baby. Some who survived were normal. Will you be among those my dearest one? Whichever, if you survive, I swear I will love you with a mighty love. If you make it, you and I and your beloved mother, will have good days to make up for these. "O God, if You are, if You can, if You wish, make her whole. Let her live to us; don't take away the proffered gift. We need her". The nurse began to retreat again and I was choked with grief, but I held it in check.

The doctor had arrived and was making preparations to enter the room. I watched him examine all the babies and then he came out to talk to me. His words were those of his colleague the previous day, only more pessimistic. He instanced the risks involved if you did live. "As high as eighty percent of such babies who survive are brain damaged. The chances are little enough, but we are not concerned at the moment in those terms. We are trying to help her survive. Then if we succeed, we will have to consider her brain condition. I just mention this to let you know the possibilities. It was nearly a miracle she survived this far at all. It took us hours to revive her. We had nearly given up trying. Another forty-eight hours will decide it, either way. Its impossible to say but the chances are poor, for the baby is still critically ill. She's fighting, but her resources are small. The damage may have been too much. Still, while there's life there's hope".

Your mother was much the same as yesterday too Antonia. She has severe pain in the wound in her stomach. It seems to be radiating throughout her body. They had to open her stomach to get you out in a hurry. We didn't talk much at all. I just told her how you were and we held hands for a long while. She got drowsy and I left. I will be back again tonight. Two colleagues, who care, have invited me to tea this evening.

Bye bye dear".

I spent the early evening with the Medical Director of the Central Remedial Clinic, Dr. Ciaran Barry and his wife Adrienne. It was a most pleasant interlude with two good friends. We did not discuss my predicament, but rather concentrated on our common interest in Gregorian music and baroque churches.

That night I again wrote to Antonia about my evening visit to the hospital.

Wednesday Night.

"Dear Antonia,

A note, to say that I didn't visit you this evening. When I went to see your mother, she was in slightly better form. There were two women sitting at her bed as I went in. She finds it extremely difficult to talk yet. She can only whisper. She knows all about you. She said one of the nurses told her that the doctors never know whether to hope the baby lived or died in a situation like this. I wanted to ask her about the operation that lead up to it, but decided to wait a day or two. She will tell me in her own good time, anyway. As other visitors came in, I could see furtive glances coming our way. On my way home dear, I was thinking about what the doctor said about you; Antonia alive but brain-damaged, or no Antonia at all; which was the better? What a dreadful thing to have to say to a daughter. The choice is not mine, my dear; in fact there is no choice; whatever it is, it rests with God. I am content to put faith and trust in Him, but above all, hope. For though I might often have doubts on faith, I have never ceased to hope. I hope for you Antonia. I pray for you, dear.
Rest peacefully tonight.

Daddy".

My last letter to Antonia was written the next day.

Thursday 15.00 hrs.

"Dear Darling Lamented Antonia, This letter is to you, in Heaven, for where else could you be now? I went in a couple of hours ago and called to the nursery. One of the nurses I had met previously opened the door and exclaimed, "Oh Mr. Jordan, will you come in". "How is she?" I asked hesitantly. I saw immediately that she was thinking feverishly of what to say. Then she said it simply and clearly, "I'm afraid your baby died this morning". "What time did it happen?" I asked. "Shortly after four o'clock" she replied. "Is she still within" I asked, indicating the little room. "No, no she's not" the nurse replied, adding that she was sorry things had worked out like this, but they had tried their best. "You know it might have been all for the best" she said. "Do you know if my wife knows?" I asked. She replied that Mary did know. Then she had some papers she wanted me to sign, allowing the doctors to carry out a post mortem. She also had a message from the gynaecologist who wanted to see me in his consulting rooms, either that afternoon or tomorrow. The nurse had been speaking to me just opposite the glass door of the smaller room. I glanced in and saw a baby in a case in the position where you had been. Was it still you? It could have been, for I could see no sign of movement

or breathing. But there was no point in embarrassing the nurse. I had seen my baby alive and would never forget you. The nurse let me out of the nursery quietly. I walked to a nearby window and put my head outside. Then it began. The tears came and I could not hold them back. My shoulders shook. I was on a public corridor but I did not care. Footsteps passed by behind me. Later a hand was placed on my shoulder, "don't trouble yourself so, son". I turned aside. A woman with a mop and bucket was talking to me. "Was it your baby?" she asked. "Yes" I said, "I am trying to regain control". Other people were passing and they looked at me. The woman said, "you're young, please God, there'll be plenty more. I had eleven myself and lost three of them. It's hard but it's God's will". As she spoke I dried my tears. "Don't let your wife see you cry now; go on into her", the kind lady said.

As I moved to go, I saw Mary come out of a nearby room. It must have been a toilet. She was barely moving, holding one hand against the wall for support. Had she heard me cry or even seen me? I didn't know. Her face was white and wan, her eyes doleful. She looked at me but kept going, struggling towards her ward. I followed her and helped her to get into bed again. I could feel the sympathy flow from the other women in the room. "You heard" she said, when she finally succeeded in lying down. "Yes" I said, "just now". "They told me this morning; it's probably for the best" she said. "Thanks be to God, it's over anyhow" I said, "Did you see her at all?" "No" she answered, "there was some question of it yesterday, but I could not walk". "She would have been severely brain damaged if she had survived" I said. "That would have been no life for her nor for us" Mary said. She seemed to regain some strength, now that she was back in bed. "Is that the first time you have walked?" I asked. "No, they took me out this morning already. I never thought I would be able to move, but I was. Did you see the neighbours?" she asked. "Yes I did". "They'll be disappointed". "Yes, they will; but the problem of the moment is to get you better and back home again". "Do you want to see my wound? You won't be able to see the actual wound but I'll show you the mess", she said. Mary eased up the bedclothes and I saw the middle of her tummy clipped together with metal pincers. There was plenty of evidence of congealed blood, a gory sight. Every so often she used to get searing pains that would leave her gasping, until they passed away. She thought it was caused by air in the wound. "I think you'd better ring home," she said. "It will have to be broken gently to our mothers". I promised I would do that and then I had to leave. I told her that I was going to see her gynaecologist that afternoon. She did not appear to be too enamoured of him. I have not met him before, but I suppose he wants to tell me exactly what happened.

I hope you don't mind that your mother never saw you Antonia. She had the hardest part to play. I saw you, thanks be to God for that. We are both in such a state that we might not know exactly what we are doing or saying. But I am writing to you, so that we will know what it was like, from my point of view. I am writing these letters to you as a bridge between us, which will last. I must close now, as I am off to see the gynaecologist.

Bye bye my love".

The Lady with the mop and bucket was my Good Samaritan.

The secretary showed me into the gynaecologist's plush consulting room. She was most concerned to let me know how distressed he was by the outcome. "It's a defeat for him, too" she said. He was a youngish man with an expensive sounding Dublin accent. He told me that the placenta through which the oxygen comes to the baby, ruptured, and her heartbeat nearly ended. A section was the only chance to save the baby. In the event, it did, but too late. He said that my wife had gone through everything, but had nothing to show. He said that when she went home she would be terribly depressed, seeing all the preparations she had made for the baby. He urged that she would be in great danger of postnatal depression and could even become suicidal. He advised me to watch her carefully, to be with her, to watch for mood swings. He was sorry for the outcome.

On my way out, his secretary told me that she had the bill ready, if I wished to pay it. This I did and received a receipt within days from the doctor thanking me, "for settling your account". I did not tell Mary what the doctor was most concerned about, but reported his regret on the outcome. It was then that she was able, with great difficulty, to outline what had happened on the morning, after I had left her at the hospital. Though it was only a couple of days previously, it seemed like a lifetime.

She had been prepared for delivery and placed on a trolley in an annex. As her labour pains increased she began to cry out, only to be 'reprimanded' by a nurse who told her that 'nobody ever had pains like you'. This continued for several hours, with Mary crying out for some sort of assistance but getting none. She knew that there was something amiss within her, but could not convince the nursing staff of this.

A doctor appeared momentarily, but when he discovered that she was a private patient, he passed on. Mary asked for her doctor to be contacted, but this was refused. She was told that he would be in at 09.30. When, after several hours of agony her doctor arrived, he examined her and had her rushed to the operating theatre for a caesarean operation. The amniotic sac surrounding the baby had burst and caused major distress to mother and baby. Hearing this, I again felt guilty that I had allowed myself to abandon her to their tender mercies.

A nurse came to the bed and told me that the Matron wished to see me. I made my way to her office. She was not there but a nurse handed me a letter. It read:

THE ROTUNDA HOSPITAL DUBLIN

Founded 1745 Incorporated by Royal Charter 1756

23. 7. 70

"Dear Mr. Jordan,

I regret to inform you that your wife's baby died/was ~~still born~~ on 23.7.70. If you wish to make your own arrangements for burial, you should notify Matron's Office as soon as possible. If you wish, the burial can be arranged for you by the Hospital Authorities by getting in touch with the Medical Social Worker the Hospital Authorities will find it necessary to proceed with arrangements.

The charge is £2. 15/- and should be paid to the Accounts Clerk between the hours of 9 a.m. and 4.30 p.m. (12.30 p.m. on Saturdays) or a postal order, together with your name and address, may be sent to the Accounts Department, Rotunda Hospital, Dublin 1.

We would ask you to instruct us promptly in order to avoid undue distress.

Yours truly,

K. Gillan
for Lady Superintendent".

A FATEFUL DECISION

I retraced my path to Mary and informed her that we had to make a decision about whether to have our own funeral or to let the hospital bury Antonia. I did not show her the letter. We had been prepared for a birth, not for a funeral. We were in no position then to consider the latter. Then we made the fateful decision, which I have regretted for the rest of my life, to allow the hospital to bury our baby.

Mary spent nine days in hospital. As she got stronger she became more eager to return home. The night before her return, I put away all the many items she had prepared for her new baby. I shed most tears over a pair of booties she had placed on the mantelpiece. She had crocheted them and we had many laughs about them.

After I paid the hospital bill, our kind neighbour again drove us back home to Portmarnock. To our surprise the neighbours had prepared a welcome home meal for us. After some brief exchanges of sadness and joy, they left us alone, but very much together. Mary was so tired and sore that she spent most of the next two weeks in bed and I had the pleasure of ministering to her.

These days were very special to me, as she was normally so totally independent. Both our families were naturally very upset when they heard the news. My own mother wanted to come to us immediately, but I advised against it just yet. Most of our own friends were away on school summer holidays. We were very much a nuclear family. Some few weeks later when I returned from school one afternoon, Mary told me that a Public Health Nurse had called to the house earlier in the morning. She had come to see how the new baby was doing.

A DISASTROUS ENCOUNTER

I began to think of the future and feared that Mary might understandably wish never to become pregnant again. She was due to make her final visit to see the gynaecologist. I formed the opinion that it was vital that he reassure her that if there were a next time, it would be quite different. I called to see him briefly to apprise him of my fears. He assured me that he would give her every reassurance for the future. He emphasised again how he felt Mary's mental health was very fragile. I told him that I had seen no such evidence. To me she seemed remarkably strong-minded. Mary saw him at the Rotunda. It was a disastrous encounter. She emerged very upset and angry. He had appeared somewhat defensive to her, and gave her to understand that he would do everything exactly the same again. What had happened was a chance in a million, he maintained. The fact that he did not arrive in the hospital until 09.30 and operated immediately had no material affect on the outcome. He rejected her view that she had been in great distress and pain for several hours, crying out for help to no avail. He told her that she had been under constant observation and monitoring and that the nursing staff would have alerted him, had it been necessary. The medical records bore this out, he said. This was another very distressing day for both of us, worse almost that any within the hospital had been. Outwardly at least, Mary appeared more and more to be able to put the whole terrible experience of losing the baby behind her. I found this difficult to understand, as I was prone to tears on a regular and ongoing basis.

ISANDS

I made contact with a small group of women whose babies had died prematurely. They were setting up a self-help group in Dublin, which ultimately developed into the Irish Stillbirth and Neonatal Death Society. I introduced Mary to them. She attended a few of their meetings at Dorothy Gunn's house in Inchicore. But she discovered that far from helping her, the regular discussions and the raising of bad memories, had the potential of setting her back. She felt that she was coping adequately and the situation was behind her. It was to be very many years later that Mary explained her rationale for this to me. In the meantime I retained a tenuous link with ISANDS, which developed into a very important support group for parents and families whose babies have died around the time of birth.

We have remained life long members of ISANDS.

P. S. 1. LIMBO?

As the years went by, there were regular reminders that served to intensify my feelings of loss. One situation was the fact that we were unsure whether Antonia had actually been baptised. This became a major source of pain, when in 1977, the Bishop of Cork, Dr. Cornelious Lucey, spoke about Limbo at a confirmation ceremony. He was accustomed to making important statements on such occasions. This time he addressed the eternal state of un-baptised persons. During his sermon he mentioned un-baptised babies, and commented that, *"they won't get to Heaven, of course"*. This infuriated me and I responded in a letter to the *Irish Times*, which had carried the report of the sermon.

My letter read.

"Sir, I read your brief report of what Dr. Lucey, Bishop of Cork and Ross, said at a Confirmation Ceremony recently. To demand as a general rule, that babies be baptised seven to ten days after birth and expect the mother to be there is indicative of an unthinking bachelor mind (who needs women priests). To state that babies who die before baptism should not be thought as being lost for all eternity, but rather will not have the happiness that they would have had, had they been baptised, is an insult to Jesus Christ who died for all of us. Who does Dr. Lucey think he is to be consigning innocent babies to a second best state? The same applies to what he has to say about non-Christians.

I am sure they must find his assertions to be too comical for comment. Of course what Dr. Lucey is about, is something we rarely witness nowadays. He is trying to frighten the faithful into doing what he thinks is the correct thing. He is speaking in a triumphalistic, dogmatic and basically un-Christian way".

Another letter, on the same day, from a Fr. Joe McVeigh, writing from the Institute of Pastoral Studies in Dundalk, simply asked.

"Sir, Does Dr. Lucey, the Bishop of Cork and Ross, think he is God?"

Patsy McGarry, the Religious Affairs Correspondent of the *Irish Times* reported on 21 April 2007 that the "Concept of limbo now consigned to oblivion". He wrote that the Catholic Church had published a document called *"The Hope Of Salvation for Infants Who Die Without Being Baptised"*. It reflected the future Pope Benedict's 2005 view, which doubted the existence of Limbo. It stated that *"People find it increasingly difficult to accept that God is just and merciful if he excludes infants, who have no personal sins, from external happiness, whether they are Christian or non-Christian".*

P. S. 2. LOCATING THE GRAVE

The brush with Bishop Lucey gave me the impetus to consider seeking the location of Antonia's grave. We both regretted bitterly that we had not buried Antonia in our own grave, instead of allowing her to go into a mass grave in Glasnevin. I had never felt strong enough previously to go to Glasnevin. But one day I phoned the cemetery to make inquiries. I gave them the relevant details, name, address, date of birth, date of death, hospital involved. To my great surprise, and even joy, they almost immediately gave me the reference number to identify the location where she was buried. They offered to give me personal assistance, if I had any difficulty in finding it myself. It was as if I had suddenly received external confirmation, for the first time, that Antonia had lived. She was on the record, albeit of a cemetery. I was very impressed and grateful for the rapidity and ease with which I had been dealt with. The code for the location was Z 303. I did not mention this to Mary. It took me a few months to make the next step and visit Glasnevin. With a little assistance, I found myself in the area where the grave was located. It was a desolate sight, consisting of what looked like waste ground, pock-marked by some miniature headstones, wooden crosses, tiny rectangular enclosures, old toys, dolls, faded flowers. My heart did not sink, for I was again close to my baby. This was sacred ground to me. Tears flowed, before I was able to compose myself sufficiently, to approach closer, and begin a detailed search. On inspection, I saw immediately that some of the fixtures had names and most importantly for me, dates. There was a clear temporal order apparent, amid the seemingly haphazard miniature fixtures. There was one rather sturdy enclosure dated July 1970. This piece of ground, I deciphered, was as close as I would ever get, to where Antonia was buried. It was an excruciating, though thrilling experience. I had made contact at last. I had identified the location of her unmarked grave.

I made several visits to the grave before I mentioned it to Mary. She expressed surprise that I was able to locate it so readily. Some few months later, I suggested that we might visit the grave as a family. By this time we had two other daughters, ages ten and five, for whom Antonia was also a very important family figure. On a Sunday afternoon, we all set off for Glasnevin. It was a sombre occasion though a very satisfying one, as we were all concerned about how Mary would react. She was quite self-contained as usual, and I felt glad that she had come. However, our afternoon was to be rudely disturbed, just after a very successful visit to our own grave. We noticed what appeared to be the current mass grave nearby. It was indicated by a large heap of freshly dug clay. We decided to take a closer look. As we approached it, we were surprised to see that the hole itself seemed to be uncovered. When we looked into the hole, we could see some of the recently buried 'coffins', or little boxes. A cursory attempt appeared to have been made to cover them with clay, but several coffins were clearly visible. I took a photograph of the scene, which upset us all considerably.

P. S. 3. A RELIGIOUS SERVICE?

In 1983 a constitutional referendum allocated rights to unborn babies.

The *Irish Times* published a letter from me, reading.

Sir, Now that the unborn have been assigned constitutional rights, could I put in a word for those babies who die at the peri-natal period? At the moment and for many years past, these babies have been disposed of in mass graves, without any clear recognition that they ever lived. No religious service would appear to be part of the disposal procedure. The hospitals offer a take-it or leave-it service, which, in the traumatic circumstances, the parents usually take. Very little religious or social counselling is involved. The parents often bitterly regret the outcome for the rest of their lives.

The last occasion I visited the current mass grave, several of the little boxes were clearly visible in the gaping hole. It is interesting to note that the Methodist Church has approved a funeral and naming service for the stillborn. A religious service would give some comfort to the family. It would confirm that a birth/death had actually happened, rather than leaving parents feeling that they were involved in a bad dream".

P. S. 4. THE HEADSTONE

Some years later, I decided that I would like to mark the grave with a little headstone. On approaching one company, I was told that they could not make such an item, as individualised memorials were not allowed on the graves.

The cemetery had earlier introduced a new scheme whereby a large stone could be inscribed with names of babies buried in the general area. We had subscribed to this scheme, but I now wanted something more personal on the grave itself. After some difficulty, I succeeded in getting a stone suitably inscribed. Then, almost surreptitiously, I drove directly to Z 303 and quickly placed it on the ground, before driving away. Later I enclosed a piece of ground with a rough timber frame around the stone. At last, we had our own grave.

There remains the possibility, if not the certainty, that in the future all these materials may be cleared, if the Cemetery Management Authority decide to recycle this area of ground for new burials. It was a most memorable day for me when I took Mary to view my handiwork. The intensity of the pain and pleasure I experienced, as I watched her bend down and rearrange some dried leaves that surrounded the stone, nearly caused my head to explode. I was amazed how calm and controlled she was, even at that moment.

I later wrote a poem, which read:

> *"Twenty winters have passed since I lay alongside you,*
> *Our first - born daughter encased within my wife.*
> *My hand pressed firmly on your mother's bulge,*
> *To feel your life deep within the womb.*
>
> *I was not there when they cut you out,*
> *Flesh of my flesh; a belated affair.*
> *The cot was empty; a red bow tied,*
> *Tied to say, to say, mother, but no child.*
>
> *Wife without words, tummy now clamped,*
> *Offspring visible within a glass box.*
> *For forty-one hours Antonia lived,*
> *Thrice I witnessed her in that incubator.*
>
> *Cleaners consoled me, nurses embarrassed me,*
> *Doctors patronised me, Matron billed me.*
> *Wooden shoeboxes exposed in a gaping hole,*
> *Received you rudely, bereft of obsequies.*
>
> *Babies who have died to a Limbo place,*
> *In faith, baptised, will see God's face."*

P. S. 5. A DEDICATION

One of the most difficult aspects of losing Antonia was the briefness of her life, the absence of time for her, the nothingness of shared experience, the absence of proof that she had really existed. I wanted it to be known that she had lived, that she was. Even the most kindly understood and sensitive contemporary letter which I received from Lady Goulding of the Central Remedial Clinic, where I worked, as it offered sympathy *"for your little baby who did not live"*, had hurt. In 1991 an opportunity arose of commemorating Antonia publicly, by dedicating my first book to her. It was a biography of Major John MacBride[16] who had been executed in 1916 and buried in a mass grave with the other executed leaders in north Dublin at Arbour Hill.

The dedication read:

> *FOR ANTONIA - WHO NEVER SAW MAYO-*
> *AND LIKE THE MAJOR-*
> *LIES IN A MASS GRAVE IN DUBLIN.*

P. S. 6. **WOULD YOU BELIEVE?**

RTE television had a programme series called, *"Would You Believe?"* They intended to devote one such programme to parental bereavement. I agreed to participate. Stephanie Fitzpatrick was the producer, with Mary O'Sullivan as the interviewer. They shot film over three days at three locations, my place of work, my home and Glasnevin. A personal interview they shot with me was a most excruciating experience. I will never forget the sound engineer who hugged me so caringly afterwards. The programme was due to be transmitted on a Tuesday night. I had alerted family and friends to the event. On the previous evening Mary O'Sullivan called to my house to tell me that, due to technical reasons, the programme I was involved in, was cancelled.

P. S. 7. In the late 1990's Orla Bourke interviewed me for a programme on bereavement she produced for RTE radio. Among other things I read a poem for her, which had been written by me in 1987. The next year ISANDS had a special anniversary commemoration at the *Little Angel's Plot* at Glasnevin. I was asked by Ron Smith-Murphy to read the poem on that occasion. That was to be a very emotional experience for me. On the day, neither my wife nor oldest daughter Judith, was able to accompany me. My younger daughter, Fiona, so aware that I could not go alone, came in from NUI Maynooth to join me for the ceremony.

The poem read:

Christmas 1987

"The stars shine brightly, on this cool Christmas night.
A red candle flames from our window.

I wave to my wife and daughter as they pass to Midnight Mass.
A white stocking hangs limply, a young girl sleeps expectantly.

Happiness wells within me, unwished for, unwanted.
So soon, by thought of you, my first-born, my cross, my joy,
The swell is overtaken.

Thrice I saw you, yet you are the measure of all I am.
The eyes fill, the tears fall on my cheeks.

It is a sacrament I receive from you, my girl in the incubator,
Who was not there, when last I called, but removed, transferred,
To a cold loose wet clay in a wooden shoebox,
Beneath a stony path, in nineteen seventy".

This poem became a template in my life, as I am the most emotional of men.
On so very many happy occasions when I witnessed my other two daughters experiencing the joys of life, that happiness was tinged with grieving for what might have been for Antonia.

P. S. 8. In 1995 we were able to acquire a Birth Certificate for Antonia. The certificate states that she was registered on the 24th of July 1970.

P. S. 9. Early in 1998 one of my nieces, Patricia Sullivan, delivered a still-born baby. On the evening we received the news, I returned home after a walk to find my wife crying. She told me that it reminded her of Antonia. She shocked me, yet thrilled me, by saying,

"If there is a heaven, she's my little angel. I don't see it as a negative experience, rather as a positive one. I don't feel a loss. May be if I had seen her it might be different".

P. S. 10. On a visit to Glasnevin in the summer of the year 2000 with Mary, I discovered for the first time, why her reaction to the experience of Antonia had been so very different from mine since the very outset. She explained, as we walked away from the little plot, that initially she had believed that Antonia had been born dead. It was only when I had seen her, that she believed that the hospital was being truthful. But the fact remained that Mary never saw her. She never 'delivered' her baby.

Antonia was thus never real for Mary, and so her absence was always mediated by that reality. She asked, how could she miss someone she never saw? *"You saw her, I did not"*, she explained.

P. S. 11. THE DUNNE INQUIRY

During that same year of 2000, a controversy arose concerning the retention by hospitals of body parts of babies who had post mortems performed on them, without the knowledge or permission of parents. All the maternity and children's hospitals appeared to be involved.

The medical establishment defended itself by stating that this was international practice and was for the common good. In 2001 the *Dunne Inquiry* was set up by the Government to inquire into post mortems and organ retention practice in Irish Adult, Children and Maternity hospitals since 1970

Prior to the establishment of the Inquiry, Health Boards and hospitals set up information lines to support families who had queries or concerns about these issues. A significant number of people came forward, according to official sources. I answered the newspaper advertisement and called the Rotunda Help Line.

I discovered that the person taking the call had not even read the advertisement and was merely offering to take details for future reference. I had earlier written to the Hospital.

My letter read.

"Secretary/Manager Rotunda Hospital 9/2/00

Dear Sir,

My wife, Mary Jordan, then of 7 Woodlands, Portmarnock Co. Dublin, gave birth to a baby girl at your Hospital on 21 July 1970. There were complications and the baby died within a matter of days. I signed a post mortem form. I would like to have any information the Hospital retains about my wife and the baby. Specifically I would like to know whether any organs were withheld from the burial carried out by the Hospital and if so what became of them? I would also like to know if the baby was baptised? I am writing on my own behalf and that of my wife.

Yours sincerely
Anthony Jordan".

I received no response to the above.

During the summer of 2003, I mentioned the above in a letter to the *Irish Times* and got an immediate and direct response from the Hospital. This resulted in an invitation to visit the hospital and discuss the matter. I did not feel up to going, but Mary did and took up the invitation. She had a lengthy discussion with two staff and found it very helpful. But she did not discover whether any organs of Antonia had been retained in the hospital.

P. S. 11. UNABLE TO VIEW THE RECORDS

In February of 2004 another advertisement appeared in the newspapers from the *National Free Phone Line on Organ Retention and Post Mortem Practices*. It said that the "Health Boards and Hospitals remained committed to providing whatever information and advice is available to families in this regard…a national free phone line will be put in place with effect from Tuesday February 3rd until Friday 20th February 2004". I responded and was subsequently contacted by a social worker from the Rotunda. It transpired that they in fact did not know whether any of Antonia's organs had been retained. Their records only went back to the 1980's. The pathologist concerned in the 1970's no longer worked there. They understood that the consultant involved lived abroad. Subsequently, in 2004, the Hospital wrote to say that it had discovered records and charts concerning Antonia and Mary. I had to write to claim them. When the two sets of records arrived at our house, I did not open the large envelope, nor have I ever been able to read the contents. Mary did read them. I have never questioned her on their content.

CHAPTER 3

DANIEL DAY LEWIS

In 1988 a tall man knocked unannounced on the door of my small Principal Teacher's Office at the National Association for Cerebral Palsy Ireland, Sandymount School and Clinic. He gave his name as Daniel Day Lewis and said he was in Dublin preparing to play the role of Christy Brown in a new film. He wished to spend up to six weeks in our school. It was a Monday morning and I was trying to organise my schedule for the day. I did not ask him to take a seat, intending to send him on his way as quickly as possible. There had been several earlier abortive schemes to produce a film on Christy Brown, and I was not about to devote any of my time talking about another. I engaged the visitor in a very brief conversation while opening the door to show him out. As an afterthought I asked him who was making the film. *"Noel Pearson is producing and Jim Sheridan is directing"*, he answered. I felt like saying, *"Well why didn't you say that at the start?"* I quickly invited the stranger to return and take a seat. In an attempt to be friendly, while his name meant nothing to me, I asked was he any relation of Cecil Day Lewis. He indicated that he was and before he could elaborate, I rashly suggested that Cecil might be his grandfather. "No, actually, he was my father", was the reply. Embarrassed, I tried to explain that Cecil Day Lewis appeared to me to be a figure from the distant past. Daniel said he was born during his father's second marriage and that his father was rather old by then.

Suitably chastened, I inquired about plans for the film. John O'Connor's son, Hugh, was to play the younger Christy Brown; Brenda Fricker would play Mrs Brown; Fiona Shaw was to play Dr Eileen Cole. Filming was due to start that summer with a schedule of nine weeks for completion. Daniel emphasized he wanted to observe the students in our school in a completely unobtrusive manner, so as to ready himself for the role of a severely disabled person. If possible, he would like the freedom to visit the school occasionally over the next six weeks.

I agreed to the request and explained the reason for my initial hesitation. I also told him I was in the process of organising a 'Memorial Day' in the school for Christy Brown. I told him of my own rather strange experience, that since my arrival in the school in 1973 I had never heard Christy Brown mentioned, despite the fact that there were still several people on the staff who had known him well.

The most prominent of those was Dr. Robert Collis, who had founded the National Association for Cerebral Palsy in 1948, and who also played a pivotal role in Christy's life. Christy died in 1981 and I decided to 'reclaim' him as a past pupil. I organised a Month's Mind Mass for him. To my great surprise and pleasure, many of his large family, as well as several friends and admirers, attended. I promised the family that at a later stage I would organise a summer school or memorial day, when we would pay attention to his life and work. It was only in Spring of 1988 that I began planning for the event. The Memorial Day was planned for the following 6th June on Christy's birthday. My visitor was very excited about that prospect. I took Daniel on a brief tour of the school and pointed out one student in particular, Mary Kiernan, who was then using her left foot to type. At his insistence of being as un-obtrusive as possible, we did not enter any of the classrooms. I later took leave of him and invited him to visit us at his own convenience. Only a few minutes later there was another knock on my door and two female teachers entered. *"Where is he?"* they wanted to know, *"where is he gone?, will he be back?"* Not for the first or last time, I discovered I lead a rather sheltered life. It appeared that Daniel Day Lewis had a huge female following, including many of our own staff. It transpired that I had seen one of his films, *"My Beautiful Laundrette"*, but could recall no resemblance between either of the two main actors in that film and the man who had just left my office. I told my excited teachers of the arrangement I had agreed with the visitor; they were very pleased. Some time later, I was told that Daniel was in a new film. I took my wife to see *"The Unbearable Lightness of Being"*. We were not impressed, and after only thirty minutes, bored by the intimate bedroom scenes, we left that cinema and instead saw, *"Crocodile Dundee"*, which was funny. Had I seen that film before I met Mr Day Lewis, I would have had doubts about the wisdom of my open-door policy with the actor.

Over the next few weeks, Daniel became a familiar figure in the school and clinic. He visited all sections of the centre, making many friends. At that time, we were experimenting with a Hungarian teaching method called Conductive Education. I can recall Daniel being very taken with those procedures. He was always as good as his word - very unobtrusive. When the media discovered that he was visiting us, inquiries and requests for photo opportunities and interviews materialised. I was placed in a tricky situation of telling white lies to some people, who, in other situations I would be seeking publicity from. The two people he spent most time with were Mary Kieran in the school and Helen Curtis in the Sheltered Workshop. Daniel's father Cecil was born in County Laois in 1904 to Frank, a minister in the Church of Ireland and Kathleen Squires. Kathleen died two years after Cecil's birth. Father and son moved to London thereafter but Cecil returned to Ireland regularly. Cecil attended Oxford, where he was a contemporary and friend of fellow poets, WH Auden and Stephen Spender. He was a member of the Communist Party. He became Professor of Poetry at Oxford and Poet Laureate in 1968. His first marriage lasted twenty-three years and produced two sons, Seán and Nicholas.

He had another son, William, as a result of an affair. In 1951 he was divorced and married Jill Balcon, twenty-one years his junior. They had two children, Tamasin born in 1953 and Daniel born in April of 1957. Cecil was a reserved father who saw little of his children, except during family holidays, which were usually spent in County Mayo. These happy occasions instilled a keen love of Ireland in both Tamasin and her brother[17]. He said that Mayo and the West became part of their secret lives as children. They continued to holiday there even after their father died. Later he made a conscious choice to continue the link with Ireland by establishing a home there and becoming an Irish citizen. Daniel said that being the son of a famous father was a burden for a young man. He was proud of the fact, while shy of it as well. He had difficulties at primary schools, and only settled down at boarding school when he came to terms with the necessity for conformity. At College he was shocked to be instructed that part of the actor's job was to chase work. He did not think he would be able for that exercise. At the start there was a sense of desperation during which he imploded while wondering whether he would ever get the opportunity to demonstrate what he could do. He said it was a dangerous time, "when you're young and you've got nothing to do. I worked it out and said I'm not going to worry about that and it did work itself out"[17a].

Early in May we had a visit by Daniel and the 'heavy gang'. This consisted of Noel Pearson and Jim Sheridan, and several people from casting, costume and scenery. They were interested in seeing whether we might have any information or equipment that might be useful to them. They were particularly interested in knowing who would be attending the 'Christy Brown Memorial Day', which was then set for 10th June. Pearson was the 'fixer' with the outwardly genial personality, who would keep everyone happy. Sheridan, who knew what he wanted and confined himself to that, was taciturn, almost blunt. Day Lewis was easy with his companions, retaining his exquisite manners. It was clear that both men valued his professional expertise highly and were most anxious to facilitate his wishes.

CHRISTY BROWN MEMORIAL DAY

An important part of the exercise for my production was to re-establish in the public mind the association between Christy Brown and Sandymount. I planned my attempt at publicity very carefully. In late May I called a press conference for Sandymount, indicating that Mona Byrne, one of Christy's sisters, would be present. All the major newspapers attended and we got some excellent photographic coverage. I also succeeded in being interviewed with one of the pupils, Imelda Nolan, on RTE's major morning news programme 'Morning Ireland'. This was an interesting experience in that I discovered that I was quite able to convey my message without being sidetracked by the interviewer. The publicity brought in a large volume of inquiries. Those who I had invited to participate on the day began to get nervous about their own contributions in what increasingly looked like being quite a public occasion. Within the school, we had several rehearsals with both staff members and pupils doing readings of prose and poetry. I had to be very selective in choosing the readings.

At the end of May I got a phone call from Noel Pearson. He was very interested to know who was being invited. He asked if it was all right for the cast and production people to attend. Then a moment occurred which I thoroughly enjoyed, then and since. He offered to organise the publicity for my 'production'. I declined, telling him that I had it under control. I was enjoying the chase for publicity for events that were being staged. Within a few days I received a generous cheque from Pearson of £100 towards production expenses.

The day started off with a memorial mass for Christy, at which I read his poem 'Good Friday'[18] as the first reading. The print media came in force; there was standing room only in the large hall. Some of those most closely involved with Christy's life attended. Catriona Maguire, whom he had known and loved since he was ten and with whom he had a long correspondence, came. Dr. Patricia Sheehan was another on whom he had depended professionally and personally and with whom he had corresponded intensely, came and gave a hilarious memorial lecture. She spoke of 'Ma' Brown and of the unquenchable spirit of the Dublin working class. Many of the Brown family attended. Daniel sat quietly in the audience with many people from the film. I chaired the day's proceedings. To my right was an annex housing a small kitchen, which thankfully was not visible to the audience. Throughout proceedings a mouse played there, making repeated attempts to run past me into the body of the hall. A part of me wished to witness the panic his arrival would cause, but I thought better of it. Every time the mouse approached my feet, I moved them quickly forcing him to retreat. I don't know if anybody noticed the unwelcome visitor. Thanks to Pearson's donation, we had an excellent reception.

One very important guest was the widow of Robert Collis. She told me that during a very difficult period in her life, Cecil Day Lewis and his wife, Jill Balcon, had befriended her. Dr. Robert Collis had volunteered to join a Red Cross mission to the continent in 1945 at the end of the war. He was among the first group into the Belsen Concentration Camp. There he met and fell in love with a Dutch interpreter named Han Hogerzeil. Collis was already married, but kept in touch with Han. Some years later in London, she became pregnant by him. He arranged for her to come to Ireland and stay with friends of his. After the birth of the baby, Collis arranged for mother and baby to return to England and stay with his good friends, Cecil Day Lewis and Jill Balcon. Collis later was divorced and emigrated to Nigeria and married Han[19]. Mrs Collis was unaware that Daniel Day Lewis was present with us that day. I sat her down with some refreshments and went to get Daniel. I had some difficulty finding him. I saw him in the playground surrounded by female autograph hunters. After some time, I succeeded in disengaging him and told him that there was a very special person I wanted him to meet. When I told him who it was, he was incredulous. He kept repeating that the Collis and Day-Lewis families had been so close over so many years, spending several holidays together at Old Head in Co. Mayo. He knew that Robert Collis had died in 1975, aged seventy-five years, and was surprised that Mrs Collis was still hale and hearty. He could not imagine that he was about to meet her. I brought him into the reception room and sat him down beside her, and asked a staff member to see they were not disturbed. An important outcome of the day for me was an offer by Caitriona Maguire and Dr. Sheehan to give me access to letters Christy Brown had written to them over his lifetime. These proved to be inspirational material, demonstrating that Brown was a great writer, a sensitive and philosophical person, but also a cunning and tough individual. The letters covered the period from the age of ten right through to his death in 1981. It became clear in the letters that Christy, even as a young man, made his own decisions. One of these decisions, it appeared, had caused some coolness between himself and Sandymount. He had decided at a certain stage that the Sandymount Clinic had done as much as it could for him and he discharged himself, much to the chagrin of the establishment. He felt that his time could be more profitably spent in writing and painting. When one of the senior staff, Dr. Patricia Sheehan, backed him in his decision she also became *persona non grata* at Sandymount.

THE MOVIE

It appeared that Noel Pearson had been having a very difficult task in raising the necessary finance for the film. He later told Michael Dwyer of the *Irish Times*, "*I had a lot of guys who put up 20 grand or 50 grand and then Granada came in and put in a million but for that, they got all the rights. One of the mistakes we made, because we were total novices, was letting Granada agree to everything. They sold the U.S. rights in perpetuity to Harvey Weinstein for a million bucks. We still don't even know exactly how much the film made although it did very well*"[19a]. It was only a pledge of £150,000 from RTE that had kept the project afloat until Granada came on board. The budget for the film was a mere £1.7 million, with a nine-week shoot planned for Ardmore Studios in Bray. As the filming drew closer a large group of our pupils and some staff got parts. Much of our old equipment was used as backdrops for some scenes. Daniel succeeded in learning how to write and paint with his left foot. Stories began to circulate of how Daniel was made up for his role each morning and remained in character all day, including being spoon-fed during breaks between filming. His attitude soon had the cast and crew feel they were involved in something very special. His method acting has become legendary. He has admitted though that when he later had his own family his tendency to stay in character had to be greatly curtailed least he frighten his children[19b]. He later told Michael Dwyer of the *Irish Times*, "*For most people I think, the most vibrant times in their lives come when they're learning about something, no matter what it is. There is no greater sense of*

Daniel, the Author, and Mary Kiernan, at the Film Premier of "My Left Foot"

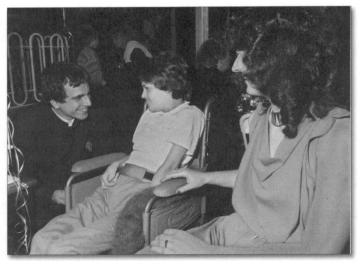

Daniel, Mary Kiernan, and Joan McNamara, at reception for "My Left Foot"

satisfaction than that. I'm always learning as I begin to approach this work. You need a shared purpose but also a shared folly as well, with the people you are going to work with. You never know if you can still do this thing, and it doesn't matter whether you've had five years off, or a few months. And whether you can find this particular thing and be true to it. People imagine there's some scientific process by which you strut this illusion. But there's no guarantee you will actually find this intangible thing that you're looking for. It always seems like you're in an experiment that could go horribly wrong. You have a sense of it, when you've found it, but the sense that you might not have found it is a very disturbing thing The moment you step out on to a film set, you're revealing yourself, not learning, and at the end of that period, of course, you feel a sense of emptiness – this feeling of 'Is that all there is?' There is a sense of loss, as well, because you're giving it up. Giving it over. There is this need for generation and this period of time afterwards is one, I think of as lying fallow. You can't use the field because it's been grazed so much"[20]. Daniel recalled the *"intoxicating sequence"* he felt when he first read the script for the film. *"It described Christy's foot in a lengthy opening sequence, reaching into his record collection, choosing a record, putting it back and picking another one, switching the turntable on, putting it on the turntable, and then delicately placing the needle on a particular place. That whole sequence was without dialogue, and I remember the very powerful visual sense Jim (Sheridan) was able to create"*[20b].

Daniel lived locally for the duration of making the film and was a familiar figure in the Sandymount area. The public did not intrude in his privacy. On one particular evening, I met him outside my house. He was full of enthusiasm for the nearby Dublin and Wicklow mountains, insisting that the best way to cross them was by bicycle. He appeared such a gentle figure himself that he elicited that aspect of people's characters. I could well imagine why women were totally smitten by him.

One particular criticism about casting Daniel Day Lewis and Hugh O'Connor as Christy Brown came from disabled actors groups. They argued that the part should have gone to an actor with cerebral palsy. There was little support for this view in Dublin, given the commercial realities involved.

It is traditional at the end of filming that the crew have a celebratory party before they all go their separate ways. I was invited to the Ardmore Studios in Bray for the occasion and enjoyed it thoroughly. I was particularly happy to meet Hugh O'Connor, his father John and his mother Mary, whom I had known several years earlier. The crew took up a donation for our school on the night. The first preview of the film, *"My Left Foot"*, took place on a Monday morning in the Savoy cinema in O'Connell Street. We took all the pupils along. Those who had been in the film were most excited. It got everybody's undivided attention. I was standing at the rear of the cinema. At the very end, Daniel, whom I had not noticed earlier, approached me almost nervously and inquired as to what I had thought of it. *"Very authentic"* I replied, *"you did a remarkable job. Congratulations"*.

He was visibly relieved. The film had focused on the character of Christy Brown, his personality rather than his life story, the details of which were often fictionalized in the movie. Some of those who had played a role in his life were sorely disappointed with the character of Dr. Eileen Cole in the film. Dr. Patricia Sheehan, in particular was most critical. She was of the opinion that the scene in the restaurant when Christy went berserk was totally out of character and seriously demeaned his reputation. She also felt that the scene in the public house where the family get involved in a major fight was Stage Irish, intended only to appeal to an American audience. In retrospect, and particularly after writing a biography of Brown, I think that Dr. Sheehan's criticisms were overstated. The premiere of the film also took place in the Savoy, with the proceeds going to the Rehabilitation Institute and the Irish Wheelchair Association. Tickets were fifty pounds each. We purchased two; three of us attended the cinema and five the reception at the Powersourt Town House. Many celebrities attended it, though it was difficult to meet everybody. Daniel gave our table a lot of attention, including, as it did, one of the important guests, Mary Kiernan. I was later most disappointed to discover that several people closely associated with Christy, including his wife Mary, were present at Powerscourt and I missed the opportunity to meet them.

The film was a popular success worldwide. It received five Oscar nominations in 1990. Daniel for Best Actor, Brenda Fricker for Best Supporting Actress, Jim Sheridan for Director, Shane Connaughton for Best Adapted Screenplay and Noel Pearson for Best Picture. Daniel and Brenda Fricker won Oscars. Daniel was astonished and made his way very stiffly to the stage to receive his award from Jodie Foster. He tried to compose himself before uttering, *"You have just provided me with the makings of one hell of a weekend in Dublin"*. He added, *"I am truly grateful to you, that in giving me this award, you are encouraging Christy to carry on making his mark"*. He described his reactions to Gay Byrne on the *Late Late Show* saying, *"I was sitting in the front row, the same row as Jim Sheridan and his wife Fran. I was sitting next to Alison Brantley, who was involved in distributing the film in the States. I had Jessica Lange on the other side. The truth is when the thing was announced I felt the blood run into my shoes and I think Allison had to push me out of the chair, because I was so stunned by the announcement. The journey across the stage to the wee table where you put the award seemed miles. The truth is that I wasn't able to enjoy it at all, because I actually felt it like being in a car accident or something. I was so shocked when the news came up. I guess that's what happens to everyone; you don't realise what it's going to mean to you until the moment arrives. All the inspiration and all the strength that we had in the making of the film came from Christy Brown"*.

I was personally sorry that Noel Pearson did not also win as he intended to begin his acceptance speech with words associated with Croke Park on All Ireland Day, "Ta an-athas orm an corn seo a ghlacadh...".

Later that night Daniel told an RTE camera crew, *"Your ears are just expecting to hear anyone else's name but your own. And when I heard my own, I think someone had to push me out of my chair, all the blood just drained out of me, you know, I feel quite overwhelmed"*. There was great rejoicing all over Ireland at the Oscar successes. A civic reception was organised by Dublin's Lord Mayor, Seán Haughey, at St. Patrick's Hall in Dublin Castle for the returning heroes. Daniel, Noel Pearson, Brenda Fricker and Jim Sheridan were presented with Cavan Crystal cups. Daniel told the gathering, *"I am so happy the weekend in Dublin has finally started. I am constantly astonished by the amazing welcomes I have had in this city. I never make plans to leave Dublin"*. Mona Byrne said, *"Christy is in heaven saying, have a great time and have a sup on me"*.

'OSCAR' VISITS

The following Monday morning I had an appointment at Ballinteer Community School. Before I left Sandymount, I told a staff member that though there had been no contact and that nothing had been arranged, I would not be surprised if Day Lewis turned up at the school that day. I asked her to 'keep an eye out', just in case. Less than half an hour after my departure, Daniel and his sister Tamasin, arrived on foot at the school. He had a duffle bag slung over his shoulder with 'Oscar' within. In a gesture that was typical of the man, so generous and unassuming, he spent the whole morning going from class to class introducing 'Oscar', meeting the children, signing numerous autographs and having scores of photographs taken. When the word went out that he was in the school, people from all over the centre arrived to witness and enjoy the occasion. When I returned to school, the party was over, and I never did get to see 'Oscar', though for the previous three years we had enjoyed being on the periphery of a great Irish adventure. Sometime later I was walking in the Irishtown Nature Park and could hear, to my astonishment, somebody running furiously downhill, calling out a strange sound, as if being attacked or attacking. I stood clear to allow this person plenty of leeway. As the person passed, I realised it was Daniel dressed in some strange 'Indian' garb. He was so engrossed and going so fast that I knew it would have been a mistake to attempt to speak to him. It was only later, when I read about his preparation for his role in *'The Last of the Mohicans'*, I realised what he had been up to that summer's evening.

Though that was the end of Day Lewis' direct contact with the school, he continued to assist individuals when he could. The following year he opened a painting exhibition at the Guinness Hop Store for a past pupil named, Clare Louise Creedon. In December1998, he launched an exhibition of paintings by another past pupil, Stephen Walsh, at the Bank of Ireland Arts Centre in Dublin. On that occasion Daniel's wife, who had only recently given birth to their first child, accompanied him. I remember introducing my daughter Fiona to Daniel. They both had spent the previous summer at Cape Cod. When he sought to establish common threads about the place with her, Fiona laughed and said, "I don't think you would have been frequenting the same sort of places as me". A rather sad postscript to the story is the that both ladies with whom Daniel had spent quite some time with in Sandymount, had naturally become very fond of him, Mary Kiernan and Helen Curtis, died soon afterwards. He was abroad on both occasions but sent large flower wreaths to both funerals.

Christy Brown paints with his left foot.

Out for a drive, (from left) Beth, Dec, Christy and friend.

CHAPTER 4

'CHRISTY BROWN'S WOMEN'

I did not delay very long in accepting the offer of Mrs Caitriona Maguire and Dr. Patricia Sheehan's letters from Christy Brown. There were about sixty letters in all. Each lady lovingly introduced each and every letter to me. Dr. Sheehan withheld at least two letters as being 'too sensitive'. When I read these letters I was immediately impressed by their authority and felt they could be a fitting testimony to his memory. Having digested the letters carefully, I returned to both women for two in-depth interviews. While both women had a deep and long standing relationship with Christy and his family, those relationships were very different. Caitriona, though becoming involved initially in a professional social worker environment, developed a deep affection for Christy. He certainly loved her and one of the most painful days of his early life was when she arrived at the Brown household wearing an engagement ring.

She tended to his youthful attempts at reading and writing. Later, as she realised the depth of his intellect, she came to be in awe of him. Dr. Sheehan never felt like that towards him. He was an adult when they first met. She retained much of a professional attitude, while becoming his sounding board for emotional outbursts.

Christy wrote to both women in some detail about the love of his life, the American, Betty Moore, to whom he dedicated his famous book, *Down All the Days*[21]. I had decided to attempt a biography of Christy. Like my earlier '*Memorial Day*', its execution was to be much delayed. I contacted Christy's widow, Mary Brown. She was very encouraging and gave me permission to use the letters in any way I wished. While there was a lot of information in the letters, I needed more sources.

I began to seek out and interview many of the Brown family, and others closely associated with the story. It became apparent that his story and the founding and early development of the National Association of Cerebral Palsy Ireland were inextricably linked. Dr. Robert Collis, the founder of the Association, had been Christy's early physical and literary mentor. He had Christy's medical condition diagnosed and put in place a therapeutic programme to ameliorate it. He had proof-read several drafts of Christy's early life story, '*My Left Foot*', which was eventually published in 1954.

In one letter to Dr. Sheehan in 1959, Christy adverts to the rumour that Collis was the real author of that book. He wrote, *"Many intelligent people believe that it was Collis who really produced that book, and I was a tag. I have met several persons, friends and strangers alike, who hold that opinion, and God bless them, I would not dream of disillusioning them by getting red faced and outraged and claiming damages for libel, in order to reaffirm my literary paternity"*[22]. In 1956, Christy took the almost unprecedented decision, for a patient, to discharge himself from the Clinic at Sandymount. He explained it to Dr. Sheehan; *"I was convinced that to remain on at the Clinic would be a selfish and unnecessary waste of both my own and the Staff's time and energy. I simply felt that I had reached my pinnacle of progress and could advance no further. Or perhaps I should say - intrepidly – that the Clinic had reached its peak of assistance and could benefit me no further... My treatment reached a point where it was all like a circus roundabout, going about and about, yet always at the same place at any given time. It was like a repeating decimal"*[23]. When Dr. Sheehan continued to give him speech therapy at his home, this caused a serious breach with Sandymount. When I interviewed Dr. Sheehan she made a remark that has resonated down the years with me. She said, *"Sandymount was always an unhappy place"*.

The other main interest for me in the letters was the relationship revealed between Christy and the lady from Stanford, Connecticut, Betty Moore. Betty was a married woman with young children, who started a correspondence with Christy after the publication in 1954 of *'My Left Foot'*. She often invited him to come and stay with her family. The idea of travelling to the 'new world' became a driving force in his life. A trip to the USA was a marathon journey and Christy realised that he would require a 'minder' for it. His enforced presence at the American Embassy in Dublin, escorted by Fr. Michael Cleary, was an hilarious exercise as the officious lady clerk insisted he sign the forms himself. In the summer of 1960, Robert Collis, who earlier had to abandon his medical practice in Dublin and move to Nigeria for personal reasons, was travelling to New York via Dublin. He offered to assist Christy on the fifteen-hour journey[24].

IN CHRISTY'S OWN WORDS

Christy wrote to Caitriona Maguire, *"Betty was there to meet us when we landed at Idlewild. You will understand this was our first meeting outside of our letters. She wore an orange dress, and as we came through the customs gallery she waved to us and lifted her arms above her head in a victory salute...she is the most wonderful person imaginable, humorous, gay, thoughtful, practical when it comes to dealing with me, oh so many things in one!"* Christy loved America and with Beth and her husband's assistance, amazed himself by becoming more independent than he thought possible. If he had a problem, America had a solution. In one letter to the Good Samaritan Caitriona, he wrote about what it was like to shed your dreams and fantasies and face reality.

He said that Beth and he had shared five astonishing years of intense and candid correspondence, and had in that time come to know and understand the peculiar nature and mould of each other's character, with a knowledge that in some aspects went deeper than 'actual', or physical experience and encounter. Then they came face to face, and the reality never matches up to the ideal. At first he was confused and frightened. Gradually he began to accept the reality. He wrote, *"The reality assumes a sweetness and vividness of its own, a keen, moving and fluctuating life that was before unknown and impossible in your dream-world of perfect living and love .You threw off the shinning cloak of dreams and put on the plain cloak of reality*[25]*"*.

After Christy returned to Dublin, he fell into a severe depression. He told Dr. Sheehan, *"it was like re-entering a prison cell after one glorious spell of freedom in the broad world outside"*. The whole purpose of his existence was to return to Beth as soon as possible. That was not to prove easy. Five years passed until they again met. Betty and her husband were on a European tour and, not surprisingly, Dublin was on their itinerary. Christy was exhilarated to discover that their love remained as strong as ever. He told Caitriona, *"I thought that after five years, and all that happened in between, but nothing had changed, nothing at all, to either of us. I knew the love would still be there; that can never alter. But it is one thing to love, and quite another to want. And that is what surprised me, dismayed me, tormented and delighted me – that we should still want each other, not just as much, but more than ever"*[26].

In the winter of 1967 Christy again visited Betty for a stay of several months. This was to be a working visit. Since the publication of his first book in 1954, he had not been able to complete a second. Betty decided that she would provide him with a suitable working environment and become his editor. It was a strained time as Betty insisted on several hours of work daily before any alcohol was provided. She also proved a stern critic, something he found difficult to take. When he suggested that some praise might be in order, she replied that he had got too much of that in the past. As the weeks passed, Beth gradually began to warm to the material Christy was producing. By early 1968, before he returned to Dublin, Christy had written half of what was to be his *magnum opus*, *'Down All the Days'*. It was published in the autumn of 1970 and carried the dedication, *For Beth who, with such gentle ferocity, finally whipped me into finishing this book..."*

Betty travelled to Dublin for the Irish launch of the book at the Bailey pub. She and Christy managed to spend a short holiday outside Dublin together. He later travelled, with his brother Seán, to the USA for the American launch. They both stayed with Betty for four months and travelled extensively with her to publicise the book. This included an interview on *'The Frost Show'*, from New York. Christy wrote to Caitriona Maguire, *"Life is now Elysian, Beth is nearby and I am happy...she's blooming. I come fully alive when she is close by. It's extraordinary, like so many doors and windows opening, pouring in the light. I'm afraid I'm a goner"*[27].

The book was proving a huge international commercial success. Back home Christy bought out the family home for one of his brothers. He himself moved out of the city and into one of two interconnecting bungalows that he had built in Rathcoole, County Dublin. One of his married sisters moved into the other bungalow. In Connecticut, Betty Moore was in some distress as details of Christy's plans for their ongoing relationship together, came to the attention of her family. She was surprised then to receive a letter from him, which to her reading, indicated that he had been discussing their situation with a third party, and was possibly having second thoughts about their relationship. He talked about the necessity for her to come and stay with him for at least one month, so that he could make a final decision. She replied that they surely had spent enough time together over the years for him to know all there was to know about her. She agreed to come to London in August 1971, to meet him and do some serious talking. They went on a motoring holiday together and never met again.

Two years earlier, Christy had met Mary, a younger and prettier woman, whose lifestyle he really did not know at all well, but with whom he had become infatuated. They were to marry the following year. Some saw Mary as Christy's Good Samaritan.

BETRAYAL

Betty Moore knew that Christy had been working on a novel based on his experiences in America. She became fearful least it invade her and her family's privacy. She sought, unsuccessfully, the return of her letters. Christy's new book had the hero reject his erstwhile literary mentor and seek to create his own fashion. He would be no acolyte of any brave, forgiving woman. At the end of everything, he wrote, they could only look at each other, like two unhappy strangers, who had shared a certain short unscheduled journey together, without anything but the most ordinary words passing between them. The story line of the new book must have hurt Beth Moore and her family deeply, but it was indicative of how selfish, even ruthless, Christy could be. The dedication of the book, titled "*A Shadow on Summer*", was to his wife and read, "*For Mab, deliverer of all my dreams, taking me ever towards morning*". The Browns lived for a time in Rathcoole before moving to Ballyheigue in Kerry. Christy, who had become an international celebrity, continued to publish novels and poetry. Later they moved to Parbrook in Somerset, where Christy died prematurely in 1981, at the age of forty-nine years. The odyssey of his short life was and will remain an inspiring story. Dr. Sheehan expressed grave misgivings to me about the circumstances of his death. When my biography, titled "*Christy Brown's Women – A Biography*" was launched at Sandymount in 1998, most of the Brown family in Ireland were present. Mary, unfortunately, could not travel from England. All the many ladies who had ministered to him during his life attended. Several spoke movingly. Peter Sheridan, who with his brother Jim, who had put on a stage adaptation of '*Down All the Days*' earlier in the year, performed the launch.

The printers had provided me with a large copy of the cover picture of Christy Brown, which was much admired at the launch. I later hung this in the school at Sandymount and had intended to leave it there on long-term loan. Within a few years Christy Brown was again to become *infra dig* at Sandymount. The Association, then called Enable Ireland, had opened a new centre at Tralee and named it the *Christy Brown Centre*. After I had completed an exhibition on Christy Brown at the Bank of Ireland Arts Centre in Dublin, I offered to mount it at the *Christy Brown Centre* in Tralee. The offer was declined. Within a short time, the centre dropped his name entirely, believing that it might have had negative connotations. When in 2000, President McAleese was formally opening the new school and clinic at Sandymount, I had placed the Christy Brown portrait and one of Pope John Paul II in a prominent position in the school. The portrait of the Pope had hung in the school for over twenty years. I was asked, however, to remove both portraits. The reasons stated were that a representative of the Muslim community was expected, and as for Christy Brown, I was informed that, *"We want to get away from all that"*. Thus once more Christy Brown had become *persona non grata* at NACPI. I later donated, on long-term loan, the Christy Brown portrait to the Dublin Writers Museum in Parnell Square. The subtitle of my book was, '*Including the founding of Cerebral Palsy Ireland by Robert Collis'*. It was, ironically, the Central Remedial Clinic which assisted with the publication of the book. The dedication was very important to me, as it afforded an opportunity to remember many friends, and make good on promises I had made to many bereaved families. It read, This book is dedicated to the memory of the following people:

"Declan Killeen, Keith Hackett, Niamh Coughlan, Donnchadha Walsh, Stephen Cruise, Niall Culligan, Michael Byrne, Rebecca O'Neill, Angela Boylan, Anne Marie Kiernan, Suzanne O'Dwyer, Nicola Duff, Eva Gannon, Ann Patricia Daly, Mary Kiernan, Joan Mary Murphy, Helena Murphy, Ann Perry, Michelle Haide, Susan Shorthall, Leon Broe, Peter Howe, Stephen Conway, Thomas Byrne, Gareth O'Kelly, John Thompson, Danny Thompson, Michael Farrell, Ken Farrell, Antonia Jordan, Keith Ryan, Derek O'Brien, Alan O'Brien, Michael Dunwoody, John O'Neill, Gary Nicholl, Mark Spandau, Robert Dempsey, Jason Scallon, David Lane, Peter Moran, Gerard Stenson, Andrew Burke, Raymond Collins Brian Kissane, Gerard Collins, Patrick Mulvey, Rebecca Kinsella, And Tomás O'Cuilleanáin".

Sometime later I did a challenging radio interview with Mary Duffy of RTE, for a programme called '*Not So Different'*. She asked me to justify my treatment of several important issues in the book. The book received a lot of publicity with a two- page extract appearing in the *Sunday Independent*. It was well reviewed in many publications. I received a large correspondence about it from people who had known Brown, and from people with disabilities. On the night the interview was broadcast in 1999, the new chairman of Enable Ireland, Donie Cashman, phoned his congratulations to my home, saying that my comments on the association were the best publicity he had ever heard for Enable Ireland.

EOGHAN HARRIS

A piece written about the book by Eoghan Harris in his column in *The Sunday Times* gave me much pleasure. It was headlined, *'Sinn Féin Risks Pushing Irish democracy Too Far'*. Harris called for the IRA to get real and wrote: *"What we need is a return to reality. We don't have to go to Goethe for it. Tony Jordan's new biography, 'Christy Brown's Women', should be required reading in republican circles. Jordan doesn't pretend that the disabled behave better than the rest of us. Brown was addicted to alcohol, adjectives and behaving badly to women – especially the American who helped him cut the verbosity from his best book, 'Down All The Days'. But Brown had one redeeming feature – that relentless realism which is the first casualty of fanaticism. For five years he carried on a romance with Moore by letter. Finally she brought him out to America. For a few golden weeks he basked in sunshine and her constant attention. But then it was over and he had to face the grey skies of Dublin. For a few days he sank into depression. But then, being Brown, he rose out of it and faced reality and himself. He wrote; "You threw off the shining cloak of dreams and put on the plain cloak of reality, and if at first the cloak was rather threadbare, the eternal and ever-changing woof of life sewed many fine and intricate patterns and colours through the otherwise sombre material"* [28].

Christy Brown in happier times with his wife Mary.

CHAPTER 5

BOYHOOD MEMORIES OF MAYO (BALLYHAUNIS)
EGALITARIANISM AND THE SPAILPÍNIDHE

In more recent times, Ballyhaunis, in east Mayo, has built a reputation for being the centre of an egalitarian society. This came about due to the relative ease with which members of the Pakistani community settled in the town, initially arriving in the 1970s, to work in the Halal factory. The green onion-shaped dome of their mosque, within a few hundred yards of St. Patrick's Catholic Church, is a familiar sight. There is now a multi-cultural cricket team in the town. But Ballyhaunis was always a rather free and easy going place, with very few levels of social strata. This has been put down to the absence of any 'Big House', or Protestant Ascendancy in the locality. We were all mostly Catholic peasants trying to survive. Ballyhaunis people have for long, unfortunately, had a reputation of not being very proud of their Gaelic heritage.

A front-page article in the *United Irishman* newspaper of the 20th of October 1900, recognised that and pointed, rather harshly, to possible reasons. It reads: "We learn from Ballyhaunis that an effort is being made there to waken up the town and neighbourhood. An excellent Irish scholar has been procured and an influential committee is being formed to further the good work. The fame which the grand old song, *Maire Bhéal Átha hAmhnais,* has for ages reflected on the town, ought to inspire all the young folk to activity in an effort which is now being made. Irish is still spoken all over the district, and as it is one of the places which supplies an enormous proportion of the *Spailpínidhe* who journey yearly to England, the existence of a strong Gaelic spirit in the town would do immense service to the cause. Our yearly visitors to England seldom come back improved by their visit. While they retained their Irish tongue and their native manners, the civilization of the Saxon had little effect on them: but since they have learned to despise their fathers' language and their fathers' ways, and attempted to ape the English, they have degenerated, in the great majority of cases, into mere boors: knowing nothing of the race from which they have sprung, imagining that it is a disgrace to be poor or to dress in anything but the style they see in England, they attempt the airs and accents of the British and render themselves ridiculous. It must be admitted that up to recently no attempt was ever made to show them the slavishness of such conduct.

Ballyhaunis, by becoming an active Gaelic centre, has now an opportunity of bringing back its young men to their senses, and by giving them some insight into the past of their country, showing them the littleness of Saxonism, compared with the pride of working to build up a self-supporting Ireland on Irish lines. Sonas do Bheal Átha hAmnais; Go n-eirighidh an obair".

Many years later when Douglas Hyde was President of Ireland, he was being driven through Ballyhaunis. As he drove down Abbey St and onto Bridge St, he noticed a group of teenagers sitting on a wall on the bridge. He instructed his driver to stop. Hyde turned down the window of the car and sought to engage the teenagers in Gaelic. They responded by mimicking and mocking him. He drove on. His secretary, who had also accompanied him, subsequently made a complaint to the local Garda Barracks. The miscreants were identified and warned as to their future conduct. I myself was confronted with this image of Ballyhaunis later in St. Jarlath's College, when a new Irish teacher inquired as to how many students were from Conamara and how many were from Ballyhaunis. These two places were fixed in his mind, as opposite poles of fluency and interest in the Irish language. I can recall feeling offended at his explanation, though I had to admit, there was some basis to it.

THE AUGUSTINIAN FRIARY
1348 - 2002

The only particular claim Ballyhaunis had to distinction was the presence of an Augustinian Friary on one of the several hills that make up the town. It survived Penal Times, being founded by Mac Jordan Duff Costello in 1348. It contains a collection of rare chalices and crosses. The fact of its existence has paradoxically been a source for some division, since the building in 1900, of a new parish church on another hill in the town. People give allegiance to one church or the other. At times the relationship between the two sets of priests was rather poor, with parish priests seeking to insist that every parishioner had an obligation to attend Sunday Mass in their parish church. In more recent times, with the drop off in religious vocations, the Augustinians experienced difficulties in 'manning' their church.

The possibility of the friary being closed and the property sold off caused consternation within the locality. This eventually occurred, in part, in 2002, when the Augustinian Order decided to cease their direct association with Ballyhaunis. They offered the church, graveyard, house and lands to the local community, if it could come up with a plan which would be consonant with the ethos of the Augustinians. The Order did not visualise selling the property to any commercial concern.

FINAL CLOSING OF THE AUGUSTINIAN ABBEY

The Augustinian Friary, after a sometimes bitter and acrimonious period, finally closed on Sunday 16 June 2002. It was a very sad day for many Ballyhaunis people. The *Western People* reported: "The dreary weather conditions reflected the sombre mood of those who ventured forth from their homes, either to attend the closing ceremony, or to participate in the peaceful protest at the Friary Gates". The controversy engendered among the locals, and within the Augustinian order itself, was echoed by the Provincial, Fr. Foley, as he apologised to both parties and prayed for, "the healing of any hurts that have been caused by our departure...these amenities and the graves of the friars who died here, will be a perpetual memorial to the Augustinians of Ballyhaunis". Archbishop Michael Neary of Tuam adverted to the tension that often exists in parishes where a public church run by a religious order may conflict with the diocesan church in that parish. Significantly, and greatly to his credit, he added: "If at times during those long centuries, the actions of the secular clergy of the Archdiocese towards their Augustinian brethren was less than friendly, less than brotherly, then we should say now, before it is too late that we are sorry for it, that we wished it had been otherwise and better"[29].

The keys of the Abbey were presented to Helen Hoban and Seamus O'Boyle, in a gesture symbolising the handing over of "the sacred space" that is St. Mary's Abbey, to the people of Ballyhaunis. The protesters on the occasion, who displayed many colourful placards, consisted mainly of dedicated members of the Friary congregation, who had been major fundraisers for the Abbey. They said that with one hundred members in the Irish province, the Augustinian authorities were acting prematurely and against the wishes of many in the Order itself.

At present a local committee is managing the building with support from Mayo County Council. The grounds are being developed into a park for the local community. The Augustinian Order has leased the property to the Abbey Partnership, which includes representatives of Ballyhaunis Community Council and Mayo County Council. In October 2006 a proposal to remove the timber pews and to have them replaced with tiered seating for concert purposes, was opposed as possibly leading to the secularisation of the whole church. The Convent of Mercy in Ballyhaunis stood on a hill opposite the Abbey.

Patrick G. Delaney wrote a poem called, *The Convent Hill*. It read in part.

Sweet Ballyhaunis of ancient grandeur,
all thy surroundings my memory fill,
and where e'er I wander my heart grows fonder,
of the dear old home by the Convent Hill.
I've roamed in childhood through many a wildwood,
round "Annagh Lake" and "Hazel Hill",
but my sweetest hours among fields and flowers,
were those I spent on the Convent Hill.

Convent of Mercy Classes circa 1948.
Author is circled centre of photograph.

1st. Class 1949
Author is circled fifth from left, front row.

The convent, too, has succumbed to changing times, as the numbers of vocations to religious orders dwindled dramatically. It was sold to commercial interests, which have developed the grounds with a house building programme ensuing. The Convent itself came to house asylum seekers from eleven countries, including Benin, Cameroon, Kosovo, Nigeria and Serbia. As is the case with many other towns around the country, there was no prior consultation with the local community by the *Reception and Integration Agency* established under the aegis of the *Department of Justice, Equality and Law Reform*. The beautiful Convent Chapel became a kitchen. However, the local Chamber of Commerce did, on receipt of official information, circulate a memo to all residents informing them of the situation. It said that, in 1991 there were 39 applications for asylum, and in 2000 this had risen to 10, 938. A policy of dispersal from Dublin became essential. Asylum seekers from over 120 countries were offered voluntary health screening for TB, HIV, Hep B and C and also vaccination, and were assessed for medical cards. They are entitled to full board and accommodation. Each adult received £15 per week personal allowance, each child £7.50 plus child benefit. The memo emphasised that the Agency had no plans for further accommodation centres in Ballyhaunis. The memo also said that it was hoped to establish a support group in Ballyhaunis to help the asylum seekers become involved in the life of the town. I understand that once more Ballyhaunis responded in an egalitarian fashion to this new challenge.

Four out of every five children born in Ireland between 1931 and 1941 emigrated in the 1950s. The main reason for this was that there was little for them to remain at home for. Society was stagnant. The emigrants wanted a future for themselves and their families. Strange to relate, alongside this massive hemorrhage, lived a prosperous business and professional class, who sometimes decried the action of their fellow citizens for leaving. The well off expected the poor to be satisfied with their lot. Some, such as James Dillon T.D., from Ballaghdereen, County Mayo, even spoke about restricting emigration to those who could prove that they were going to relatives abroad. Other politicians and officials did not believe that Ireland would ever be able to cater economically for all its citizens. They thought it better that high emigration occurred, so as to preserve the quality of life for those remaining at home[30].

The new Inter-Party Government set up a Commission on Emigration in 1948, which reported in 1954. It found that 'the fundamental cause of emigration is economic; the search for a higher wage and better living conditions than at home'. Remittances home had positive and negative effects. Sometimes they allowed other members of the family to remain at home, but in other instances they provided the means for others to emigrate[31]. During that first Inter-Party Government of 1948-51, Seán MacBride argued for a move towards industrialisation[32] and the Industrial Development Authority was established and economic planning accepted as essential government policy. In the early 1950s, Ken Whitaker pointed out that even employed people were leaving their jobs to better their prospects in Britain.

Author left watches as John Biesty holds the Sam Maguire Cup in 1950.

Josephine, Paddy, Bernadette, Tommy, Anthony and Jimmy Jordan at front, 1950.

Author with Mary Guilfoyle 1958.

Author's father Thomas Jordan 1894-1947.

Seán Lemass finally convinced the establishment that emigration was indeed caused mainly by economic forces and that Ireland must industrialize and create jobs. Much of the above experience was to be replicated in my own family's record. It has been calculated that during the 1950's-1960's Irish emigrants sent monies home to the value of 1.6 billion euro.

THOMAS JORDAN AND DELIA KEDIAN

My father, Thomas Jordan, was born in Cummer, in the parish of Aughamore, Ballyhaunis County Mayo, on 6 December 1894, to Anthony Jordan and Margaret Murphy from Mountain, Aughamore. They had been married on 14 February 1893. Thomas was one of six children. Urlar Lake separates the family home from Urlar Abbey, founded by the Carthusians in 1400. As the youngest son on a small farm, there were no prospects for him at home, so as a very young man he emigrated first to England and then to Detroit city. There he worked in the Ford Motor factory, manufacturing munitions during the war years of 1914-1918, returning to making cars thereafter. He later worked as a tram operator. Having accumulated quite a large sum of money, he left the USA shortly before the Wall Street crash of 1929. Back in Ballyhaunis, he tried to buy a small farm within a mile of the town, but was 'encouraged' not to make a bid, as a local man believed that he was entitled to buy the farm. Some time later he was able to buy another farm in the same village. He also purchased two sites on the edge of the town at Knox St. On one of them he built a substantial house, with five bedrooms, a shop, and large sheds at the rear accessible to carts and traps.

During the construction, on which he worked himself with the building contractor, Dennis Sloane, he noticed and was noticed by a lady cycling in and out of town to work. Her name was Delia Kedian. She was born on 11 October 1903 to Patrick Kedian and Margaret Kilkenny of Scrigg. They had been married on 3 February 1894. Her half brother, Thomas Kedian, a Lance Corporal in the Lancashire Fusiliers, had been killed during the battle of the Somme on the 7th of July 1916. His body was not recovered but he is commemorated on the Ulster Tower at Thiepval. A second cousin of mine, Private Billy Kedian, was the last Irish soldier to be killed in the Lebanon in 2000.

The Kedians came from Moneymore, a tiny village about two miles from the town. Mammy was beautiful and talented. She worked in B.T. Lynch's garage business on Main St as a bookkeeper, where her script and head for figures were highly regarded. She had been approached to marry a distant cousin of hers, but expressed no interest in that match. Instead, she inquired about the 'Yank' who was building the house on Knox St. He made similar inquiries. Soon an introduction was arranged at a crossroads dance at a village near Cummer, called Crossard. A man about to set up a shop needed someone who understood business and would be capable of managing such an operation.

A woman who had spent several enjoyable years working in the town for someone else would find the prospect of owning and running her own business very desirable. He was a shy man, while she was an extrovert. Soon, they fell in love and were married in the local church of St. Patrick's on 3 March 1930. They both had done well. Over the next seventeen years they had six children. The shop prospered, selling bicycle equipment, groceries, and large quantities of foodstuff for human and animal consumption. Tom Jordan rarely entered the shop but confined himself to working the farm. Their marriage was an extremely happy one. I was the second youngest child of the family of two girls, Bernie and Josephine, and four boys, Paddy, Tommy and Jimmy. But my experience within it was that of a one-parent child. My father died before I was five and I, unfortunately, have no memory of him. He died during the blizzard of 1947, when coffins had to be taken to the graveyard by sleigh. £1,200 remained in his bank account. The local paper, 'The Western People', carried this pious, though comprehensive, notice about him. I was happy to locate it, as it lists all the family connections.

OBITUARY OF MY FATHER

It is indeed with great regret we announce the death of Mr. Thomas Jordan which took place at his home Knox St., Ballyhaunis, on 20th February. The Deceased, who was about 50 years of age, was a native of Cummer, Aughamore, and for years carried out a successful cycle business in the town. The late Mr. Jordan was a man of exemplary character, and his gentle and unassuming manner gained for him the wide esteem and respect of a wide circle of friends. During his illness the deceased bore his suffering with resignation to the Divine Will and on the date mentioned passed peacefully away to his reward fortified by the rites of the Catholic Church, of which he was a devout member. To his sorrowing widow and young family we express our sincere sorrow on the great loss they have sustained. On the evening of his death the remains were removed to the Parish Church. On Friday, solemn High Mass was offered by Rev. John Lyons (recently ordained), assisted by Rev. Fr. Jennings C.C., and Rev. Martin Kenny, African Missions (cousin). Very Rev. Chancellor Prendergast, P.P., was master of ceremonies. After Mass the funeral took place to the new cemetery. The chief mourners were: Mrs Delia Jordan (widow); Paddy, Josephine, Tommy, Bernadette, Anthony and Seamus (children) ; Mrs Boland, Mrs Dolan, and Mrs Lowery (sisters); Anthony Jordan (brother); Mrs Finn and Mrs A. Jordan (sisters-in-law); Martin Boland, James Dolan, Patrick Lowery, John and James Kedian (brothers-in-law); John and James Dolan, Peter Lowery, Patrick Boland, John and Tony Jordan (nephews); Noreen Finn and Margaret Lowery (nieces). (American papers, please copy).

My brother Paddy, who was aged sixteen years then, would become my father figure. He fulfilled this role very well, as I was never conscious of any deficit in my life due to the absence of my father, until I was in my late teens. I had become very friendly with the Holmes family. I used to play golf regularly with both Michael and Conor. We would often call to each other's houses. On one occasion, while I was in their house, most of the family were present, except for their father, Bob. When he arrived in from work, I became conscious of a qualitative change his presence effected in the family grouping, something I had never preciously experienced My boyhood memories up to the age of thirteen or so, are of an almost idyllic existence. In summer we made the hay on our farm at Carrowrea, having earlier saved the turf on the nearby bog. Tea and sandwiches never tasted so good as in the bog or in the hayfield. I remember one catastrophe when the cattle ate our food. I often got the task of trampling on the cocks of hay as they were being built by my brothers, and then at a certain height having to jump clear as the apex was completed. One of two firm rules was that hay forks had to be stuck firmly into the ground when not in use, and rakes should not be left flat with their teeth protruding upwards. Of course, the rain intervened regularly and work already completed with dry hay had to be undone and reworked. I loved guiding the donkey as he pulled his cart, always fascinated by the reported significance of the cross on his back. I remember cutting turf myself on our farm one year, when my brothers had gone to England. I brought it home with the ass and cart during winter. I recall the wheel of the cart slipping into the ditch outside John Morley's house in Kilmannion. I sought John's held and he assisted me to lift it out onto the road. The whole operation was a nonsense exercise, as the turf was 'spaid' and burned like paper when put onto a fire. My brothers later kept cattle on the farm and it was my job to 'keep an eye' on them. Either Paddy or Tommy would then come home from England, when the cattle were due to be sold. I recall walking cattle to the fair in Kilkelly with Paddy, and standing around all day until they were sold. The notion of having to walk the cattle home again unsold was a nightmare scenario. On another occasion with Tommy, we nearly lost a beast in a bog hole. The more it struggled to get out, the further it sank. It was only with local help and by tying ropes around the beast that we managed to extricate him.

FAMILY HOLIDAYS

I usually had three holidays each summer. We invariably went either to the seaside at Salthill in Galway or Enniscrone in Sligo for one week, as a family group. In Enniscrone, we stayed at MacAvan's guesthouse. A seaweed bath at Kilcullen's, which dated from 1912, was considered a delicacy. I usually spent a few weeks on my Aunt Mary's farm in Errif, about two miles off the Knock road. There I collected the eggs and fed the hens and generally made a nuisance of myself. Once a week I waited expectantly for Aunt Mary to return from shopping in the town. She brought sweets to me.

The most pleasant memory of those holidays was that of being allowed harrow the ploughed ground behind a horse, amid the swelter of excited seagulls and crows. The methodical and symmetrical routine of team horse, harrow and human, breaking up the ground into smaller particles and extracting large stones from the clay, was very satisfying. It was so simple yet so effective. It was an experience in low technology, that has made me suspicious and resistant to high level technology.

CATHOLIC BOY SCOUTS

The third element of my summer holidays lay with an organisation that played a huge part of my early life. The Catholic Boy Scouts of Ireland had a troop in Ballyhaunis since 1942. It was named the 4th Mayo. I was a member for many years. During the winter we met weekly in the Scouts Den to practice a variety of skills. In summer we went on several weekend cycling weekends to Cong or Pontoon. We also had a major camp, lasting for a fortnight, in such places as Killarney, Dungarvan, Dublin, Enniscrone, Louisburg. We usually indulged in the game of cricket during these camps. In later years I became a keen admirer of the game and often nominated the forty minute confrontation between Michael Atherton, captain and opening batsman for England, and Allan Donald, the fast bowler from South Africa in the 1998 Test Match at Trent Bridge, as one of the greatest gladiatorial contests I ever saw. Atherton writing about it later said, *"Amid the intense emotion, the sledging and the noise of the crowd, both of us remained calm and focussed. There is a lot of talk about cricket being a team game, but in essence it is a battle of individuals, of batsmen against bowlers"*[32a].

One year we went to an international Scout Jamboree at Buckmore Park near Maidstone in Kent. The weather was so bad we christened the place Muckmore Park. My younger brother Jimmy was on this trip. On another occasion we camped at Glenstal Abbey in Limerick. The first night there, it rained intensely. I was in a two-berth bevy tent with John Biesty from Knox St. As the rain lashed down I dozed off. The sound of John's hand touching the ground around the tent awakened me. "Jesus, Anthony" he said, "we're being flooded". The water was seeping through the tent as it made its way down the steep incline. The scout motto was *"Bí Ullamh"* or *"Be Prepared"*. So we slipped on our raingear and dug a trench around the tent to catch the rain. We then dug a gully to redirect it away from our tent down the incline. Back in our warm sleeping bags we huddled together and listened to the incessant rain. Within about ten minutes we discovered that our trench had not been dug deep enough as it filled up, overflowed and saturated the inside ground. Before we could decide on further action someone clapped on our tent with orders to evacuate to the Abbey. The Boy Scouts had an estate in the Dublin Mountains called Larch Hill. It overlooked the city and at night the vast array of lights resembled the Milky Way to boys from the country. I spent many happy times there, occasionally doing overnight hikes across the mountains. We usually kept a close eye out for the Devil, while passing the eerie hulk of the Hell Fire Club. Paddy Forrie from Knox St., John Morley from Kilmannon and the inimitable Seamus Durcan from Abbey St., were the Scoutmasters during my happy time in the 4th Mayo.

I attended the *Morris Tribunal* in late February 2007 to hear Jim Higgins MEP giving evidence. He explained how he had referred to an ex-Garda as a Garda, by saying, *"Once a boy scout, always a boy scout"*. A smile passed my face as I heard a fellow Ballyhaunis man, and a fellow boy scout, refer to an era where he and I, and so many others, had such fun.

YOUTHFUL PLEASURES

I attended the local convent school in Ballyhaunis until I was seven. The one memory I have of that is of Sister Oliver, who had beautiful pale skin. I met her in 1999 and she still retained her good looks. After First Communion, segregation began as the boys attended their own school on the edge of the town near the graveyard. There were three teachers there. Mrs Fahey, a kind motherly figure. Mr. MacNicholas, a man with a penchant for cruelty, as he often insisted a pupil place his hand on the table as he was being slapped. Bill Mulligan was the Principal. I discovered in later years that he got his post ahead of a neighbour of mine, Michael A. Waldron LLB[33], due to the fact that De Valera's Fianna Fáil had not come to power a few weeks earlier in 1932. His main interest was in cattle. He lived on his farm about three miles outside town at Coolnafarna. In the mornings we could track his car as it made its way towards the school. He was a binge teacher. He could spend several weeks concentrating on the same subject. Mathematics or 'Cow Sums'. *"If a man went to the fair to buy or sell a cow"*, as we used to refer to them, was his favourite subject, with history in second place. He used to season his caning rods up the chimney. Pupils had to contribute five shillings or quantities of turf to heat the school.

Many attended school barefooted in summer. I can recall a local curate examining senior pupils in catechism before a Confirmation ceremony. He attempted to cane one boy and chased him round the classroom. As Bill Mulligan guarded the door, the pupil made good his escape by jumping out through an open window. At my own confirmation ceremony, on 4 March 1951, only the brighter pupils were sent up to the altar to be examined by Archbishop Joseph Walsh. The rest were examined in their seats by visiting clergy. About twenty of us approached the altar as if for Communion. I remember that the row of older boys in front of us were all put back for further examination by the Archbishop, as some had not answered satisfactorily. He asked me to explain the term, 'wrath'. There was a boy in our class from Holywell, named Tommy Biesty. His father, Bob, kept stallions. Bob Biesty regularly brought one of the stallions to the back yard of Dillon's public house on our street. There the stallion 'served' a variety of mares. I was always fascinated by this spectacle and it was my first introduction to sex. The majesty of the stallion, immaculately groomed and preening, as he went proudly about his work was an awesome sight. Of course, at first, he had to be careful that the mare was receptive and often had to initiate a ritual foreplay. The violent thrusts of the stallion, mounted on the mare, always made me wonder how she could endure such violence.

Sex was a constant fascination for us boys. I encountered human sex on an early occasion. A common 'game' was to trace a courting couple and to get as close to them as possible and 'see' what happened. Bertie Dillon and I once followed a couple down Knox St. where they turned in the New Road and lay up against a grassy bank. We climbed inside the bank and crept along until we were directly inside their position. We could hear the man trying to coax the woman to allow him to "do it", as she asked him not to. Bertie and I were almost in hysterics with suppressed laughter. Eventually we had to retreat lest we be caught. The couple knew both of us well and the man would have given us an awful hiding if we were discovered. All during my boyhood, I understood that there was a house on the periphery of the town, where married men could go to buy sex. A man who lived on our street was wont to offer us boys one shilling, if we would hold his exposed erect penis in our hands. I often encountered his offer to groups of boys, but I never witnessed anyone take the shilling.

Some of my school friends' families, like myself, had shops. On one occasion three of us, Bertie Dillon, Tommy Moran and myself, volunteered to supply cigarettes for an illicit smoke in the loft of the Scoutmaster Paddy Forrie's house on Knox St. This was to be a real smoke, with inhaling compulsory. As we sat expectantly on the upper floor, I inhaled one and a half *'Player's Please'* and got violently sick. I never wished to smoke again. A butcher on our street named Brody Morley had his own particular game at our expense. He would put a penny in the palm of his large hand and place his thumb on top of it. We were then invited to try to prise it free. No matter how hard I tried, and I often did, I never succeeded, nor did Brody ever let me have one of his pennies. How he enjoyed annoying me, especially when I cried in exasperation! I should have kicked him on the shins!

STREET GAMES

We played street games of all descriptions. There was no differentiation between the boys and the girls. The term 'street games' is accurate because most of them were played on the street or in a field called the 'Lochan' just off the street. There was little vehicular traffic on Knox St., so it really belonged to us. Football, hurling, rounders, handball, conkers, tick, fighting, hide-and-go seek, all had their season. Eamon O'Toole, Teresa Moran, Noreen Morley, John Morley, the Rattigans, the Dillons, and above all Tony Greene, were among my closest companions. During autumn we collected hazel nuts and blackberries from the woods near the *Giant's Hollow*.

This was a symmetrical cavern, the size of a football field, deep within which we played rolling games, yet always ready to escape fearfully, when someone decided to scream that he could hear the giant's steps lumbering towards the hollow. After the October Devotions, which consisted of the Rosary and Benediction, we played with the girls in the bushes in the churchyard.

When I met one of those girls, Fionnuala Leetch, some forty years later at a reception in the Conrad Hotel, after a coming out recital by Maria McGarry in the National Concert Hall, she authenticated my memory by asking, did I remember the fun we had with those games after the October Devotions?. Just the other day as I walked past Sandymount Green in Dublin, I noticed many unclaimed chestnuts on the footpath. I mentioned this to my daughter Fiona as a metaphor for the changing times. She replied that the children of today were too busy with their play stations to bother with chestnuts.

INTROIBO AD ALTARE DEI

I spent several years as an altar boy in the parish church. It had its advantages. We got to dress up in uniform on a regular basis. When we served at High Mass for a funeral, we often got a shilling from the sacristan or the undertaker. We also got released from school for the morning. The liturgy and ritual of the High Mass was of great beauty. Four priests participated, one of them usually a Friar from the Augustinian Abbey, each standing behind the other on the ascending altar steps. I can still hear Fr. Tom Rushe intoning the '*Dies Irae*' with great gusto. We had to learn the Latin responses for the mass. The priest began '*Introibo ad altare Dei*' and the server responded, '*Ad Deum quae laetificat juventutem meam*'. The 'Stations' were another perk. This consisted of a Mass said in peoples' houses attended by all their friends and neighbours. This was a custom which begun during the Penal Days. The Stations were held on a rotational basis, usually in the country. Afterwards, there was a meal provided. The servers got a full day off school for the occasion. The Stations happened only at specific times of the year and the priest would announce their location at Sunday Mass. I always thought the names of the villages concerned rather romantic; "Scrigg, Leo and Coiltibo", "Cave, Togher and Carrowrea", "Dernacong, Brackloon North and Sackahard". When Tom Leetch became Head Server, he instituted a prize for the 'best server'. My namesake, Jarlath Jordan from Upper Main St., (who is now a neighbour of mine in Sandymount and an daring world traveller) and myself shared first prize.

DEATH OF A CAT

The most traumatic event of my boyhood, and something, which still causes me pain, concerned our family cat. He was a sleek black prowler, whom I loved. The archway leading from our yard directly onto the street was most dangerous, unless one stopped to check if the roadway was clear. The cat had used several lives before he was eventually run over by a truck and had his back legs mangled into smithereens (little pieces). The cat then disappeared for a few days before, in desperation, reappeared for food. As soon as I got a good look at his terrible state, I knew what I had to do. I prepared a canvas bag and weighed it down with several stones. With a saucer of milk I enticed the cat to approach me. When he did, and began to sip the milk, I grabbed him and pushed him, resistant, into the bag and tied it with some twine.

Then I began my sorrowful journey along the tree-laden path, on which we played, at the back of the houses on Knox St. It was the way we went to the river in summer to swim. But this time I continued further along the path, towards a bend in the river at the bottom of a hill near the Augustinian Friary, carrying my live load. He continued to seek a way out of the bag. I did not speak. I dared not. I remained rigid, determined, single - minded, moving purposively ahead. At the deep water's edge, I dropped the bag into the river and forced it beneath the water with a broken stick. While I still held the top of the bag, the cat fought fiercely for escape, for air, for life. I denied them to him and he gradually weakened, until suddenly all struggle ceased.

I released the bag into the running water. I did not watch it float away. As I turned to come home, I stood upright and screamed, shouted aloud, howled and cried profusely. Then I ran along the path hitting protruding branches, not caring if they hurt me, knowing that I had done a terrible deed, which should be punished. I did not run directly homewards but turned towards another part of the river, where we used to swim in summer. I ran through P.A Waldrons's field, Webb's field, Johnny Gilmore's field, still screaming, mad, for what I had done; mad for what I knew I had to do. On reaching the river again, I fell on the grassy bank and pummelling it with my fists, I cried for my sleek beautiful black cat.

"THE BRILLIANT FIFTIES"

My brothers had racing bicycles and later motorcycles from an early age. Tommy was a mechanic and Paddy a joiner. Riding pillion and holding on tightly to them, as we sped along the roads was thrilling. Once, Tommy and I went on holidays to Salthill. We went for a spin in Conamara and we came to a dead end on a roadway. I always thought roads went on forever. My brothers were excellent footballers. It was always thrilling to see them play for Ballyhaunis. Paddy, who was a most tenacious footballer, later played senior football for Mayo, Westmeath and Meath.

Indeed during the summer of 2004, when Westmeath made their historic breakthrough by winning the Leinster Championship in Croke Park, I immediately phoned Paddy at his home in Solihull to tell him of that victory. Both brothers insist that the 1950s were exciting times for them. Mayo won the All Ireland championship in 1950 and '51. A neighbour's son, Seán Flanagan, captained the team. Trips to Dublin were common, as Mayo people walked tall. I know of nothing which inspires a county's people more than winning an all Ireland senior title. Unfortunately I was too young in the early fifties to appreciate it. Mayo has not succeeded in winning one since, despite some valiant attempts to do so. In the fifties dances in McGarry's Hall on Clare St. went on until the early hours of the morning. There was no shortage of female company and though wages were low, Guinness was cheap. My brother Tommy soon graduated to cars. He had a succession of them in the mid 1950s. I remember all the older members of the family, including my mother, driving to the Irish Grand National at Fairyhouse in County Meath one Easter Monday.

John McGahern recalled that era as he wrote of Patsy Conboy who set up a dancehall near where McGahern lived: *In spite of being denounced from several pulpits it prospered and Patsy Conboy became a local hero. People came by bus, by lorry, hackney car, horse trap, on bicycles and on foot to dance the night away. Couples met amid the spangled lights on the dusty dance floor and invited one another out to view the moon and take the beneficial air. "There wasn't a haycock safe for a mile around in the month of July"*[33a].

Mayo played in the senior All Ireland football finals in 2004 and again in 2006. Some counties would regard this as a measure of success, but Mayo cannot. Ignominious defeats convulsed Mayo folk.

Keith Duggan of the *Irish Times* came up with an entertaining theory. He wrote after the 2004 defeat: *"In a real sense, Mayo are a giant of the game and they can be relied upon to always produce attractive, and fairly regularly, exceptionally talented teams. But God above! There are times when they are as tragic as the Native Americans. So why have Mayo not won more All-Irelands? My theory is that it might come down to good manners. There is an aristocratic bent to Mayo society. They will never quit on this. That is what allows Mayo to retain their aristocratic air, their pomp. The castle may have been ransacked many times but the family was never evicted"*.

Until Mayo win another All Ireland senior football title, the people of that county, worldwide, will continue to feel bereft and not fully reconciled with modern Irish society. The place of sport and particularly Gaelic football, in the cultural life of the majority of Irish people, is of enormous import. This is in no way to minimise the remarkable achievement of the Mayo ladies football teams in winning four All Ireland titles in recent years. Indeed my two daughters and I have enjoyed to the full our visits to Croke Park on those memorable occasions.

ANNAGH MAGAZINE

The Ballyhaunis parish of Annagh has been producing a high quality magazine for the last twenty-five years. It has documented the local history of people and places and events. I began contributing to it in a strange circumstance. In 1984, to celebrate the founding of the GAA, it carried an article on those people from Ballyhaunis who had won All Ireland medals. My name was omitted by some error. My good friend, Tom McCormack later suggested that I contribute to the following year's issue. I set out to write about what Ballyhaunis then meant to me. To my surprise I discovered the answer lay with the people whom I had known and grown up alongside. Then I had to face the fact that most of those were either dead or no longer living in Ballyhaunis. The people that I had known no longer existed there. Thus Ballyhaunis had little current meaning for me. I was shocked by this discovery and decided that I could not conclude my article on such a note. I have contributed a variety of articles to *Annagh* during subsequent years and always await its publication with eager anticipation.

3rd Year Students, St. Jarlath's College 1957/58
Author is 5th from left front row.

CHAPTER 6

ST. JARLATH'S COLLEGE TUAM

CLERICAL POLITICS

For the boys who were boys when I was a boy

When I was thirteen or so, much of the fun and innocence in my life seemed to disappear abruptly. Up to then, it had been all thoughtless action with never enough hours in the day for me to do all the things I wanted to do. Two factors came together almost quite simultaneously to change all this. Three of my older siblings, Josephine, Paddy and Tommy, decided within the same year, to emigrate to England. They had each been gainfully employed, but yearned to travel and avail of the opportunity to better themselves economically. The family was shorn of its most vital members. In that same year of 1955, I was consigned to a boarding school, where the annual fee was about fifty pounds. Why this happened I do not know. My two sisters, Josephine and Bernadette, had attended the local girls secondary school, while the boys went to the local Vocational School, as would my younger brother Jimmy. There was no secondary school for boys in Ballyhaunis. As I would discover later from the Prior of the local Augustinian Church, their Order had been refused permission by Archbishop Walsh to open such a school in the town. The Prior said it was a matter of church politics taking precedence over local need, with the Archbishop protecting the diocesan seminary of St. Jarlath's from possible Augustinian competition.

Fr. Kieran Waldron, a Ballyhaunis man, working from the diocesan archives in Tuam, has done an invaluable service by documenting this unhappy episode in his excellent book, *Out of the Shadows: Emerging Secondary Schools in the Archdiocese of Tuam*, published in 2002. He writes that the Provincial of the Augustinian Order, Fr. Thomas Cooney, wrote to Archbishop Joseph Walsh on 2 May 1944, making a formal request to open a day school for boys in Ballyhaunis.

The Archbishop replied; *"I regret very much if I did not make it clear that the question of setting up such a school was a matter entirely for the Chancellor as Parish Priest. But should he decide to set up a school, or should any other Parish Priest come to such a decision, I should ask the Parish Priest concerned to have the school run by diocesan priests. We have quite a number of priests of the diocese trained – indeed we are in the fortunate position at present to have a number of our priests in England, America and Australia who will be returning to work in the diocese"*.

Fr. Waldron writes, surprisingly, that the Parish Priest in question, Archdeacon Geoffrey Prendergast[34], "did try to enlist the help of the De la Salle Brothers sometime in the 1950's to set up such a school". A diocesan run, boys secondary school was eventually opened in Ballyhaunis, in 1961. Thus, unfortunately, did many generations of boys from the Ballyhaunis district, miss the opportunity of availing of a secondary education, due to clerical manoeuvrings. However with the advent of free secondary education, for all in the late 1960's, a social revolution began which enabled most young people to access middle and later higher education. Thus the inherent qualities of the Irish nation were liberated for the first time.

ALL ABOARD THE BUS FOR TUAM

A big brown suitcase was purchased in Fordes of the Square in which to carry all my new belongings. The item on the prescribed list, which seemed strangest of all to me, was a laundry bag, which had to have my name stitched on to it. There were about ten boys from the town going to St. Jarlath's College for the first time. A visit to Archdeacon Prendergast P.P. was *de rigeur* for each of us. Because most people did not have motorcars, the journey to Tuam was made on the CIE bus, which travelled on to Galway. We waited outside Bertie Curley's shop near the Square for its 08.30 departure. Our suitcases were loaded on to the roof of the bus, where an indented shape gave them a secure hold. The bus conductor then covered them with tarpaulin in case of rain. Hurried goodbyes, some tearful, were made to parents and siblings by the first year contingent. The bus moved off and turned into Bridge St., out under the railway bridge to Devlis and right - handed at the fork in the road for Cloonfad. For some it was like going on a picnic but others, including myself, were full of apprehension. After passing through Cloonfad, County Roscommon, we came to Dunmore, County Galway, where several more boys joined us.

The first sighting of Tuam came at a right-angled bend on the road about three miles from the town. The tower of the cathedral came momentarily into view. It was to be a moment of nervousness on every occasion I witnessed it for the next five years. As the bus entered the narrow streets of the town, some experienced students approached the bus conductor, requesting the bus to stop at the Cathedral near the College entrance. This would have facilitated us by ensuring that we only had a short distance to carry our suitcases.

The bus driver, however, refused to stop and drove on through the town to the authorised stop at the railway station, over one mile from the College. There the luggage was unloaded and we boys had to begin the arduous task of retracing our way encumbered with heavy suitcases. We arrived piecemeal with sore hands, heavy hearts, and very vulnerable. The college did not appear so formidable from the outside. But within were long corridors, large panelled windows and huge bare soulless rooms called dormitories. First Year pupils, dubbed '*Connors*', were assigned to two such rooms.

The one to which I was directed had about sixty beds divided into three rows. It was nicknamed '*Kip*'. '*Paradise*' and '*Horse-box*' were names of other dormitories. There were literally no furnishings in the dormitories apart from about twenty wash hand basins and mirrors along one wall. All of my belongings had to remain in my suitcase under my bed for the year. No privacy was possible. In today's parlance it would be described as 'open plan'. For most this would have been their first time away from home and often their first occasion to wear pyjamas and underclothes. The only positive thing about '*Kip*' was that another boy from Ballyhaunis, Edward Moran, choose the bed next to me alongside a wall. We would be tennis partners during our sojourn in college.

THE DEAN OF DISCIPLINE

The bell rang the next morning at 06.30. We had twenty minutes to wash, dress and get down two flights of stairs, on our way to the Oratory for Mass at 07.00. If you were late you stood the risk of being accosted by the one sadistic priest it has been my misfortune to encounter. He was the Dean, Christy Langan. He was a good looking, meticulously coiffured man in his forties. He lived in a room on the first floor, strategically positioned near the stairs. If you were guilty of a misdemeanour, or if you were in the company of one who was guilty of a misdemeanour, or if you or he was thought to have been or might be guilty of a misdemeanour, you and he were invited to take up a position outside Christy Langan's door. There, in due course, vicious punishment might be meted out, using a long walking stick. He was charged with looking after our care and welfare. We young boys were completely at his tender mercy. Of course, most of the priests including the Archbishop knew of this harsh regime but nobody shouted stop.

A local barber used to visit the College once weekly. He would bring contraband sweets or '*mag*' for sale to the students. When Christy Langan discovered this on one occasion, he immediately ordered the barber off the premises. The student, whose head was half shorn, was instructed to accompany the barber to his premises in the town, to have the haircut completed. After Mass there was breakfast at 08.00.

The food was a real disaster. There was little of it, and it was mostly bread. I was hungry on a regular basis and as time went on survival was achieved only by the regular arrival of parcels from home. In the Refectory we sat on wooden benches, fourteen to a table. We rotated by one position each day, which meant that a different boy was at the top of the table each day. This was of enormous strategic import as the person occupying that position, divided the food and had first choice of the portions. To be at the bottom of the table often equated to very meagre rations.

Hogan Cup Champions 1959/60

Refectory St. Jarlath's 1950's

With breakfast eaten we had a free period, to take some air and exercise. This usually meant going on the '*Walks*'. The latter consisted of a tar macadam pathway, circumnavigating three football pitches facing the College. About six boys could walk abreast and it was the most common form of 'putting down time' in the College. You walked with your friends, waiting until such a group formed or arrived for you to join. Tradition decreed that boys from each year generally walked together, though mutual interests or common locality might occasionally dictate otherwise. One rather poor effort at a joke by myself and some of my friends held that the more frequently you 'did the walks', the quicker the holidays would come. Many did not appreciate it. From 08.30 to 09.30 we had morning study. This was a most important feature of College life, as it afforded a last opportunity to prepare work for early delivery, which might have been neglected for whatever reason. The Study Hall was another large room, which accommodated over three hundred boys. Each had a desk wherein books copies etc were stored in relative safety. Each year's grouping sat together. The Hall was patrolled by a Dean of Study, who was usually a young priest and thereby someone capable of a reasonable outlook. From 09.30 to 12.30 classes were held in forty-five minute periods. There were two streams to each year, with about thirty in each class. I was in the 'A' stream, as was my bedside partner. Some sets of twins were split on results based criteria. I was not aware of any distinctions being made between the two streams, except that in the 'A' stream, all took honours subjects in the Certificate Examinations.

The teacher of Irish was a priest from just outside the town of Ballyhaunis. His pedagogical philosophy was demonstrated early and often by his regular dependence on the use of a large leather strap. He identified himself, regularly as, 'a country boy from outside 'Bally-have-niss' and not a townie'. In 1958, to the great relief of many students, he left the College and in 1969, became a distinguished Archbishop of Tuam. When I read in his obituary in the *Irish Times* in March 2001, that he was 'a skilled teacher', I smiled ruefully. His successor in St. Jarlath's College began proceedings in our class by identifying the number of boys from Ballyhaunis and the numbers from Connemara. It appears that he understood both locations to be opposite poles for expertise in Irish. Indeed I had to smile ruefully on the morning of 20 July 2006, as I read a report from the previous day's proceedings from the McGill Summer School in Glenties Co. Donegal.

Senator Jim Higgins MEP, a native of Ballyhaunis and a contemporary of mine in St. Jarlath's College spoke about his own attitude to Irish. He said that Irish was his least favourite subject at secondary school and that he despised the language when he left. He said, *"There was the absolute insistence on grammatical precision. One could accept that there had to be a reasonable grasp of the nouns in their five declensions, but the verbs were beyond me for the most part... If you did not manage the gymnastics of grammatical correctness, one's jaw was likely to be met by an open hand as if he was hitting a half-solid against the back wall of an alley. Is it any wonder I hated Irish?"*

However, as an adult, Jim said happily, he had come to genuinely love the language. I have written my daily diaries in Irish for more than forty years and regard the language as one of the most fundamental aspects of our culture. Unfortunately the way Irish has been taught has put people off speaking it.

"BALLAGHDEREEN IS IN COUNTY MAYO?"

I was responsible myself for coming to the attention of another teacher, Fr. Colin Canavan of Conamara. He was a native Irish speaker, whose English I found extremely difficult to understand. He taught History and Geography. While listing the towns in County Roscommon one day, he included Ballaghdereen. This was contrary to my local knowledge and though I was only in the College a few weeks, I immediately sought to correct the 'mistake'. His reply was that the book stated Ballaghdereen was in Roscommon, so there! To the amazement and amusement of my fellow students I did not accept that as the final answer. In fairness to the teacher he allowed me to state my case. I indicated that during the previous summer I played juvenile football for Ballyhaunis in the East Mayo area championship. My *coup de grass* was to tell the class that among the teams we played was Ballaghdereen. I concluded, therefore, that it must surely be in County Mayo. At that, the teacher declared the matter decided, according to what the book said. I am amused at least once a year, when Patsy McGarry of the Irish Times pens an article seeking to put the record straight.

PV O'BRIEN

In general the level of teaching expertise was very low in St. Jarlath's. As I would discover for myself later, the Higher Diploma in Education, which was the recognised qualification for teaching at second level, did not equip one at all with the skills necessary for teaching. The one teacher who engaged me by his own personal enthusiasm for his subject was PV O'Brien. I still retain and use the copy of *Palgrave's Golden Treasury* we used with him all those years ago. As I read it, and I do regularly, I am listening to his remarkable voice. He told us that during 1958-9, he was going to ignore the Leaving Certificate Syllabus for 1959-60 and *"delve into the glories of English literature"*.

This did not meet with total agreement, as some students, who were intent on getting high grades in the Leaving Certificate, felt that we should be concentrating on that exercise and not wasting our time on frills. When Fr. O'Brien died in 1989, the *Tuam Herald* published an obituary stating that he had been born in 1921 and had taught in St. Jarlath's College from 1947-1968. He had been a leading figure in amateur theatre in the West of Ireland and a long time friend of Ray MacAnally, who had died only a week earlier.

Alongside the obituary, the *Herald* published a short letter from myself, which read: *"I see the death notice of Fr. Patrick Vincent O'Brien P.P. in this morning's paper (24/6/90). My mind goes back just over thirty years to St. Jarlath's College where the vibrant "PV O'Brien" taught English to a generation of Western boys. He never made free with his pupils but nevertheless was respected as a great teacher, in the classical mould. He attempted to expose his pupils to English literature through his own obvious love for it. His was no mere interest in helping people to pass examinations. I never met him in those thirty intervening years. But only yesterday as I was reading some poems from my 1958 copy PF Palgrave's Golden Treasury, the voice in my head was that rich western voice of "PV". Ar dheis De go raibh a anam".*

The teachers did not generally engage with the students, outside the classroom. There was no sense of an organic Catholic school community, growing together, as modern parlance might put it. A student quoted in the authorised College's Bi-Centenary publication of 2000, says: *"There was one thing lacking in my day. The priests were very much removed from the boys, and very formal in their dealings with them. Rarely would a boy be called by his Christian name and surname would be called out, but more often, the boy's Christian name would be unknown to the priest..."*[35]

After a dinner of some potatoes and tracings of meat, there was another short break before classes resumed until 15.30. Then the most satisfying period of the day, lasting for two whole free hours intervened. There was a different football pitch for each grade, minor, junior and senior. I was lucky enough to be big for my age and a fairly good footballer. I loved the game as it allowed me to express myself in a variety of modes, aggression, subtlety, comradeship, skill and a desire for success. I sometimes believe that I did little else during those five years except play football. During Saturdays and Sundays I might play as many as three games each day. Leagues of all kinds were organised to keep us busy.

The second period of study ran from 17.30-19.30. It was a long session. The Dean of Studies did not interfere unduly at whatever activity you pursued at your desk, provided that quietness was observed. One piece of entertainment practised regularly against the Dean was that of flicking a fountain pan full of ink onto his black soutanne, as he paraded up and down the hall. He would only become aware of it, if his hands came in contact with his wet garment. A vital piece of equipment in the hall, especially if one was involved in any nefarious activity was a hand mirror, to monitor the Dean's position. His most advantageous position was at the rear of the Hall or else up on his podium in the middle of the Hall.

The only place you could expect some privacy was in the toilet. But even that could not be guaranteed when Christy Langan went on the offensive against smoking. He would rush into the toilets and jump up on the chamber of any empty cubicle to peer over the wall into an occupied booth. Many students, including myself, read their correspondence there in relative privacy.

St. Jarlaths School 1959
Enda Colleran, Pat McGrath, Author.

Photograph of Leaving Cert. Class 1960
Author is 5th from left, front row seated.

Flushing toilets were a novelty for many of the boys, whose homes and schools would only have had dry outside toilets. Toilet paper was almost an unknown quantity, with students having to scavenge for paper to clean their bums. Supper at 19.30 consisted of tea and bread. We resumed study again for an hour from half past eight. Then it was time for the rosary in the Oratory followed by bed, with lights out at ten o'clock. The Dean usually patrolled all the dormitories at night, where the boys were at their most vulnerable. More boys got beaten in their beds more often than at any other location. A past student is quoted in the Bi-Centenary book;

"Discipline was strict, but the regime was relatively humane. You'd get 'batters' if you were caught smoking, for playing cards, for prompting at study and, in instances, for missing something in class. But when you got 'battered', you didn't mind, you accepted it. Mostly you acted the hard man, and pretended that it didn't hurt you. Four was normal, six was considered a bit much, eight was unusual, and anything more meant that the person had lost it"[36].

Five Monitors, supervised by one Procurator, assisted with general discipline each year. Padraic Concannon, Tom Glennon, Kevin McMorrow, Martin Newell and Vincent McGagh were the Procurators during my five years. They were 'trusties' in penal parlance, but fine people in their own right. A Procurator is defined as 'a civil official of the Emperor's administration in ancient Rome, often employed as the governor of a minor province or as a financial agent'. Though I received relatively little physical punishment in College, I remain full of righteous anger for those who fell victim to a surfeit of such cruelty. I believe Christy Langan was a sick man. But the entire teaching staff knew what was afoot. The genial President, Con Heaney, to whom I was a favourite, allowed it, as did Archbishop Joseph Walsh. In fairness, none of those priests choose to be teachers and did not see their vocation fulfilled by teaching.

MARTIN O'GRADY

A civilised and humane regime descended on the College during the 1957-8 academic year, when Fr. Martin O'Grady, from Kinvara, became Dean, after being ordained at the Irish College in Rome. Unlike others, he would actually talk to the students about themselves, about himself, about anything. He was no saint, but set out to avoid inflicting physical punishment on any student if at all possible. He was a stylish footballer and joined those playing on the senior pitch. There he gave as well as he got. I remember being the subject of what I considered rough play from him on one occasion. I amazed myself, by warning him aloud, within the hearing of several clerical team mentors, that if he repeated the offence I would 'flatten him'. I expected some later retribution, but none ever materialised. He was a delightful, an exasperating, but a truly fine human being. What a change! He died tragically some years later in a car accident. He was a Good Samaritan.

FOOTBALL LORE

St. Jarlath's is almost synonymous with Gaelic football. If the place had a soul, it was round and made of leather. Those who played for the College teams were highly regarded by their peers. It was on a circuit of the *'Walks'* with two of my class mates, John Geraghty and Mattie Greaney, that I was first informed that I had been selected to play for the College Junior Football team in the first round of the Connacht Championship. I did not express any excitement because I did not believe the news. I thought that the messenger, John Cosgrove, was joking. I was only a third year and as most fourth years were still eligible; the team was normally composed mostly of fourth years. My two companions, who were also good footballers, were very excited on my behalf. Within moments, the word spread around the *'Walks'* and boys from my year shouted their congratulations. The boys from my hometown of Ballyhaunis were particularly vociferous. The bell rang for study and we all trooped into the large Study Hall. Once the priest in charge had said the prayer, quiet prevailed for the two-hour period. I tried to concentrate on my work, but my mind continually wandered. I was still sceptical, as the team captain had said nothing to me. I found myself selecting the Junior Team in my own mind. I couldn't find a place for myself on a team for under seventeens.

There was a semi-official method of communicating during study. It consisted of writing notes and passing them along to the designated person. But before the note commenced its journey, the sender always sought to make eye contact with the designated recipient, so that the latter could ensure no student hijacked the note en route. The Dean of Studies tolerated the practice, but felt entitled to intercept and read any note, and confiscate it, if he so wished. I got a nudge that a note for me was about to commence its journey. I had to turn around to identify the sender. It was the captain of the Junior Team. He winked at me and smiled. I watched the progress of the note, all the time keeping an eye on the location of the Dean. Many other eyes were also watching the transaction. It would be a boon for our class if any of our number made the team. The note was shoved into my grasp. I opened the lid on my study box and threw it inside. I checked that the Dean was not observing me and then took the note out again and read, " *Anthony Jordan is on the Junior Team at left half back; Eddie Geraghty is left full back; Liam Campbell right back, Pat Sheridan is right full-forward Pat Donnellan full forward. Pass this note on to them"*. All named were third years. My selection was a sensation, as far as I was concerned. I had no idea that I was even in the reckoning. I couldn't imagine what Fr. Kavanagh, the team selector, was thinking. I showed the note to those around me, and then readdressed it and nodded it on its way to Pat Donnellan. I was dumbfounded. I couldn't cheer or scream or cry. I had to sit quietly and pretend that I was studying. I knew that my family would be proud. But my main thought was one of continuity between my hometown and the county of Mayo, football and St. Jarlaths. I was aware of a great tradition, and now, at the age of fifteen, I was part of it.

Our first game, on 24 November 1957, was in Ballinrobe against the local Christian Brother's School. I played well and we won handsomely. The team that day was: Seamus Kilraine, Liam Campbell, Martin Hannon, Eddie Geraghty, Gerry Maher, John Boland, Anthony Jordan, Michael Folan, Michael Lyons, Pat Sheridan, Jimmy Walsh, Jim Nestor, Ger Griffith, Pat Donnellan, Eamon Gavin. In our next game, St. Enda's of Galway defeated us before a crowd of many thousands in Tuam stadium. The crowd, which included the famous RTE commentator, Michael O'Hehir, had come to see the second game, a National League match between Galway and Louth. The latter had recently been crowned all Ireland champions, with such famous names as, Stephen White, Dan O'Neill (a Mayo man), Kevin Behan and Dermot O'Brien. Unfortunately when O'Hehir went on air, he spoke about the Colleges match. He said that he had mistakenly presumed that St. Jarlath's was the team which was winning by a landslide. During that game, for the only time in my career, I came very close to being sent off by the referee, Rev. Leon Ó'Móracháin. He did not appreciate my attempt to collide heavily with my opponent's right ankle. The latter was the St. Enda's free taker and was scoring from all angles. *"Try it once more and you're off"* Fr. Ó'Móracháin warned[36a].

The following year I again played for the junior team as we reached the Connacht final against Summerhill of Sligo. It was due to be played at Easter. That Spring, however, saw a major outbreak of influenza in the country. Within the College it became an epidemic with all classes suspended. The boys not affected together with some of the priests, notably Fr. Paddy Williams, ministered to those smitten. One pupil, from Ballyvary, died in the Infirmary. My diary for 26th January 1959 reads, *"Fuair PJ Lenehan bás inniu. Chuir mé mo lámh trí a ghruaig agus bhí sé go h-an fuar"* (PJ Lenihan died today. I ran my hand through his hair and it was very cold) I remember Pat Donnellan and myself helping to lift his body from the bed into the coffin. Later, though I did not have the 'flu', I took to bed and got the 'flu'. Within weeks, those, who had recovered were allowed home to recuperate for three weeks. I was one of those. On returning, I discovered that the delayed Junior Final was scheduled for the next Sunday, and I had lost my place on the team, but was listed among the substitutes. I got the opportunity to play a few practice games and prove my fitness. One of the corner backs, Enda Colleran, got injured and was replaced at half time. I was lucky enough to be the substitute chosen by Fr. Kavanagh and Seamus Leyden, the team captain, as we won the match.

I owed a lot to Fr. Kavanagh throughout my football career in St. Jarlath's. But I always felt uneasy in his presence. He taught science. After third year, a choice had to be made between doing science or Greek. There was never any question but that I would choose the latter, simply due to my feelings about the teacher of science. The main 'reason' I can give for my feelings, relate to the shock I suffered when, during a football outing in my third year, some of us had occasion to use a urinal. Fr. Kananagh came in to use the toilet and I was shocked to see him go through the motions of relieving himself, just like anyone else.

I suppose it was evidence of the huge divide between students and priests and the shock of discovering that they were just like us in this fundamental way. During the last term of fourth year, when the Gaelic football season was complete, I opted to concentrate on playing soccer rather than athletics, which Fr. Kavanagh coached. He was not amused, as I had potential as a good sprinter. At the start of my final year I realised that there would be a surfeit of boys vying for positions on the senior team's defence. My position there could not be guaranteed. I approached the new team Captain, Pat Sheridan, and discussed the matter with him. I suggested that I would initially be willing to try my luck in attack. He discussed it with Fr. Kavanagh and on the first team sheet issued for senior pitch, an event eagerly anticipated by all students, I was positioned at right half forward on the 'A' team. I had never previously played as an attacker and found the style of play demanded there, totally different. When you got the ball in the forwards, you had to use it constructively in the prevailing circumstances. This meant thinking, weighing up various options before playing the ball. Previously, you could and often had to act instantaneously and instinctively. My direct opponent on the first day was John Morley from Knock. It took me a little while to weigh up the new situation. As I got the ball, I was easily dispossessed on several occasions. I was taking too long to decide what my best option was. Soon I decided that I should revert to what I knew best. When I next got the ball, I began to immediately attempt a score forgetting about my team-mates. I ended that game by scoring one goal and four points. Pat Sheridan told me that Fr. Kavanagh was quite impressed. Luckily I retained that position on the team for the full season, as we won the All Ireland Hogan Cup, beating St. Colman's of Newry in the semi-final at Croke Park, and St. Finian's of Mullingar in the final at Athlone by 3-10 to 3-7.

A FATAL FLAW

I can recall, quite early on in that campaign, losing my early courage in attempting to score from various positions on the field. During one particular game against St. Mary's in Pearse Stadium, Salthill, I received the ball out on the right wing. My instinctive reaction was to try to score a point. But the thought ran through my mind that I might miss. I then decided to play safe and lob the ball into the centre. That could have proved a near fatal flaw for my career as my potential as a scoring forward ended at that moment. I have seen this occur to many forwards since and I recognise, if not sympathise with, the syndrome, particularly with those playing for teams for Mayo. Luckily for me, Fr. Kavanagh persisted with my selection, despite being offered contrary clerical advice. Another affliction occurred during that season which also inhibited my play. My diary entry for 17 September reads, "Bhi mo chos go dona". I developed almost permanent slow cramp along the front of my right foot from below the kneecap to my ankle, while playing. This made it very difficult to kick a high ball.

Fr. Kavanagh could not understand why I always kicked low balls, even when in a good position to kick a point. I did not confide in anyone, lest I lose my place on the team. I recall some years earlier, having a problem with my knee which necessitated having my leg from the ankle to above the knee in plaster for a few months. On one visit to the local doctor I encountered Frank Stockwell, the gifted Galway footballer, who surprisingly advised me to quit football.

The style of football played in St. Jarlath's was similar to that of successive successful Galway teams. It was a short passing game, thoughtful, with slick and quick movements. We practised regularly with the Galway senior team, which were runners up in the all Ireland of 1959. It consisted of such household names as Seán Purcell, Frank Stockwell, Frank Evers, Mattie McDonagh, Mick Greally, Jack Mahon, John Nallen, Mick Greally, and Joe Young. We often opposed the entire senior Galway team. Several of our own 1960's team starred on the famous Galway three in a row 1960's team.

John Geraghty our stylish and fearless goalkeeper is the only one of those yet unmentioned. The fulcrum and brains of our team was the captain, Pat Sheridan of Mayo, a born leader. The late John Morley from Knock played at centerfield. He was later to be murdered, (together with a brother of two of our class mates, Tom and Damian Byrne of Knock) by the IRA, while carrying out his duties as a member of An Garda Síochána.

Eddie Geraghty was a powerhouse in attack, while Gerry Prengergast punted beautiful passes along the right wing to me. These balls dropped over the heads of my marker as I ran on to them at pace. The player whose style I remember most clearly, was the high-fielding centre half-back, Tony Ryan from Milltown. He appeared to climb early, float for a moment, and flick his hands to receive the dropping ball and then slide gracefully to the ground. The steady Liam Campbell from Ballinlough was full back. Three boys from fourth year were also on that team, Seamus Kilraine, Larry O'Brien and Jimmy Staunton. The rest of the panel included, Seamus Forde, Vincent Greaney, Vincent McGagh, Mick Staunton, Seán Brennan, Joe Jennings and Charlie Walsh. While football was the main sport in the College, other sporting activities also figured. In 1959 a College team consisting of Michael and Myles McEvilly, Michael Balfe, Charlie Walsh and Seán Burke won the All Ireland Life Saving Competition. Tennis, swimming, handball and athletics were popular, with an All Ireland medal being won by Martin Clancy, of our year, for long jumping in 1959.

MAYO MINORS

Unfortunately there appeared to be an inability or reluctance among the mentors of Mayo football teams to realise the full potential of footballers who had played for St. Jarlath's. In the 1960 Connacht minor championship, neither Peadar McGee nor myself, who had won All Ireland medals with St. Jarlath's, were selected for the

Mayo minor team to play Galway in Tuam. During the second half, when Mayo were well beaten, a Mayo mentor shouted back to the row of substitutes, asking was there any forwards among us. Peadar McGee identified himself as one and was ordered into the team. Some time later a similar inquiry was made and I identified myself as a forward and was consigned to the field of play. The nucleus of that Galway minor team provided the later, great Galway senior team of the 1960's.

BALLYHAUNIS GAA

I played football for the local teams in Ballyhaunis at all grades but won only one medal during my career, an East Mayo Junior medal in 1964 The ethos pervading Ballyhaunis football was to win at all costs. This was echoed by our supporters, who when their team was being beaten, as it often was, would barrack the referee and on occasions, attempt to have the game abandoned by threatening to invade the pitch. Despite my transferring to the forwards in College, I continued to play in the backs at home. The players I remember most playing alongside for Ballyhaunis, were Gerry McGarry, Jim Higgins and Kieron Benson. They were most zealous in harrying the opposition and utterly reliable colleagues. Ballyhaunis won very few county championships. The exceptions were the minor title in 1951 and the senior title in 1958. The team that latter day consisted of: Charlie Phillips, PJ Moran, John Healy, B. McGrath, Jarlath Fahy, Noel Waldron, G. Mulkeen, P. Moran, John Dillon, John Biesty, Michael Ryan, Peter Waldron, Val Byrne, Tom Langan, P. Moran.

CULTURAL MATTERS

The top storey of the most recently built wing of St. Jarlath's College, which comprised of one very large hall, was given over entirely to entertainment. It was the venue, during first term, for rehearsals for the annual light opera production. The productions during my time in College were, *Iolanthe, Patience, The Student Prince, The New Moon and The Yeomen of the Guard*. PV O'Brien and Christy Langan produced, with Charlie Scannell and Gabriel Charles as musical directors. I was 'a dainty little fairy' in the first named show and a 'gentleman' in the latter[37]. The operas were performed publicly in the town cinema, the Odeon, for three nights prior to the Xmas holidays. There was great status attached to being a Principal in these shows. There was always much innocent hugging and handholding with 'female' members of the cast by other boys backstage. During our last year Con Heaney, the President, announced that he had many reports from past pupils that an inability to do ballroom dancing proved a major obstacle when they started going to dances. He decided therefore, that, we were all going to learn the various routines common to ballroom dancing before we left college. He provided taped music and supervision. The students were then left to teach themselves.

*St. Jarlath's College
Magazine Cover.*

*Sureshot!
Author with Trophies.*

Paddy Jordan and Mena McGee, marry 1958.

As there were no females available, we had to learn the female as well as the male roles. This exercise proved a great success, with most boys becoming quite expert at careering around the dance floor and piloting their partner to do likewise. In later years I often invited my female dancing partners to assume the dominant role, much to the amusement of onlookers and my partners. On Sunday nights we often had a film in the Hall. There, in the dark, you sit close to your best friend and allow the movie to transport you both into the escapism of a romantic world. As the picture ended, and we faced the trek downstairs along the corridor, upstairs to the dormitories, with the prospect of 06.30 Monday mornings on the agenda, a terrible feeling of anticlimax pervaded the hundreds of students. We would wait until all the credits for the film were completed and the screen went blank, before we moved. To this day, when I attend a film, usually with my daughter Fiona, I stick to this practice, though the rest of the audience may have long departed. I also have had a lifelong aversion of going out on a Sunday night ever since.

During the last two years of College, it became possible to engage in an exercise which supplemented the meagre diet available. There was a reserve army corps, '*An Fórsa Cosanta áitiúla*' or *FCA* for short, attached to the college. It held practice sessions monthly and afterwards the participants were provided with a meal in a local café in the town. I joined at the first opportunity. We were provided with uniforms and heavy-duty army boots, which were ideal for traversing the '*Walks*' and intimidating any group, which might be slowing down our onward progress towards vacation. On some occasions, as I found myself reminiscing sympathetically about St. Jarlath's, in the company of other past pupils, it has been pointed out to me that as I had been on the various College football teams, I had been a favoured student. That had never occurred to me and I was never conscious of it.

1960: Front Row: Padraig Forde, Tony Greene, Officer, Seán Cleary, Seamus Forde. Back Row : Anthony Jordan, Seán Mulhern, Paddy Moran, Michael Regan.

CLERICAL CAREER GUIDANCE

There was no career guidance in St. Jarlath's College. The only discussion I can recall on the subject, and one which had a major influence on me, occurred during last term in Greek class. Fr. Paddy Williams, the genial teacher, decided to invite each boy to indicate what he was 'going to do' when he left. I must have been very naïve, as during the five previous years, I had never given the slightest attention to such a matter. I was keen, therefore, to hear what the others were going to say. Some were going to work on the family farm or shop. Others were going to university. Some hoped to do primary teaching. But the largest group by far indicated that they were going to 'sit the *Concursus* for Maynooth'.

I did not know what this involved but found it a convenient answer to Fr. Williams' question. It appeared subsequently that it was regarded as a great achievement and honour to be accepted to study for the priesthood at Maynooth, as places were limited. Students who failed the *Concursus* went on to study for the priesthood at other colleges[38]

I thus found myself a candidate for Maynooth through sheer ignorance and chance. But the excitement and sense of elitism involved among those successful in the *Concursus* was very enjoyable. It was only later that I discovered the close relationship that existed between our College and Maynooth. A student quoted in the College Bi-Centenary publication says.

"The whole place, anyway, was focussed on Maynooth at that time, probably too much so. If you had any talent at all, you were expected to go to Maynooth, to give it a try anyway. It was very much a minor seminary. It was never clear who might have leanings towards the priesthood. It was never obvious. There was an expectation that the high achievers would go on to the priesthood. And they did, so the expectation was not groundless. But I never discerned any real difference between the guys who became priests and the rest of us... there were thirteen boys anxious to go to Maynooth in my time. We sat a special exam called the Concursus and, of the thirteen, only four were allowed to go to Maynooth. The others went to All Hallows, Clonliffe and other Colleges"[39]

ESTABLISHMENT OF ST. JARLATH'S

It is ironic that when, in 1800, a decision to establish St. Jarlath's was made by the Catholic Archbishop of Tuam, Dr. Dillon, he had to send his nominee as first College President, Rev. Oliver Kelly, to the Protestant Archbishop of Tuam, Dr. Beresford, for the requisite permission to set up the College. This resulted from the fact that the established church was charged by law with maintaining a system of education. It is clear that the main purpose in establishing the College was, "as a preparatory school for Maynooth". The official document emanating from Dr. Beresford to Oliver Kelly on 17 October said, in part.

"...We, therefore being satisfied as to your abilities and due qualifications in discharging your duties therein, and having, therefore, accepted as such, the appointment of the said Rev. Edward Dillon, do by these presents, grant and confirm unto you the office or employment of schoolmaster of the said preparatory school for Maynooth..."[40]

Due to the relative poverty of the Irish Catholic Church and Irish Catholics in general, it was not practical to run junior seminaries solely for the education of candidates for the priesthood. Such colleges therefore enrolled both lay and clerical students. By and large St. Jarlath's gave a good though a somewhat narrow education. When in 1947, anticipating the 150th anniversary of the College, Archbishop Joseph Walsh, issued a pastoral letter seeking funds for St. Jarlath's, he praised the contribution it made to the West of Ireland. He said that College bursaries and scholarships made it accessible to those less well-off.

He recounted how hundreds of College students had gone forth across the globe, "always keeping up the highest standards of the Catholic priesthood". He added, "Not less honourable nor less religious are their class-fellows who chose a secular career, their fine Catholic spirit testifies to the excellence of the training they have received"[41]. One former student, writing from London, took issue with Dr. Walsh. His criticisms concerning accessibility and curriculum echo my own experience, though I note, with surprise, that the author of the bi-centenary book, John Cunningham writes that "between a quarter and a third of St Jarlaths' students were being supported, to a greater or lesser degree by various foundations associated with the College"[42]. The former student wrote.

"I was somewhat amused by His Grace's reference to the sons of 'poor' parents receiving education of the 'highest class' in his seminary, where, as is common knowledge, only children of well-to-do farmers, teachers, and merchants are boarders. The sons of poor parents in the archdiocese save those with easy reach of a few secondary schools in some of the towns have to be content with primary education... the archbishop's allusion to the 'highest class' of education provided in St. Jarlath's college sounds very piquant to me who went through that mill. I never saw a play or opera staged by or for the students. The truth is that the curriculum of the 'college' was arranged to suit the minority of 'students' who intended to proceed to Holy Orders, though of course the parents in general paid the cost"[43].

RONNIE DELANEY

One very annoying aspect of College life, for me, was the unavailability of newspapers and radio. I was very interested in world current affairs from an early age. I was conscious of the traumatic events of the Hungarian Rising in 1956 and how the Hungarians had been led to believe that if they rebelled against the occupying Soviet army, the Americans would come to their rescue. They rose out and were slaughtered by the tanks, while they waited in vain. The invasion of Suez by the British at the time provided the Americans with the excuse to do nothing. Within St. Jarlath's I felt very frustrated at my inability to get reliable information. I have a picture of 'the Butcher of Budapest', Marshal Zhukov, in my scrapbook. On that never-to-be-forgotten day in 1956, when Ronnie Delaney was running in the 1500 metres Olympic final in Melbourne, we received the result just after breakfast, when Fr. Charlie Scannell pinned a piece of paper on the notice board, reading, '*1. Delaney, 2. Richtzenhain, 3. Landry, 4. Tabori, 5. Bannister, 6. Jungwirth, 7. Scott, 8. Boyd*',

I had an arrangement with my mother that she would retain all the daily newspapers during term time. Then, when I got holidays I had the luxury of reading them at my own pace. Those piles of *Irish Press* or *Irish Independent* gave me many days of sheer pleasure as I followed the chronological development of various stories. I began to keep scrapbooks at that time and am still surprised at my interests.

There are reports of the death of Margaret Burke Sheridan, on the Dalai Lama and the Chinese take-over of Tibet, the new President De Gaulle in 1958, the EOKA War of 1958 in Cyprus, Pope John XXIII meeting President Eisenhower, Burnley being Champions of the First Division and Aston Villa, Division Two Champions. I followed the IRA campaign of the late 1950s, keeping reports and memorial tributes to Seán South and Fergal O'Hanlon. The *Irish Independent* headline read: *"Two Men Dead Following 15-Minute Gun Battle"* on the 2nd of January 1957. Among the names I notice in those cuttings, as being imprisoned are, Tom Mitchell, Cathal Goulding, and Seán Stephenson, while those interned included Frank Maguire, William McKee, Joe Cahill, Patrick McClean, Seán Keenan. I also acquired one of the first copies of the ballad commemorating Fergal O'Hanlon and Seán South.

"Twas on a dreary New Year's Eve, as the shades of night came down,
A lorry load of Volunteers approached a border Town,
There were men from Dublin and from Cork, Fermanagh and Tyrone,
Their leader was a Limerick man, Seán South from Garryowen".

The words of that ballad would later play a significant part in my later life.

BALLYHAUNIS TO ENGLAND

When I left Ballyhaunis in September 1955, I little realised that I would never again spend another full year living at home. I was removed from my native habitat into an unnatural and precarious environment. The boys I had grown up with and played with, but more importantly the girls I had grown up and played with, were now at an ever-increasing remove. A scattering occurred, with many displaced permanently. Almost as important, we were also removed from our physical environment, the trails, the paths, the woods, the bushes, the rivers, where we played Cowboys and Indians, chasing and fighting, gradually disappeared from our kin. With most of my own family in England, I began to travel there to work during the summer holidays.

I would stay with my brothers or sisters in Manchester or Birmingham. England was a culture shock, despite the Irish clinging together for mutual support. Coming out of a local church in Manchester after Sunday Mass, I would sometimes meet as many people from Ballyhaunis, as if I was at home.

I first went to England in the summer of 1956. My sister, Bernadette, who had been anxious to go also, was given permission to accompany me, ostensibly for a few weeks. My first job was at a WH Smith magazine stall at Victoria Station, Manchester. It included an early morning newspaper delivery round in the locality. Another year I worked in Stockport in a menswear section of a large department store. It was there I learned the fundamental nature of advertising. The shop took a large advertisement in the local Friday evening paper for Saturday's shoppers. Men's suits were always featured at a very cheap price. Before we left the store that evening our manager would identify the sole suit available for the advertised price, and then only until 10.00.

"The important thing is to get them into the store", he would say. On one occasion an English female colleague of mine was slightly overpaid. I rejoiced, saying how lucky she was. To my amazement, I failed to dissuade her from approaching the cashier and returning the excess payment. She could not understand my attitude. One summer I shared a flat with my brothers over the Astoria Ballroom, which was the main dancing centre for the Irish. I would often walk to my sister's flat near Platt Fields Park by way of the Northern Hospital. Prostitutes who were then free to solicit openly on the streets frequented this area. I got to recognise them by their particular beats. One sight of an Irish person I witnessed in England has stayed with me. It occurred one Friday evening on the upstairs deck of a bus travelling from Picadilly. A young Irishman sat alone near the front, quietly drunk, contentedly eating sweets from a very large jar, in which shops kept their sweets. I could imagine him, opening his pay packet and deciding to indulge himself in a fashion he always wanted, by buying the full jar.

The girls I encountered during my working holidays in England compensated for the increasing breach with local girls caused by attending a boarding school. I remember vividly falling in love with a gorgeous girl named Valerie. She had a most attractive figure and was almost boyish in her impishness and speed of movement. I always thought Cliff Richard's song, *"Living Doll"*, could have been written about her. The only teenager I can recall in those days having a regular girlfriend in Ballyhaunis, was Tom Leetch. But Tom was always a loveable *avant-garde* figure.

CHAPTER 7

MAYNOOTH 1960-65

In 1960 it was deemed a great honour for any family, and parish community, to have a member accepted for Maynooth. My own family was quietly very pleased. As with going to St. Jarlath's, a long list of necessary items was furnished, the most exotic of which was a clerical hat, which I kept in a box. The fees at Maynooth were reputed to be much higher than at St. Jarlath's, but there was a vague hint among the candidates, that these could be negotiable. One of the big surprises I immediately encountered, was the discovery of how closely modelled on Maynooth, St. Jarlath's had been. The two regimes were almost parallel. Unlike some other boys, I had never previously been aware of the role of St. Jarlath's as a junior seminary and almost a preparatory school for Maynooth. The student population there, in 1960, was five hundred and sixty eight. The college was organised rigidly on separate house, diocesan and class divisions.

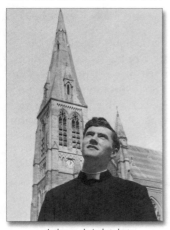

Author as clerical student.

There were thirty-seven students from the archdiocese of Tuam there, with ten in first year. Four of the more senior students were from Ballyhaunis. The accommodation for first and second year students, in buildings named, *Rhetoric* and *Logic*, comprised 'Junior House', from which there was very little contact with the middle or senior students. The number of students by year, were, 72, 54, 68, 80, 84, 85, 106, with nineteen postgraduates[44]. The one hundred and six first years, were each assigned a numerical seniority order, from Dennis Curran of Kerry to Thomas Walsh of Cork. This dictated the order and alongside whom, a student operated for most communal activities e.g. seating, in the refectory, chapel and class. I was placed at forty-one between Joseph Collins of Derry and Patrick Kilcoyne of Achonry. These youths and others adjacent like Donal Musgrave of Waterford and James Doherty of Derry, were people with whom I would have most interaction during our first year and possibly beyond. This system ensured the fracturing of any special diocesan friendships and compelled students to mix.

BRIEF HISTORY

The Catholic hierarchy established St. Patrick's College Maynooth with the eager assistance of the Irish Government in 1795. The latter, which was essentially 'a Protestant Parliament for a Protestant people', under George III, King of Great Britain and Ireland, (whose bust now adorns the College library), believed that it was better to have students studying for the priesthood in Ireland, rather than on the European continent, where the government could exert little influence over their education and outlook. The need to placate Irish Catholics in the face of the American Revolution and the challenge from the Volunteer movement at home persuaded the British government that the Penal Laws should be liberalised. In earlier times candidates for the priesthood served an apprenticeship form of training. The Council of Trent had exhorted bishops to set up seminaries more suited to the purpose.

The Irish Catholic Church had then sent its seminarians to train in the Catholic countries of Spain and France, where eventually a network of 'Irish Colleges' developed. These offered about five hundred places for clerical students, but due to the repercussions of the French Revolution many of these were lost and the Colleges confiscated. Britain went to war with revolutionary France and was glad to be able to enhance its influence over the Catholic clergy in Ireland by supporting the establishment of Maynooth. However, the bishops had to accept a governing body, the trustees not exclusively ecclesiastical, and a board of visitors not exclusively Catholic[45]. Maynooth soon began to depend heavily on the government for current expenses, which could be and were withdrawn, if the College or the hierarchy were in disfavour with the authorities.

An example of this occurred in 1845, when Parliament voted to cancel establishment grants, providing for two hundred and fifty free places in the College. These were later reinstated and increased to five hundred places. All grants were cancelled for two years in 1871, but were gradually built up to three hundred, to mark the centenary of the college in 1894. This mechanism together with a series of private foundations for bursaries established by clergy and laypeople from 1806 onwards meant that many clerical students had little or no college fees to pay. One example was the 'Mooney Fund', set up by the Parish Priest of Ringsend in Dublin in 1915. By 1960 the income from that fund, enabled twenty-seven students to have their fees paid in full. This facility meant that Maynooth was open to all social classes, as fees were not an insurmountable problem. The interdependence between successive governments and the Catholic Bishops was to cause ongoing conflict with advanced Irish nationalists, who felt that the latter were not playing their due role in the quest for national independence.

In 1912 Major John MacBride wrote that, *"It is a regrettable fact that most of the Irish Bishops, being Maynooth bred, aid the British Government in the effort to denationalise Ireland"*[46]. I had been unaware that Maynooth was an actual university like those in Dublin, Galway and Cork, where people went to study for degrees for teaching or other professional qualifications. I was amazed to discover that I was doing First Arts in anticipation of spending three years taking a Bachelor of Arts degree. It was only then it dawned on me why it took seven years to become a priest, as four years of theology followed the university degree. Maynooth suited me fine.

The two things I was most interested in were readily available there, books and sport. The great joy of my sporting life became soccer. In the Tuam archdiocese fraternity, we would play several games some days. Unlike my difficulty in adapting from the backs to forwards in Gaelic football and the consequent requirement to play tactically, I adapted to the same requirement in soccer without difficulty. In fact that very quality of the game became its greatest attraction for me; holding the ball at my feet before seeking to play an astute pass, became my *raison d'etre* on the soccer field. I still continued playing Gaelic football as required, and reverted to my old position of left halfback. But the physical ferocity employed in Gaelic football at Maynooth made it less attractive to me. I dabbled in rugby until on one occasion, instead of a hand-off from an opponent I received a clenched fist in the face from a blond Corkonian. One of my most cherished sporting memories came in 1973 at Lansdowne Road, when the English rugby team took the field to tremendous applause, after both Scotland and Wales had refused to turn up the previous year.

The other game that began to fascinate me in Maynooth was croquet. It was played in summer term. No more than cricket, many Irish people think croquet is a game for old ladies or wimps. I have rarely seen so much antagonism engendered in any game, than in croquet. The kernel of the game consists of putting your ball through a series of hoops, but also, and crucially, thwarting your opponent from doing likewise. It can be head to head combat, with mallets in hand.

READING MATERIAL

There was a very small general library available in the College, though not a lending library, which to my great pleasure, was little used by most of my fellow students. Quite often I would be the sole occupant. The books were of good and diverse interest. Among the books I read during my early years there were;

To Katanga and Back, by Conor Cruise O'Brien, *The Status Seekers,* by Vance Packard, *Cry the Beloved Country,* by Alan Paton, *Of Mice and Men & Cannery Row,* by John Steinbeck, *The Loneliness of the Long-Distance Runner,* by Alan Shillitoe, *Exodus* by Leon Uris, *Children in the Sun & the Devils Advocate,* by Morris West, *The Spanish Civil War,* by Hugh Thomas. I made detailed notes of several of those books, including Cruise O'Brien's book, which I would use many years later.

Even at this time remove, I am somewhat dismayed with myself that I do not know who was responsible for providing such a range of books. Only one other boy from our Hogan Cup team came to Maynooth, John Geraghty. He remained a very special friend and we saw a lot of each other, especially as he, too, took to soccer, constantly refining his daredevil goal-keeping skills.

I was friendly with all the Tuam boys, having already spent five years living with them. Every county in Ireland was represented among the first years. I became friends with some, but others I could barely tolerate. The youths with whom I found it most difficult to adapt were in general from Ulster. I found then to be more argumentative and in-your-face. I had some difficulty acclimatising to their rapid speech patterns, though this applied equally to some from Cork and Kerry. One youth from Omagh in Tyrone confirmed me in my republican views, when he said that we in the *Free State* (the first time I had heard that term articulated), had got our freedom in 1921, but the nationalist people within the Six Counties were still fighting for theirs. I must beware of generalisations, as the most genial and kindest boy I encountered in Maynooth, was from Derry City, one James Doherty, now alas deceased.

The strictness of the regime presented little difficulty to me after St. Jarlath's. The only addition consisted of a combination of silence, meditation and spiritual reading, lasting daily for one hour. The academic course for me consisted of Philosophy, Logic, Gaeilge, Latin and History. I had little interest in any of them except for history, where we had an inspired lecturer in the person of Fr. Tomás Ó'Fiaich of Armagh. He was an open and endearing man, who was loved by the students. There was little enthusiasm among the general student body for secular academic study. Most did not see the acquisition of a degree as a high priority, save for being essential for continuing towards the priesthood. Very few were keen on pursuing an honours degree regarding its acquisition as negative. This could be seen as cultivating an anti-intellectual atmosphere at Maynooth. It was explained to us that priests who had an honours degree invariably found themselves teaching in the junior diocesan seminary for many years after ordination. This was a prospect, which had little attraction for those who felt they had a vocation to the priesthood. This perspective might explain to some degree why many of the priests teaching in the junior seminaries were such frustrated people. Thus most students treated the acquisition of a degree in a minimalist way. I ended up doing Gaeilge and Latin for my degree, two languages which I would only come to admire and appreciate very many years later.

Maynooth College General Science Class.

Maynooth College Class 1963.

PRESSURE TO LEAVE

Two main differences between Maynooth and Tuam were the absence of corporal punishment and each student having his own room. The experience of having to exist on one's own in a little room was a huge change for most of us and was very challenging. It enforced a certain degree of solitude and solitariness as visiting another student's room, was strictly forbidden. There was a constant pressure applied to the students, as there were rules laid down for all eventualities and situations. Nothing was too trivial for the Deans. Strict adherence was required whether it was for silence, deportment, hygiene, dress, attitude, care of college effects, visiting arrangements, modesty, humility, and application.

One Dean, Paddy Muldoon of Donegal, who was a very weird man, was notorious for emphasising that "Silence is the norm, Meester. You may only speak when it is allowed". One ex-student recounted more than thirty years later, that he occasionally had nightmares populated by the prowling Paddy Muldoon. There was a formal mode of serious reprimand for unacceptable behaviour, which entailed receiving a *caveat* or warning from the College. These were colloquially referred to as 'cats'. If you got three 'cats', you were automatically expelled. Silence was observed during meals, as one student read aloud from some favourable text for our spiritual or aesthetic improvement. It was during one such exercise in November 1963, that a student, Pat McGrath, whispered to me that John Fitzgerald Kennedy had been assassinated in Dallas. Only after the official prayers was one allowed to speak. Adherence to these rules was regarded as affording an outward sign of an inward vocation. If a student erred in any serious way or in a series of minor ways, he was invited to leave the College. This was a regular occurrence even for the most trivial of reasons, like smoking, having a newspaper or book which was not countenanced. We would only hear of an expulsion after the student had packed his bags and departed. We were continually invited to leave voluntarily, if we felt we did not have a vocation. The front gates were always open and intended as a permanent invitation to leave, should anybody wish. The College did not want a single student to remain unless he was absolutely sure he had a vocation.

PETER CONNOLLY VERSUS TOMÁS Ó'FIAICH

One student expulsion occurred over letters written to the *Irish Press*. These had originally emanated from two professors, Fr. Tomás Ó'Fiaich and Rev. Peter Connolly. Their public disagreement on cultural nationalism created a storm and much merriment among the students. Another contributor attacked Fr. Connolly and the College, demanding to know where it stood. The College President intervened and both priests agreed to desist from the public debate. At that point another letter from a third professor appeared in the paper defending Fr. Connolly. When the President spoke to the third professor he had no knowledge of the letter that had

Judith & Fiona Jordan at the launch of the Yeats Book, Westport 2004.

The Author is introduced to Chad Varah by Director Mary Bryans 1994.

The Samaritans 112 Marlborough St. Dublin.

Antonia's grave at the Little Angel's plot Glasnevin Cemetery Dublin.

Fiona tends Antonia's grave.

Our beloved dog, Murphy.

The Author's mother with baby Judith.

Judith, Anthony, and Fiona Jordan at the Little Angel's Plot Glasnevin 1980.

Daniel Day Lewis, Fiona Jordan, Anthony Jordan, 2004.

Daniel Day Lewis visits Sandymount School with Oscar, 1989.

The Farrellys, Jordans, Pringles at RHK 1999.

We celebrate W.B. Yeats' birthday in Sandymount Green 2001.

The Author, President Robinson, Judith and Mary, at Áras an Uachtaráin 1994.

President McAleese with the Author at Sandymount School.

Anthony Jordan, Ambassador Sutherland, Sir Patrick Mayhew at the British Embassy, 1995.

Enda Kenny TD launches Cosgrave book in Gallery 4 Sandymount.

Pat Wallace, Liam Cosgrave, and the Author at lecture series given by him on Cosgrave book at the National Museum 2007.

Sean Dublin-Bay-Loftus, Minister Jim Higgins TD and the Author at Ratra House Churchill Exhibition 1995.

Judith, Jimmy, Mary, Tommy John & Fiona Jordan.

Jimmy, Paddy, Josephine Connolly, Author, Tommy 1986.

Friary closes, 12.8 02.
L. to r. Joe Keane, John Forde, Seamus Durcan, Anthony Jordan, Fr. Kieran Waldron, Pat Higgins.

Marion Coy, Enda MacDonagh, Bernard O'Hara.

*The Author presents Christy Brown letters
to Noel Kissane and Gerry Lyne at the National Library 2002.*

The Author, Han Hogerzeil-Collis, with Rabbi at Anne Frank Exibition.

MY LORD AND MY GOD.

JESUS MERCY

MARY HELP.

Remembered With Love
GARY NICHOLL
81, BROADFORD PARK,
BALLINTEER, DUBLIN.
Who died on 24th September, 1981.
Aged 9 years
— R. I. P. —

He gazed amid the little ones,
And stopped to pick the best;
Dear Gary was the chosen one,
With Jesus now he rests.

A much loved pupil,
the late Gary Nicholl.

Photo montage of Sandymount Pupils
who died 1973-2001.

Michelle McQuinn, Anthony Jordan, Marie Heaney, at Children of Lir Mural Sandymount.

Sandymount School
Anthony Jordan, Cristine Kiernan, Rosaleen O'Halloran, Joan McNamara, Yvonne Kidd.

Staff Sandymount School.

Ordination Class Maynooth 1967

Author, Ursula Scanlon, Miriam Dermody, Yvonne Kidd, Joan MacNamara.

Eaton Mongey's Funeral 2007.

Enda Kenny TD and the Author.

Bernie Duffy.

Cardinal Tomás Ó' Fiaich.

appeared in his name. The next day's *Irish Press* carried a declamatory letter. It appeared that students had written it. An investigation occurred and my diary entry for 24 October 1964 states, "Cuireadh xxxxx as an gColáiste ar maidin. Bhí sé ag imeacht amárach ar aon nós"[47]. Fr. Connolly entered further controversy in the following April. The *'Irish Theological Quarterly'* published in Maynooth carried an essay from Connolly's entitled, *'The Moralists and the Obscene'*. It sought to set criteria for distinguishing between pornography and a legitimate treatment of erotic material. The Trustees of the College, i.e. senior members of the Hierarchy, did not approve and censured Connolly and the Board of the publication. Though Connolly was a dedicated and orthodox priest, his freedom to pursue his legitimate professional work was not to be permitted.

At a reading in the Writer's Centre in Dublin in 2007, I ascertained from Edna O'Brien that she had been aware and was grateful to Connolly for his defence of her writings. That Fr. Connolly was an independent thinker was illustrated many years later, when he was on a radio panel with Dr. Declan Kiberd, Professor of Anglo-Irish Literature at UCD. Kiberd recalled: *"I remember a radio programme in 1980 with Fr. Peter Connolly. He was a great liberal critic of the censorship in Ireland in the mid-twentieth century. He said one very strange thing. He said that when religion would go in Ireland, it would go fast and no one would know what was happening"*. When he said this, we just thought he was being provocative. We were so shocked that no one responded on the programme and then we asked him afterwards, when the microphones were turned off, what he really meant. He pointed to the fate of the Irish language as proof that when Irish people no longer find something useful, they are not slow to purge themselves of it[48].

ECCE SACERDOS MAGNUS

The one somewhat unnerving aspect of taking a degree at Maynooth was that the results became known by being published in the daily newspapers. *'Maynooth Exam Results'*, the headline read. The ignominy if one failed and the consequences for one like me, who was entirely happy at Maynooth and wished to continue there, caused great nervousness. A complicating factor was that there were two Jordan names to identify, one A.B, and the other A.J. Luckily both names appeared in the papers during the summer of 1963. Many students, who had earlier decided that they did not have a vocation, made the pragmatic decision to remain on and finish their degrees. Arriving at such an initial decision was often a traumatic one. It also applied pressure on those who intended staying. The authorities regarded this in a positive way, as they were adamant that they did not want people continuing unless they were absolutely sure of their vocation. One third of those who started in 1960 had departed by 1963. As we were approaching the end of that year one farsighted student, Patrick E. O'Keeffe, circulated an autograph book among the class, inviting each to sign their names and make an entry. Mine read, *"I have long thought it one of my country's misfortunes, that so much that is best in the Irish Church departs for the mission field, while among those who remain at home, there will always be some whose favourite music is the anthem, 'Ecce Sacerdos Magnus'."* This was a quotation from Conor Cruise O'Brien's book, *'To Katanga and Back'*, and was my reflection on a few of the College professors, compared to the many activists I had encountered, who spent their priestly lives, serving abroad, never seeing themselves as great. As in St. Jarlath's, the Deans had responsibility for discipline. In Junior House, we had Tommy Finnegan from Sligo as Dean. He was an affable man with a civilised manner and outlook. In Middle House, we encountered the aforementioned Donegal man, Paddy Muldoon. He treated the students as morons, constantly hectoring us about the most obvious and trivial matters. His was a most insufferable officious personality.

He would have been regarded as a total misfit in any other walk of life. But he reigned supreme in his domain and took harsh action against anyone foolish enough to challenge any of his numerous *ex cathedra* pronouncements. This insistence on absolute obedience to superiors may not have served the Church that well. It certainly did not suit those who abandoned Maynooth for secular life burdened by a tendency towards undue servility. In Middle House we ended our university period and begun our theological studies, for which we had originally come to Maynooth. We studied Fundamental Theology under Kevin McNamara of Clare, later to be Bishop of Kerry and Archbishop of Dublin, before dying at an early age. He was a diligent, serious man, who when it was suggested to him that we spend some time considering other religions, dismissed it out of hand. We referred to him as 'Kevy Mac'.

ENDA MCDONAGH

Enda MacDonagh from our own diocese of Tuam lectured on moral theology. It was worth going to Maynooth just to have come in contact with this man. He was civilised, intelligent, open minded, and a Christian. His devotion to the person and example of Jesus Christ was exemplary. There was nothing closed about him; he was open to all possibilities; the ultimate sanction was conscience, an informed conscience. It was clear from him that what passed for Christianity in the Irish Catholic Church sometimes bore little relationship to Jesus Christ. We had studied the theology of marriage in great detail. I recall in one class with MacDonagh, when the higher calling of virginity in celibacy was being discussed, I stated that I regarded the calling to the married state as being, at the very least, an equal calling. After severe disapproval from some classmates, MacDonagh, who stated that we had to remain open to all possibilities, rescued me. He also added that he would not necessarily disagree with my view.

MacDonagh had earlier given cause for some concern among the hierarchy, because of his association with mediating to a grouping of homosexuals. Speaking about this he said; *"There were a couple of difficult instances – one after I spoke at the first public meeting of a gay and lesbian group in Dublin in 1972. There were a lot of objections from bishops, priest and lay people. No hotel in Dublin would host the meeting and we ended up in Trinity College. A number of people came over from England for that first meeting and they went a bit wild. Conway (Cardinal) deflected a lot of the outrage. I thought he was the only real leader in the Catholic Church in Ireland in the last fifty years. He was a politician. He had a sense of goals and strategy and he worked at it"[49].*

The controversy over artificial contraception raged during those years as Pope Paul VI dithered on the issue, before finally rejecting the advice of his expert Commission, to accept the inevitable and correct position of allowing contraceptives. Enda MacDonagh became associated with a group of theologians who questioned the wisdom of such a stance. In my opinion one of the greatest tragedies to befall the Irish Church in recent times, was its inability to harness the messianic qualities of Enda MacDonagh in a leadership role. But his role of 'outsider' in the Church has played a vital role for many. In June 2007 St. Patrick's Cathedral Dublin, in an historic move, appointed Fr. MacDonagh an ecumenical Canon to its chapter. He was installed at the cathedral as the Prebendary of Clondalkin. Enda is a true Samaritan.

SECOND VATICAN COUNCIL

Professor Frank Cremin of Maynooth and the diocese of Kerry was a trusted *peritus,* or private theologian to Archbishop McQuaid for the duration of the Vatican Council. In Maynooth he often quoted John Charles McQuaid's infamous phrase, on arrival back at Dublin airport, that *"Nothing has changed".* This resounding guarantee of his orthodoxy failed to secure his episcopal promotion. Cremin saw the see of Kerry first go to Kevin McNamara and then to Eamon Casey. It later emerged publicly that Cremin had been a theological advisor to Noel Browne during his battle with McQuaid and the hierarchy in 1951 on the *'Mother and Child'* scheme[50]. As late as the mid 1980s, when Noel Browne was preparing his autobiography, Cremin was not prepared for his earlier link with Browne to be documented. Even the in-house Maynooth journal, *The Furrow,* edited by the venerable Fr. J G McGarry came under suspicion, as McQuaid told Bishop Browne of Galway that it 'was doing harm'[51]. One of the early initiatives to flow from the Council is noted in an entry in my 1965 diary for 6 March, which says, *"Bhí an t-Aifreann nua i mBéarla againn ar maidin don chéad uair le an t-Athar Harty. Thaithnigh sé liom".*

Dr. McQuaid was very suspicious of Maynooth and sought to exert control over the staff there, directly and indirectly, through his brother bishops. When he was not being successful enough, he began to promote his own diocesan college at Clonliffe, as a more reliable center for the formation of priests and religious and lay missionaries, and where he could exert total control. This surely indicates some level of paranoia in McQuaid, rather than evidence of any great independent intellectual activity at Maynooth. For the sad fact is that throughout its history, Maynooth has not distinguished itself in that field, except in very rare exceptions.

TWO BY TWO

The one practice at Maynooth which caused me some concern was the routine by which students approached the altar to receive Holy Communion. Like most official activities, it was done with great uniformity. Each row of students stood up in their pews and exited onto the central aisle to form a queue approaching the altar. This meant that if one student, for whatever reason, did not wish to receive Communion, he was immediately isolated and remained visibly so, until those sitting next to him, returned to throw a cloak of anonymity round him again.

The logical inference for someone not approaching the altar was that he felt he was not in a state of grace. In those times, this was almost automatically taken to be some matter related to the sixth commandment, as the Church was obsessed about such matters. It required some moral courage to stay put in such circumstances. I find it ironic that, currently, when Confession appears to have become but a memory, that that uniform Maynooth practice, has become almost standard in all Catholic churches.

Each diocesan group had its own football and croquet grounds in the senior part of the College. It also had what was termed its own position or '*pos*', where, during brief recreation periods, its students gathered to stand in a circle and socialise. Though there were extensive *Walks* in Maynooth, the '*Pos*' was the main focus of diocesan camaraderie. It was very unusual for a student to fraternise within another diocesan '*pos*'. The very small diocesan groups amalgamated within their own archdiocese to form viable '*Pos's*'. The term '*Pos*' was the abbreviation of the Latin word, '*postis*', and meaning doorpost. Our *pos* and football pitch were adjacent to the Crucifix rockery at the entrance to the college cemetery. No burial took place there during my term in Maynooth.

Some of the factors which made Maynooth so congenial to me were its physical beauty, the ritual practice of the Catholic liturgy, and a sense of being a part of Irish history. St. Joseph's Square facing onto the Gothic Revival style of the famous Pugin College Chapel must be one of the most peaceful places in Ireland. The Chapel itself remains awesome in its scale and decoration, despite a lifetime of visitation. Memories of participating in liturgies there help to sustain me in this era of the demise of Latin and Gregorian chant. The College itself is historical, as are the ruins of the Fitzgerald castle 'outside the walls'. It was possible for students to visit Dublin, if they had a reasonable excuse. Many students exercised this option for a variety reasons. I was so content within the College that I only visited the metropolis on one occasion during my five year stay and then only to meet my sisters, who were returning to Manchester after a holiday at home.

Newspapers became available to the students about 1964. But you could never get a complete paper in your hands. It had to be split up into its separate pages to satisfy all those waiting to read it. Henceforth a complete newspaper has remained a luxury for me, and I remain very reluctant to part with any section. On one 1st of April, the *Irish Times* printed an editorial saying the Government was introducing Prohibition. A student from Cavan, whose parents ran a pub got very angry before someone asked him to reflect on the day's date. Radio was not officially available. But I recall two science graduates of my own year, manufacturing and selling tiny radios, which could pick up Radío Éireann. There was a constant market for those at three pounds each. The students produced a journal each year, called *'The Silhouette'*. I wrote an article for it on the historical split in Irish athletics. I enjoyed seeing my work in print. We also had a Bulletin Board on which chosen topics were treated in both visual and written format. I looked after that for a period and enjoyed the researching and writing involved. I ran into some criticism once, when using propaganda material from the South African embassy in London, I produced a Board defending the apartheid system.

MINOR ORDERS & MAJOR ORDERS

There were a variety of stages, during the last four years, on the road to receiving the Holy Orders of priesthood. These consisted of the minor orders of *Tonsure*, *Lector*, *Acolyte* and the major orders of *sub-Diaconate* and *Diaconate*. The reception of these in chronological order was a sign that the College authorities believed you were a suitable student. Any transgression, even very minor, and your name would be omitted from the appropriate list for the end of year's orders ceremony. Having a visitor in your room, or being such a visitor, was a major transgression. Tardiness or sloppy dress, were minor offences. The lists of Orders were published in the annual *'Kalendarium'*, which was the official book giving all details of College life. Each individual's status was clear for all to see, especially the diocesan authorities, who were often, at least part - funding one's College fees. At the end of my first year in theological studies I had embarked on the Minor Order of *Tonsure*. These were of little importance in themselves. But at the end of my fifth year, I could be faced with the prospect of being called to the order of *sub-Diaconate*. This involved taking vows of obedience, poverty and chastity. It was only during that year of 1964-5, when faced with such a momentous decision, that I began to seriously consider my own situation. Despite witnessing the departure of so many of my peers, who were referred to as *'cuts'*, including five of the ten boys who had come with me from St. Jarlath's in 1960, I had remained on automatic pilot, almost oblivious to the seriousness of my position.

BALLYHAUNIS TIES

During my five years in Maynooth, I always spent the Christmas and Easter holidays at home. During summer I usually spent a considerable period in England. In Ballyhaunis my routine continued as previously. I played football for the local

GAA teams. I was heavily involved with the Boy Scouts. I began to use their estate at Larch Hill in the Dublin Mountains as a base for hitch hiking excursions around Ireland. One summer I hitch hiked through Scotland with a fellow student, Des Walsh. I was surprised to discover I could converse in Scots Gaelic with people in Oban. On our first night in Scotland we camped on a hillside outside Kilmarnock. During the night I awakened to find myself alone in the tent, I lifted the flap to see that my partner had rolled out of the tent and was asleep under the stars, further down the hillside.

I remained friendly with some of my female school friends. I recall seeing two of them, Mary Nally and Bernadette Concannon on Main Street one summer's day. There was another attractive girl with them, whom I did not recognise. As she left them, Bernadette and Mary crossed the street to speak to me. They told me their friend's name was Margaret Mulkeen. I told them that I was going to Croke Park to see Down play Kerry in the All Ireland final of 1961 at the weekend. Bernadette gave me the keys to her flat in Rathgar, saying it would be empty for the weekend. (Many years later, while exiting from Star of the Sea Church in Sandymount, I was approached by a lady, who introduced herself as Margaret Rafferty nee Mulkeen. She was the attractive lady from Ballyhaunis and remains a good neighbour of mine). I became a keen golfing enthusiast during those summers on the local nine-hole course. Among the people I played with regularly were Seán Smith, Ian Wilson, Michael and Conor Holmes, Fr. Bart. Delaney OSA. The course at Coolnaha had a sandy-drumlin base and was quite a testing course which challenged the player at every stroke. It was a most beautiful setting, which was a boon for the local community.

DECISION TO LEAVE MAYNOOTH

I was quite content with my life but realised that decision day beckoned in Maynooth. I did not panic as I realised that I had the full academic year to make a decision. I usually leave major decisions to the very last and then live with the consequences. Naturally it was the celibacy element of the vow which concerned me. During the previous four years, I had been very busy and females played little role in my life. It was during the autumn of 1964 that we studied in great detail the morality of marriage. I felt that such a study would be useful to me, whether or not, I left or stayed. After returning from Christmas holidays I began to consult my spiritual advisor, Fr. James Doherty C.M., or 'Jimmy Doc' as we called him. The main outcome to these discussions was his advice, whatever decision I came to, would be the will of God. I had decided that Easter was to be my deadline I assessed the various reasons for and against. Among the former were, idealism, safety, and trivial mindedness of secular life, security; among the latter were my immaturity, possible failures, and attractions of married life. I went home for the Easter vacation without making a firm decision.

During that holiday I was at a film in the Parochial Hall It was called *"Move Over Darling"*, starring Doris Day and James Garner. There was one scene, a very modest and wholesome scene, as one would expect from Doris Day, where as a married couple, the pair sat in bed. There was a quality discernible, a tender feminine mutuality that appealed to me. In that instant, I can recall deciding that I would follow the married state and pursue such an ideal in my life. I returned to Maynooth for final term in a very contented state of mind. I met with 'Jimmy Doc', who blessed my decision. He alone in Maynooth was to know what I intended.

On 10 June 1965 I wrote in my diary, as Béarla: *"It is difficult to know what is best to do or why I want to do what I expect to do –leave. Am I just throwing in the towel? One never knows one's motives really, and this is a matter of utmost import, so it seems better to avoid the heights least one be crushed at a fall from there. The prospects outside seem fair but getting started will be difficult. Teaching seems to be the only obvious outlet. But I hope to try and write something printable at all costs. One could really fulfil oneself in that line if one could write. Radio work appeals to me but I don't think I would make the grade and I am sure the competition is very keen. I think I have been very happy over the past five years. Life here definitely suits me very well and the company is excellent, though I doubt if that is as true as I think. Enclosed life has had many defects for my character development, as I know. I doubt whether I will ever be as happy again and yet I feel I must go. I hope my motives are not base. I feel I wouldn't live up to the requirements so necessary in the priesthood and might only shipwreck my own and others' lives, though of course the same could happen in the secular life, sine gratiae Dei"*.

I decided to finish out the term to the end of the academic year. I also decided to inform each of my family simultaneously. I wrote six letters and posted them together. None of the family had any problem with my choice. In replying to my letter, my mother expressed thanks and joy that I had come to a clear decision. She said that it was better to have tried out Maynooth and got it out of my system, than not to have tried at all. I was the fifty third student of my original class of one hundred and six in 1960, to leave. Though I had come to my decision in quite a leisurely fashion, I had not developed any clear plan of what I might or could do subsequently. I was almost totally ignorant about job prospects. I did not even know that a Higher Diploma in Education was a prerequisite for post-primary teaching. So it was, I left Maynooth in as almost a vague and ignorant state as when I had arrived. My own decision to leave Maynooth was not the only major family decision to be made in 1965. My brother, Tommy, who had lived in England for over ten years, had decided that he and his family would return to live in the family home at Ballyhaunis. When I arrived home in June, Tommy was just about to commence a new business of delivering milk directly to households around the town. I accompanied him on his very first round of deliveries. I was later to introduce him to the pleasure of playing the local golf links, where he has remained an active and successful member ever since.

P. S. 1. Some twenty years later I was contacted about the showing of a film called *"Men for the Harvest"* in the Irish Film Centre. Chloe Gibson had made it at Maynooth during the winter of 1963, for Telefís Éireann. We had seen it at the time but it had no sound track. It had recently been 'discovered' at RTE and a soundtrack added. I attended a packed Film Centre, with many other ex-Maynooth men. Afterwards there was a discussion on it. My reaction was very negative. It portrayed in black and white a staged Maynooth, the elements of which I recognised, but that for me conveyed an overall picture of a place and a time I could not acknowledge.

Despite the familiar faces of Joey Hamill, Mick Harty, John Charles McQuaid, John Cleary, Padraig O'Connor, John Cosgrave, Tom Savage, Donal Musgrave, Pat O'Keeffe, Paddy Kilcoyne, Jimmy Doherty and myself, I repudiated the film as not portraying the place where I had spent five happy years. When in 2007 I received a DVD of this film my reaction had changed, and I was quite happy that the picture it portrayed was indeed authentic.

P. S. 2. Leaving Maynooth removed me from contemporary events there. It was not until Patrick Corish's bi-centenary book, *"Maynooth College 1795-1995"*, was published, that I read about events there in the immediate two years after my departure. I was surprised to read of how the senior students had pressurised the College to make major changes in the disciplinary life of the students. Corish writes of the President reporting to the Bishops of *"disturbing tendencies"* and the fact that *"some relaxations had been granted but others were simply being taken"*. He repeated his conviction of the *"urgent need for a planned and far-reaching reform. What in fact was happening was like a pressure-cooker lid too long screwed down giving way under the pressure that had built up...Things sacrosanct for generations just went"*[51a]. The only one from our class of 1967 to become a bishop was Gerry Clifford, Auxiliary Bishop of Armagh. Of the five men from the archdiocese of Tuam who were ordained from that class of 1967, none remain in the ministry.

Maynooth College

CHAPTER 8

ST. PATRICK'S COLLEGE DRUMCONDRA
TOMÁS Ó'FIAICH ASSISTS ME

"Coláiste Phádraig Manuat
Co Chill Dara
Dé Luain

Dear Anthony,

I was sorry to hear that you are not coming back to Maynooth, but I am so used to losing good friends every year in this way that I am never surprised nowadays, when I hear that so and so is not returning. I wish you God's Blessing and every happiness in your new career. Yes, I remember you quite well from your chub year[51b]. If my memory serves me correctly, you sang a rebel song in the Christmas free class of that year and I don't mind admitting that this gave me a soft spot for you from then on. I even remember where you sat in class – along the wall on my right looking down. I rang St. Patrick's Drumcondra this morning after receiving your letter... I know that the College authorities conduct interviews with prospective students at the beginning of September and it is necessary to have your name down for this in good time. The report on studies and conduct, which they will get from Maynooth, when you make formal application, will carry a fair amount of weight and the interview will then clinch the issue. The interview includes also I think, a test in oral Irish. However when Fr. O'Hegarty comes back I'll get full particulars from him and shall then write to you again.

I hope you have a nice holiday and are not working too hard in Birmingham.

Gach beannacht

Tomás Ó'Fiaich".

I communicated my decision to leave Maynooth to Archbishop Walsh of Tuam and to the local parish clergy. I had thought that they might be in a position to advise on alternate career options, but this did not happen. The local parish Administrator, Fr. Tom Rushe's, only advice to me was to recompense the diocese by whatever sum it may have supported me during my time in Maynooth. I got a reference from the President of St. Jarlath's College, Fr. Michael Isaac Mooney, where he deemed me, "a satisfactory student in every respect".

BUS CONDUCTOR ON COVENTRY ROAD

After a few weeks at home in Ballyhaunis, I followed the family tradition and emigrated to England. I went to stay with my eldest brother, Paddy and his family, then living in Birmingham. At that time in England, most public services operated to a higher standard than in Ireland, and it was a pleasant place to live. I became a bus conductor with Birmingham City Transport, working out of their Coventry Road Garage, near Birmingham City football ground, on the number fifty-eight and sixty routes, from the city centre towards the airport. The work was congenial and the early morning shift of 04.30 to 11.30 suited me fine. I finished work shortly after most people began their working day. There was plenty of time for reading and sports activity. I was quite happy as a bus conductor, but the fact that I had a university degree meant that there was an expectation from my working colleagues, who were most congenial people, and my family, that I should be doing, or at least aspiring, to something else.

Teaching was the obvious career, but I was in the ridiculous position of not knowing how to access that career. As the weeks went by, I recalled hearing an anecdote in Maynooth that one of the priests there, Fr. Tomás Ó'Fiaich, had once directed a student who had left towards entering primary teaching. I decided to write to him. I told him that he probably would not remember me, but that I had been a student of his during the academic year 1960-'61. I outlined my current position and indicated that I hoped that he might be able to direct me towards primary teaching. I was not very hopeful of a response, since it was mid-summer, and he might be away. I had not known him particularly well and it was some years since I had been a student of his. I expected that he would not remember me. But to my surprise and great pleasure I soon received a reply, which indicated otherwise. His letter of reply began this chapter. The song that he remembered me singing during that Xmas free class of 1960, was the one I quoted earlier, as being in my scrapbook from the late 1950s.

Fr. Ó'Fiaich had indicated that he would write again after he had succeeded in speaking directly to his contact in Drumcondra. This he soon did, which was just as well, as technically the official date for applying for entry in the autumn had passed. This time his letter came from *"Crossmaglen, County Armagh"*. He had gone to great trouble to illustrate exactly the kind of information I needed to produce for my application to the Department of Education and St Patrick's Drumcondra. He ended his second letter:

"I hope everything is clear in that, and that you will be successful in getting in. Let me know how things go.

With all good wishes for a pleasant holiday
Agus gach beannacht ó Dhia agus ó Mhuire ort".

I followed in detail the procedure Fr. Ó'Fiaich had advised and after a very rigorous interview, singing and oral Irish tests, I enrolled as a 'graduate student' at St. Patrick's, Drumcondra, in October. There were about ten graduate students; three had recently left Maynooth, Pat. O'Keeffe and Pat Burke, classmates of mine, together with Michael Joseph Lyons of Louisburg. Some twenty years later, I acquired a letter concerning myself, written by the President of Maynooth, Michael A. Harty to the President of Drumcondra, Fr. Donal Cregan C.M. It was dated 17 September 1965 and read;

"I confirm that Anthony Jordan (Tuam) took his B.A. degree in Maynooth in 1963. He then studied theology for two years and decided to leave last June as he felt that he had no vocation for the priesthood. He was a satisfactory student and we can readily recommend him from the point of view of character and academic ability".

Tomás Ó Fiaich was my Good Samaritan.

ST. PATRICK'S COLLEGE, DRUMCONDRA

The Vincentian Order managed St Patrick's College Drumcondra. The teacher-training course there lasted for two years, with most students aged between eighteen and twenty years, having recently completed their Leaving Certificate Examinations. They regarded the Graduates as mature and learned people. The latter spent one year in the College, concentrating in the main on the methodology, philosophy and practicalities of teaching. The College was situated about two miles from the city center and adjacent to Croke Park. New residential blocks had just been completed and the modern single room living accommodation with a large common room was most congenial. Previously, students had lived in boarding school type communal dormitories. Freedom of movement was only curtailed by the necessity of attending lectures. I liked the College and the students. It again provided ample sporting and reading opportunities for me. But I soon came to believe that the system in place did little to challenge and extend the majority of the students. They had all done extremely well in their Leaving Certificates and were bright. They entered Drumcondra ready to work hard and broaden their horizons. But they soon discovered that the course did not make challenging academic demands on them. They found it quite easy. This led gradually into complacency and a false impression of their true abilities. Many of them, after two years in Dublin, went back to rural Ireland without interacting with the cultural possibilities of the capital city. At home again, they were not extended or challenged intellectually. It was a great opportunity missed for the people directly concerned, their own families, and their future pupils. However, that said, it is widely accepted that primary school teachers have made an enormous contribution to very many aspects of society in Ireland.

The female of the species fared even worse. The regime in Carysfort College still remained quite restrictive and while producing excellent primary teachers, rarely extended their vision of themselves. My most intense intellectual pleasure in Drumcondra came from an English lecturer, John Killeen, through our mutual love of poetry, particularly that of the war-poet Wilfred Owen.

The most important thing I got from that year was the ability to teach, to organize and deliver a lesson in such a fashion that most of my pupils would have a good opportunity of understanding and accessing the material involved. Drumcondra certainly delivered the art or science of teaching very well. It was hard work, with painstaking preparation, apprenticeship and closely monitored performance, and detailed evaluation. If you did not succeed in teaching practice, you did not become an accredited teacher. During my years there, the person in charge of 'teaching practice' was the father of Derval and Neil Jordan of Clontarf, affectionately called 'Cluichi'. I also used the year to have several intense female relationships. We were impecunious students and so were many of the females we encountered. An inexpensive venue for dancing was provided by Kevin Street Garda Station, where close contact on the dance floor was termed 'lurching'. I was on a learning curve and needed all the experience I could get. During the year I maintained one continuous, though modest, relationship with a girl from Clonmel, with whom I would attend the annual dress dance in the Shelbourne in June. That was the last occasion I met her. One of my 'graduate' friends, Michael Lyons of Louisburg Co. Mayo, played the violin. He persuaded me to accompany him to the nearby St. Francis Xavier Hall to attend the 'Studio Concerts', which were played by the Radió Éireann Symphony Orchestra on Friday nights. The fact that these were free proved a great incentive. I became addicted to classical music and it has remained a major part of my life since. My wife and I are regular season ticket holders for the National Symphony Orchestra. I also began to frequent Trinity College and UCD. I participated in several student activities, especially debates at the '*Hist*' Society and L & H. I attended '*Waiting for Godot*' at the Gate Theatre. I read Edna O'Brien's, '*The Country Girls*' and '*The Girl with the Green Eyes*'.

JOHN McGAHERN AND THE INTO

I had already read John McGahern's first novel, '*The Barracks*'. His second book, '*The Dark*' caused a furore in 1965, when the Censorship Board banned it. The sad and indefensible action of depriving him of his post in a primary school in Clontarf was taken. His first book had been highly acclaimed and he got a year's leave in 1964 to avail of a Macauley Fellowship to write '*The Dark*'. It contained very explicit details on sexuality, particularly male masturbation. This frightened the clergy and the fact that he had married a foreign woman in a London Registry Office made him unacceptable as a primary teacher in the archdiocese ruled by Archbishop John Charles McQuaid.

His trade union, the Irish National Teachers Organization, did not back him, due to a technical matter that he was not then a currently paid - up member. Noel Ward, a former executive member of the INTO, writing in the *Irish Times,* under the headline "*When a teacher was engulfed by 'The Dark', and his union failed him*"[52], discounts this excuse, writing, "*First of all it is clear that he was sacked*".

He had been in a permanent post in Clontarf from which he took approved leave of absence. Second, McGahern was an INTO member of long standing. His INTO card, seen by this writer, records his membership successively of Athlone-Trim, Drogheda and Dublin City branches… the affair only became public in February 1966. The final sentence in the January 1966 INTO minutes say 'No action was taken'. Some years ago, John McGahern was invited to read at the Teacher's Club in Dublin. The INTO President said welcoming the author was both 'pleasurable and penitential' and acknowledged that the union's role in the McGahern dismissal case had 'not been heroic'[53]. Many years later speaking on RTE, McGahern recalled JJ Kelligher, the Union secretary saying to him, "*If it was just about the book, we might be able to do something about it, but why did you have to go and marry that foreign woman?*" The Parish Priest, Canon Patrick Carton, told McGahern, "*The Archbishop told me to get rid of you*". In an interview with John Cooney, MacGahern said, "*I heard privately, but there was no way you could prove this, that John Charles McQuaid said if the INTO backed me, he wouldn't give them any support in pay negotiations that were coming up for the Department, and that he'd back them to the hilt if they would have nothing to do with my case*"[54].

Though a victim initially, McGahern survived and achieved deserved literary successes, before his early death in 2006. He had been able to take a very benign view of his treatment. He said remarkably, on RTE, "*I have nothing but affection for the Church. The Church was my first book and my most important one*". But the message sent out to primary teachers, with the connivance of the INTO, on that occasion was a stark one: freedom of thought and action was subject to those who owned and controlled the schools, namely the clergy. This occurrence was to have a very direct effect on me within the next few years. Among my contemporaries in Drumcondra were Joe O'Toole and John Carr, who both subsequently became General Secretaries of the INTO; Brian O'Shea became a T.D.; John Dennehy was later Secretary-General of the Department of Education and Science; Alan Titley became Professor of Gaeilge at Drumcondra and later UCC, as well as a witty journalist. Though I did not know him, I feel John MacGahern was a Good Samaritan.

SPIRIT OF 1966

One strange occurrence during the 1916 Commemorative year of 1966 was a representation by the Minister of Education to the President of Drumcondra about the ethos of the College. It appeared that an article in the College magazine, '*Dochas*', during the previous year had criticized the College for being 'West British'. This had received much publicity and the Minister of Education intervened. Fr. Cregan, the President, told the students that an improvement was being demanded in the current year. One immediate result saw the College give official recognition to Gaelic games over foreign games, though the urbane and far-sighted Fr. Cregan emphasized that he had no objection to a Rugby club being established in the College.

It was in this context that the student President of the English Society encountered some criticism from Fr. Cregan for inviting Owen Dudley Edwards to speak at the Society. A most enjoyable event during the year was the pageant organized by the Gaelic Athletic Association to celebrate the fiftieth anniversary of the Easter Rising. It was titled, "*Seachtar Fear – Seacht Lá*" by Bryan MacMahon. This was a massive operation produced by Martin Dempsey, with a cast of hundreds and performed over three evenings in Croke Park and once in Belfast. Many of the College students, including myself, participated. Among the cast were Brendan Caldwell, Des Nealon, Niall Tobín, Edward Byrne, Ronnie Walsh, with Rinnceoirí Inis Ealga. A programme note said that the first pageant to be held at Croke Park was "The Defence of the Ford", which was written and produced by Padraig Pearse. It was staged on 9 June 1913. It was also during Easter of 1966 that the IRA sought to demolish Nelson Pillar in O'Connell St., and succeeded in blowing up the top half. Most of the students hurried in to town that morning to see the result. The Irish Army later completed the demolition, with their first attempt causing much collateral damage on the street. Luckily I had climbed the Pillar on several occasions.

MY FIRST TEACHING POST

In the 1960's, the official school year began on 1 July, with the summer holidays following within a week or two. It was therefore vital for new teachers to have acquired a post, any post, for that date. It meant that you were then on the payroll for the holidays during July and August. It was in that context I received a letter from a school principal on 20 June 1966, which read;

"*Daingean Co. Offaly*

Dear Anthony Jordan,

This being the first time to hear of your appointment I wish you a Céad Míle Fáilte. The school opens at 9.30 and closes at 3 p.m. Lunchtime is from 12.30 to 1 p.m. and Christian doctrine time is from 12 to 12.30. You have not mentioned digs so I understand you have got them, and a reasonable price is fixed. Holiday time is not fixed yet but the summer holidays maybe given about the 8th of next month.

Hoping this will be helpful.

Is mise le meas Séan Ó Conaill".

So on 30 June I traveled by train to Tullamore and hitched a lift the few miles to Daingean. I survived the following week but found it very tiring. My principal was very helpful as were several ladies who taught in other local schools and with whom I shared digs. But Daingean itself frightened me. It consisted of just one street and as soon as you stepped outside the house, all eyes appeared to follow your limited movements. I knew that I could not long survive in such a place.

The close proximity of females, surprisingly, did not appeal to me. In fact I found it most disagreeable to share so many of the mundane functional operations of life with them. But the appeal of a cheque at the end of the summer made up for the discomfort. I returned to Daingean on the 1st of September with the firm intention of securing another post elsewhere. There was little difficulty in this and within a few weeks I had two interviews arranged: St. Peter's in Little Bray and Coláiste Mhuire in Parnell Square. I interviewed for Bray first and was very impressed by the principal, Mr. Murray. I then decided to make a private pre-interview visit to Coláiste Mhuire, never having encountered Christian Brothers previously. I did not like the ambience there, and cancelled my interview. Within a few days I was offered and accepted the job in Bray. I informed the Parish Priest during lunchtime one day, giving him one week's notice. He was annoyed, but said, *"I can't hold you"*.

MY SECOND TEACHING POST

In Little Bray, an area north of the Dargle River, I discovered that my classroom, a prefabricated room, was not ready. I shared a classroom with Tom Raftery, who had been a classmate of mine in Drumcondra and whom I knew well and liked. He was a Galway man and a great raconteur. Two others on the staff, Michael MacMahon and John Dennehy, had also been classmates of ours in Drumcondra. Con Murray from Donegal, who later went to South America as a lay missionary, and Larry Weir, who became a barrister at the Four Courts, completed the staff. Mr. Murray from Longford was a gentleman who always insisted that any parent wishing to see a teacher was obliged to talk to him first. This proved to be of great mutual value to both parents and teachers. I spent a full academic year there and enjoyed it immensely. The contact and interplay with intelligent boys was most exciting and challenging.

T.C.D. or U.C.D.

That same month of October also saw me register at University College Dublin for the Higher Diploma in Education, which I learned was the recognized qualification for teaching in a secondary school. I had earlier applied to Trinity College Dublin for a similar course but my application was late. I regretted that very much, as I had come to regard Trinity, as having the ethos and ambience of what a university should have, unlike UCD. However UCD had historical associations with James Joyce and Cardinal Newman and was the location for the Treaty Debates. I later received the offer of a place at Trinity, but by that time I had paid my fee to UCD. I regretted very much missing the opportunity of attending Queen Elizabeth's Dublin establishment. One very pleasant surprise at UCD was the presence on the course of several people I knew well. There was Pat O'Keeffe, with whom I had been in Maynooth and Drumcondra. Edward Moran, with whom I had been at primary and secondary schools, and who had arrived in Dublin by way of London, Columbia University and

Kenya. Another Ballyhaunis man, Frank Fahey, a famous Mayo minor footballer was also there. Lectures took place three afternoons a week, after school. This proved very tiring. The course itself was totally uninspiring and certainly did not fulfill its primary function of preparing its students on how to teach. It compared very poorly with the course in Drumcondra. If the equivalent courses in the other universities were of the same quality, post primary education was being very badly served. One lecturer actually read his notes aloud and never engaged in eye or verbal contact with the students. As a result, attendance at lectures was usually quite sparse. The head of Education at UCD, Professor Ó'Catháin, would occasionally announce a roll call in advance, and on those occasions, the Physics Theatre would not be able to seat the entire attendance.

Maynooth Football Team 1961. Author is extreme right front row.

Ballyhaunis Football Team 6/9/1964. Author is 4th from left back row.

CHAPTER 9

CANON JAMES HORAN
IN PRAISE OF WOMEN

Monsignor James Horan became a national figure when he succeeded in building an international airport on top of a 'soggy, boggy mountain', in remote Mayo. He had made his name locally in the 1950s by building a dancehall in the rural half-parish of Tooreen and promoting it vigorously. He spent nine months during 1950, traversing American cities collecting £8,000 for the project. As Vincent Power writes in his history of that era,

"Monsgr. Horan believed there was room for the small operator who knew the market and did his business properly. That brought him into competition with the Reynolds' empire. The monsignor booked top bands for his hall at Tooreen. He ran a thriving business and threatened the survival of other halls in the region. He took crowds away from McGarry's Ballroom in Ballyhaunis. But McGarry's fought back by offering their premises to the Reynolds'. The idea was that Albert would transfer some of his bands to boost the Ballyhaunis ballroom. Then, news spread that the Devil, no less, had been sighted in Horan's ballroom in Tooreen. The finger of suspicion pointed in one direction. "I was credited with it as an opposition tactic" says Albert Reynolds, "I never took away from the fact. Mgr. Horan even said it to me on the day that we talked about building an airport in Knock. I don't know whether he really believed it – but he certainly remembered twenty-five years later. I was always blamed for it"[55].

In the summer of 2005, a local artist from Coolnaha, Ballyhaunis, Eilis Murphy mounted a multimedia exhibition in Dublin on "The Devil in the Dancehall". I knew Fr. Horan moderately well, having played golf with him at the local links, which was half way between Ballyhaunis and Tooreen, on several occasions. I often went to dances in Tooreen before going to and after leaving Maynooth. Fr. Horan was very proud of the fact that there was an almost alcohol free atmosphere in his hall because there was no public house in the locality. He has written,

"No hall in the country was as well run and as strictly supervised as Tooreen. I supervised the hall personally on all occasions... a very decent and select crowd danced at Tooreen"[56].

I was to have personal experience early in 1966 of how true his words were.

On this occasion I had met a rather special lady at a dance there. The band was playing a slow foxtrot. I was dancing very close to my partner; when I was tipped on the shoulder by the good priest and told, 'mind your dancing'. I had gone to the dance with my brother Tommy, his wife Mary and my sister Bernie. There, amid a phalanx of women on the opposite side of the hall from where the gentlemen assembled, I saw a most beautiful girl. As the next dance was called, I joined the throng of men advancing across the floor and burrowed my way through the advance guard of ladies, to boldly take her hand, asking, *"will you dance please?"* We made our way around the back of the massing throng to the dance floor, where I took her right hand in my left hand and placed my right hand around her waist, and off we sailed. Her boyish figure and soft gentle voice enamored me. My most recent and remote experiences had tutored me, that if you met a lady you fancied, it was better to seek to persuade her to continue to dance with you. That was usually a good sign of reciprocal interest. We remained together for the rest of the night, save for me excusing myself briefly, to get the keys of my brother's car. Advance planning was important as that night demonstrated, when we spent some time in the rear of Tommy's Morris Minor, engaged in rather modest foreplay. She was home from England to visit her sick father. I told her that I usually spent some time in England each summer and would like to call on her. She gave me her address, to which she was returning within a few days. As soon as we got back home to Ballyhaunis, I wrote the address in my *Eason's Diary*; "224 Colne Road, Briarfield, Burnley".

John Waters has written in his own original way of the show band era, dominated at first to a great extent by the Catholic clergy. He saw it,

"As a central element of what we now speak of as the modernization of Irish life… On Sunday morning the faithful trooped into Mass to be told why they should abstain from company keeping, self abuse and mutual gratification, and on Sunday night they handed over their pound note to the same priest, to be allowed into the local Dionysian citadel in the hope of finding a sexual partner for the night"[57].

Monsignor James Horan, Mayo Dancehall and Airport Builder.

I still find it hard to understand how I was able to exclude, for the most part, all carnal thoughts of women from my life, for five whole years, from the age of eighteen to twenty three years. Many would think it unnatural if nigh impossible. Yet it happened to me. I was not living in a monastery. I spent several months each year away from the College in a variety of environments. But when I left Maynooth, I decided that I had a certain leeway to make up and set about acquainting myself with as many females, as my rather meagre outgoings would allow. I soon fell into the habit of having several girl friends at the same time.

One of them, a demure civil servant from Clonmel, with whom I dallied for a full year, insisted on being treated modestly on all occasions. I reckoned that this was good training for me, and though she fed me well, it was not enough. A lady from Galway, whose brother was a priest, was more liberal. Then there was another civil servant from Mayo, who was game for anything.

There was also, among others, a lovely ex-nun from Cork, who held me so closely yet tenderly. To earn some badly needed money, I had become a collector for the Augustinian Missions Weekly Draw. This involved collecting one shilling each week from a list of people at their home addresses, which were supplied to me by an agent for the draw. I received three pence out of each shilling collected (twelve pence to one shilling). My area covered Rathmines. One Friday evening I knocked on a flat on Leinster Road. One of the female occupants let me in, saying that my client was in bed and that I should go in to her bedroom. I collected the shilling and sat on the bed for a chat, for I knew my customer fairly well from previous calls. On this occasion, to my surprise and consternation, she requested me to pleasure her. I made no return visits to that bedroom to collect a shilling.

WORKING FOR GEORGE WIMPEY

One of my sisters, Josephine Connolly, lived in Manchester. I went there in the summer, to afford myself the opportunity, should I decide to exercise it, of visiting the lady I had met in Tooreen. I got a job with Wimpy Construction at a large new housing estate they were building at nearby Middleton. I had to leave the house at seven in the morning to get to work for eight. It was hard rough graft, where a labourer like myself could be given any manual task.

At one point I got the job of cleaning out completed houses of all extraneous matter. This meant sweeping all the floors and dumping everything outside the front doors. When I was close to completing a house, I would look outside and if there was no sign of the ganger, I would proceed to scatter all the material around the lower floor and recommence sweeping as slowly as possible. This was adhering to the well known principle that when you got a congenial task, you spun it out for as long as possible, lest you be given a pick and spade and ordered into a trench to 'dig deep and throw back far'.

During one week's work a general 'tidy up' of the entire site was ordered, as officials from Head Office in London were due for an inspection. Consternation ensued after it was belatedly discovered that one row of six houses were built facing the wrong way. To disguise the mix-up, the front and rear windows of the houses were gutted. A large hole in the ground was excavated to dump damaged material in. I often wondered how the Company could make profits on such jobs.

MEETING MY LIFE MATE AGAIN

After working about a month with Wimpy, I wrote to the lady in Briarfield, informing her that I proposed to visit her on the following weekend. Her reply said, "I received your very unexpected letter to-day. I shall be pleased to see you on Sat". She gave me clear directions. I proceeded on a forty-mile bus journey over the bare Lancashire moorlands to Burnley and then on another bus, to the East Lancashire town of Briarfield. It was a small town of narrow streets flanked by stone houses.

Overlooked by Pendle Hill, it was a bleak place, even in high summer. I did not know quite what to expect as I knocked on 224 Colne Road. The lady might be in digs there; she might be living with relatives or friends. However, she greeted me herself on the stone floor and made me welcome. Being quite nervous, I soon found myself acting foolishly, by reciting, what I considered, some suitable verses of a WB Yeats' poem. I was later to discover that this caused much disquiet to the lady, who wondered whether I was 'the full shilling'.

She chided me for the threadbare quality of my clothes, wondering aloud as to what her neighbors might think if they saw me. She was living alone in the house. Her brother, with whom, she had been sharing the house, had emigrated to Canada recently. She did not immediately invite me to stay the night, but as the evening went on and my behaviour improved somewhat, I felt that I would be so asked. I left the following evening, without as much as touching her, but with an invitation to return the next weekend, if I wished.

I invested in a new dark green suit for my return trip. It was commented upon favourably and with some relief, as she had decided to take me dancing to nearby Blackburn on the Saturday night. Back at the house in the early hours of the morning, I felt that another chaste relationship would not be to my interest or advantage. She did not spurn my advances as we kissed and cuddled. But suddenly she became quite agitated and pushed me away roughly, becoming, I thought, quite hostile. I was taken aback and as she refused to discuss what was amiss, I retreated to bed, somewhat confused. She did not speak of the incident the next day, but I indicated that I was somewhat startled by her strange reaction. We parted on good terms, as I began what was the start of my return journey to Ireland. Within a few weeks, I received a letter postmarked Burnley & Nelson. She told me that the Joan Baez LP, I had brought to her, had become her favourite record, though she had not liked it at first.

The reason for her letter was to say that if I did wish to write to her, to do so directly to Briarfield and not to her Irish address, as her mother would be very suspicious. She added, *"I have a rule, I never tell her little things like that"*. She also apologized for alarming me on my last visit. I was later to discover the reason for her strange reaction that night. I knew, even at that early stage, that she was a unique individual, who I would be very lucky to capture. It was obvious that she was entirely her own person, one who would come to her own decisions in her own time.

We exchanged letters over a few months before I returned to Manchester for my sister Bernadette's wedding to Michael Duffy. I spent the weekend at Colne Road, where we resumed our rather tentative relationship. Thereafter I began to send reading material to her, including books by Edna O'Brien and John MacGahern. As we continued to exchange letters on a frequent basis, I became more certain that she was the woman for me, if I could capture her. She was the most self - contained, honest and straightforward person I had encountered. She knew who she was and what she was, and what she wanted. She was mature, direct and confident.

In a later 1967 letter I mentioned that a friend of mine was trying to talk me into going to Africa, to teach for a few years. I intimated that I was thinking about it. I did not receive any reply, which was unusual, so I wrote again. She replied from Manchester, where she had recently moved, saying:

Dear Anthony,

"I received your very welcomed letter to-day. I did get your letter and book last Monday week but you upset me and that's the reason I didn't answer it. Well Anthony, in one letter you say you are stopping in Dublin another year and in the other you are going to Africa or Canada. You can please yourself where you go, but I certainly would not write to you to either of those places, for a number of reasons. If this is what you have in mind please don't answer this letter. It is bad enough you being in Dublin and I in Manchester, but at least we can see each other once in a while, but I couldn't see any sense to you being in Africa and I in Manchester. I would rather forget. Why didn't you mention this to me when I saw you, or is it your mate who is getting the better of you? It's so difficult to sort things out like this in a letter. I understand why you think about this but even so. Well Anthony, enough of that, I am enjoying life here quite well. I am very happy at work and that's the main thing. The reason is that the girls I work with are excellent; we have lots of laughs and chat and no falling out. One of them said to me the other day very seriously, "Mary, do you get depressed when you think you're getting older?" She said that she does. I said, "No, I am wishing I was eighty". She asked, "Why?" I said, "Well I'm sure to be nearer to the grave then, if not in it". She said, "I wonder what we are put here for; is it to make somebody happy?" I replied, "Well I don't know"...

I re-read all of her letters yesterday, the 10th of August 2004. It was an exquisite experience to realize that the magic she created for me then, remains as vivid as ever, because she has not changed.

There was one other girl, a Corkonian, a more experienced person than myself, with whom I was 'great' during those years. Our relationship was a strange one, in that I think I could have loved her, but she did not express her true feelings for me, until it was too late. I presumed that she was not overly concerned whether our usual weekend meetings happened or not. I used to phone her at the last moment. We never spoke about our feelings for each other. She would not entertain such a topic. And we spent so many, many hours together, some of them quite passionate, and wonderful. She had a suitor down at home. Early in 1968 she proposed to me "as it was a leap year", but I did not take her seriously.

On one, almost last occasion in July, two friends had seen me off for England at the Dunlaoire ferry terminal. They then left to walk down the pier to watch the boat sail out of the harbour. As I passed through the embarkation point, my Cork friend came rushing up to me, past the protesting ticket checkers. There, in a few moments, she poured out her feelings for me, detailing all the occasions, when she had wanted to speak but could not; how she waited for my telephone calls each Friday night, denying herself the chance of going out with friends. It was dramatic and traumatic. The time was short. Many thoughts rushed through my mind, many words I could have said, some critical and all sad. She told me that she would emigrate for a year or else accept a proposal of marriage. I continued my journey and as agreed, unfurled my black Maynooth umbrella, as the boat passed out of the harbour, identifying myself to my two friends, Ann Malone and Pat O'Keefe, standing on the edge of the pier, unaware of the recent drama.

Dunlaoire Harbour, departure point for many of the Author's forays to England.

CHAPTER 10

LADY GOULDING'S CENTRAL REMEDIAL CLINIC

Lady Valerie Goulding founded the Central Remedial Clinic with Kathleen O'Rourke in 1951, in an attempt to counter the challenges of a polio epidemic then raging in the country. It began in a house on the corner of Pembroke St. in Dublin 4, before moving to Prospect Hall in Goatstown, which was officially opened by President Seán T. O'Kelly in 1954. A special day school was established in 1956. As polio was contained, the Clinic began to concentrate on the early treatment and management of children with Cerebral Palsy.

I became a member of the school staff at Goatstown in 1968. Later that same year, the Clinic moved to a new purpose - built campus in Clontarf, which was officially opened by President Eamon DeVelera. Lady Goulding's father, Viscount Monckton of Brenchely, had been a close advisor to King Edward VIII at the time of his abdication in 1936. Valerie, then 18, acted as a messenger between the King and his lover, Mrs Wallis Simpson. She was a witness to the unfolding drama involving Winston Churchill and the Prime Minister Stanley Baldwin. She later said, *"I couldn't understand the attraction of Wallis Simpson"*.

As Valerie Hamilton Monckton, the 20-year-old daughter of a Tory minister, she came to Ireland in 1939 for the Fairyhouse Races and met Sir Basil Goulding. The head of his family's fertilizer business, Sir Basil was then a prince of Irish industry. They married quietly in Downings, Co. Donegal. At the outbreak of the war, they both went to England. Basil joined the RAF and Valerie became a first lieutenant in the Artillery Training Unit. They returned to live in Ireland in 1946, at Dargle Cottage, near Enniskerry, Co. Wicklow. She never settled down to a life of conventional domesticity.

A decisive and kind woman with a strong sense of duty, she needed a cause. For several years in the late 1940's she worked as kitchen help at Marrowbone Lane health clinic. *"The poverty of the Dublin slums, the malnutrition, unemployment, abysmal social conditions; tuberculosis was rife; there were barefoot children, and that really got me,"* she said. She met Kathleen O'Rourke, a fitness instructor, who was giving exercise classes to young housewives in Bewleys' Café, Grafton Street. Following her father's influence, Lady Goulding converted to Catholicism in 1962 and remained an ardent Catholic for the rest of her long life.

PRINCIPAL AT GLENDALOUGH

Prior to my joining the Central Remedial Clinic, I had been Principal of a two-teacher school in Glendalough for one year. I had been so appointed by the local parish priest, while working in England earlier in the summer, without any interview. I had to abandon my flat in Dublin and take the St. Kevin's bus, which was the only mode of public transport into the mountains of County Wicklow. I decided to get off at the village of Roundwood to collect the school keys from the parish priest, for the following morning. I had no digs arranged, so the parish priest instructed his curate to put me up for the night. I was on my own after that. Being an old boy scout, I had come prepared to fend for myself, with sleeping bag and cooking utensils. The school consisted of one large room, divided by a portable partition, to create two teaching spaces. For the next few nights, I slept in the school, which did not have electricity or running water. By then, some of the parents had organized digs for me in the nearby village of Annamoe. The assistant schoolmistress, on whom I was depending for all kinds of procedural advice, drove through Annamoe on her way to school and was able to give me a lift to and from school. She was commuting from her home on the North Circular road in Dublin each day. We agreed very shortly to pool traveling expenses and I returned to sharing a flat in Ranelagh with the Dillon brothers from Ballyhaunis. Such an ambience held more allure for a young man without wheels, than the rugged beauty of Wicklow. Although, when schoolwork was particularly frustrating, it was very relieving to be able to walk out into the schoolyard at Laragh, and look down on the beautiful valley of the two lakes. The manager of the school was a very civilized and congenial curate named Fr. Tom Stack. He visited occasionally and believed in forward planning for official paper work.

The first task each morning, when the weather got colder, was to light an open fire, using turf and sticks. The boys were very adept at this. I decided that I would cook my dinner on the fire. On the first such occasion, as the smell of bacon and cabbage wafted through the room, the Schools Inspector, Nicholas de Rís, arrived. Before I had time to panic or offer any explanation, he commented approvingly, "tá an boladh sin go deas" (That's a lovely smell). On a later occasion when he came to examine my teaching proficiency for my diploma, the local parents put on a fine meal for us. Such a function was aimed at lessening the time available for the conduct of the examination. He was very impressed with the playing of my tin whistle band. I did not tell him that I could not play myself and had 'taught' the class, by getting them to copy one pupil who could. When teaching an arithmetic lesson and questioning the class on the best way to complete the task, the inspector asked me to complete it myself on the blackboard. As I approached the board, I had a mental blank and could not remember how to do it. Luckily Mr. Rice changed his mind and asked me to go on to the next lesson. Even though there was only a distance of eighteen miles between Bray and Glendalough, there was a huge difference between the respective pupils and their attitude to education.

In Bray they were eager and forward. While in Glendalough, education was not such an important priority. The children there were shy, though delightful. During first term, the assistant mistress moved out of Dublin to Greystones, to shorten her commuting time. I had little option but to follow suit. From there our journey took us to Newtownmountkennedy and up Slaughter Hill to Roundwood, through ever changing nature schemes, to Glendalough. In Greystones I lived in a self-contained flat in a house occupied by an elderly lady named Mrs Palmer. She had five children and said quite seriously that if she were to have her way over again, she would have had five cats instead. She maintained that she would have got more satisfaction out of the latter.

On a couple of occasions when the assistant mistress could not travel, neither could I, so the school remained closed. If there was any hint of snow in Greystones we did not travel, on the correct assumption that the roads would be impassible on higher ground. On one of these occasions, I made the mistake of phoning the parish priest. He told me that opening the school was my responsibility, as principal teacher, and that I should not bother him again.

My own lack of transport and the lure of the fleshpots of urban living, made me decide to start looking for a job in Dublin. I answered an advertisement from an establishment that I had never heard of previously, called the Central Remedial Clinic School. It was situated in Goatstown very close to my old base in Ranelagh. I interviewed, but they decided the appointment of a lady was more appropriate at that stage. However soon afterwards I received this letter:

Anthony Jordan, Esq,
Ripley, New Road,
Greystones
28th February, 1968.

"Dear Mr. Jordan,

You will remember that in a previous letter I mentioned the possibility that we would require a third teacher. It now appears certain that we will need one from 1st July. We are applying to the Dept. Education for official sanction for this appointment. Assuming this is forthcoming we would be very happy to offer you this appointment.

Accordingly, I would be very glad to know if you are still interested.

Yours sincerely

R. McLoughlin.
Administrator.

P.S. I would mention that we hope to move to the new premises in Clontarf during the summer holidays".

THE CENTRAL REMEDIAL CLINIC

The Central Remedial Clinic, (originally known as the Dublin Remedial Clinic) in Clontarf occupied a Scott-Tallon designed glass building. It soon became a most exciting place. Lady Goulding, due to her title and her close links to the British establishment, as well as her eccentric businessman husband, Basil, drew all types of people to the Clinic and became a celebrity in her own right. The rich and the famous paraded regularly, to be photographed with the children and relieved of plenty of cash by Lady Goulding. It became very fashionable to be involved with raising money for disabled children. I can recall a young Tony O'Reilly becoming involved in providing shoes for children there. Lady Goulding was a hard-working Chairman. Though always minimizing her own intellectual capabilities, she realized where her strengths lay and had no compunction in using her position to fundraise enthusiastically for the Clinic. Like many others from Ireland, her first port of call had been to the United States of America, when she had a most adventurous journey to Boston, on the Irish Pine in 1952.

Her most famous fundraising coup was to persuade George Annesley to donate £100,000 for the privilege of having the Clontarf premises named after his deceased daughter, Penny. He had laid down two additional conditions for his donation. The Government had to match his money and he wanted the freedom of the City of Dublin. The latter proved unattainable, even for Lady Goulding, but at a lunch in his honor at Maxim's in Paris, Annesly handed over the cheque. Jimmy Saville summed up the basis of the special ethos of the Clinic very well, when speaking on an RTE programme to celebrate the 50th anniversary, he said, of Lady Goulding, *"She leads from the front. She's inexhaustible. She has a charisma all of her own. Everyone wants to be on her team"*.

Lady Goulding had earlier sought to enlist the support of Archbishop John Charles McQuaid for the Clinic. Despite the fact that Kathleen O'Rourke was a niece of his, McQuaid refused. He explained that he only became involved with organizations, which were entirely Catholic. Lady Goulding was a Protestant at that time. The next most important person at the CRC, in my opinion, was the Medical Director, Ciaran Barry. He was a Donegal man, who had been headhunted by Lady Goulding in London. He demanded and generally got the best from staff. He could be abrupt, because essentially he was a shy man with whom I developed a special rapport. He and I were the only males among the professional staff. Some of the females deemed him a misogynist. Generally speaking, women did not interest him. When eventually he did fall for one, he expressed his amazement to me that it had not happened earlier. He was determined that he would capture the lady's heart, and he did. Some jealous medical peers referred to him as looking like a Jesuit. His early and sudden death was a tragedy, but by that time the Clinic was renowned internationally as a 'centre of excellence', regularly hosting international conferences.

*Kathleen O'Rourke, co-founder of The Central Remedial Clinic
welcomes clients and guests at the official opening in 1968.*

*Lady Valerie Goulding and President DeValera,
at the official opening of The Central Remedial Clinic.*

The Principal of the School was Maureen Hughes from Westport. She was a shrewd, intelligent lady who treated her staff with great dignity. She was successful in ensuring that the unique role of the school, within a predominantly medical establishment, was understood and respected. I can recall the school staff having a meeting with Dr. Barry to discuss the status of the teachers within the Clinic. He was astute enough to realize that it was vital that all categories of staff felt empowered and their roles acknowledged.

SPECIAL EDUCATION

Special education was a new concept to me. Its basic aim was to establish the individual needs of a pupil and deliver them to him/her in a structured way. Schools for the mentally handicapped were recognized for the first time in 1955. Schools for children with physical disabilities came slightly later. But one could not always make clear-cut distinctions between the two, as so many children had multiple disabilities. It was a very different kind of teaching from what I had known. The amount of visible progress could be minimal with some pupils. This required a facility for detailed and methodical teaching, often without the incentive of any spark of intelligence or mutual understanding. If a teacher could not adjust to such a regime, he/she could scarcely continue to work in such a school. But there were many incentives. The children themselves were very special people, as were their parents, and in general it became a privilege to know and serve them both. But there could always be a danger of complacency and a failure to challenge the children sufficiently. Our main attitude was to try to treat the children as closely as possible to what we would do in an ordinary school. An ongoing difficulty was that clinicians saw them as 'patients', while we saw them as 'pupils', and sought to minimize the debilitating aspect of contact with medical personnel.

As Dr. J. Boyd Dunlop, one of the first medical people associated with the CRC has said, 'the tendency in 1950 was to keep children in hospital for treatment. The basic aim of the Clinic was to avoid hospital treatment'. The difficulty of trying to get different professional disciplines to work together is well known. Health and education appear to be very distinct fields, with a lack of mutual understanding commonplace. It appears that there has long been a Standing Committee between the Departments of Education and Health in Ireland, where disagreement was often the norm. When, on occasion they have been able to agree on common projects, the matter of who pays has often led to paralysis.

In later years the placing of children with disabilities in separate schools from their peers became an ideological matter for many, despite the resources sometimes available. The civil rights movement in America had repercussions throughout the western world. New trends came to Britain first and from there to Ireland. Often, when America and even Britain were discovering the mistakes they had made, we in Ireland were just adopting these same practices.

Lady Valerie and guests admire blow-up of photograph below.

Clients and Staff photograph of the era.

There was a terrific buzz about working in the Clinic. Everyone knew of the CRC. It had a high profile. It was a happy environment. Staff was respected. Postgraduate study was encouraged. A well-funded research programme was inaugurated. There was an ethos of success about the place. Because of the huge publicity and fundraising campaigns, staff were regularly invited to attend all kinds of functions. Parties for staff were commonplace. A knock on the classroom door could mean the entry, accompanied by Lady Goulding, of almost any high profile person in Ireland or internationally. Barry Fitzgerald, Bing Crosby, Eamon Andrews, Jimmy O'Dea, Group Captain Leonard Cheshire, Jimmy Saville, Aidan O'Hara, Gay Byrne, Noel Purcell, Jack Cruise, Maureen Potter, James Mason, Dickie Rock, Chris Curran, Pat Taaffe and many leading politicians crossed our threshold.

CHARLIE HAUGHEY

One such politician was Charles J. Haughey. He was the son-in-law of the Taoiseach, Seán Lemass, and had been passed over for the post of Taoiseach by that cute Corkonian, Jack Lynch. In 1970, while Minister for Finance, the *Arms Crisis* saw Mr. Haughey dismissed from office and apparently sent into political wilderness. Lady Goulding, however, saw Haughey's difficulty as an opportunity for the Clinic to enlist him as a major fundraiser. She was quite open about her strategy, as she knew that Haughey could use the position as a means for political rehabilitation. She told her biographer, Jacqueline Hayden, *"It probably sounds rather nasty but it was good for the Clinic"*[58]. *The Clinic was based on Dublin's north side, Haughey's own area. He headed a fundraising committee of eight people, holding short, focused weekly meetings at Gouldings' Fitzwilton headquarters"*. Lady Goulding said that, *"He was great and there were just so many people beholden to him. He'd roped in a lot of help, businessmen and henchmen"*[59]. His target was £350,000. Lady Goulding, commented in 1987 that, *"but for Charlie, we'd have no centre today"*.

In an interview with RTE television in 2000, as a prelude to the publication of a book on Mr. Haughey, Terry Keane said that she first met Charlie Haughey at one of his CRC fundraising ventures. He attended one Christmas party in the CRC and entertained all by his pursuit of a beautiful lady who was on the staff. After dancing with her most of the night, he repaired to the reception area to escort his partner away. There were two exits from that area. As Charlie covered one exit, she swept through the other and into the waiting car of one of the doctors. Too late, Charlie saw his fate. He returned to the bar and growled to the barman, *"give us another fucking gin"*. On 23 September 1980, I attended a function at the CRC where Charles J. Haughey, An Taoiseach, was officiating at an opening ceremony of a new facility. In the audience I was surprised to see, Monsignor James Horan, then of Knock Basilica and Papal Visit fame. I spoke to him of our games of golf in Ballyhaunis and wondered why he was present for this occasion. With his knowing and cunning grin, he said, *"I'm meeting Charlie for lunch later. I'm trying to persuade him to build an airport for us in Knock"*.

He also told me that the current Chief Executive Officer of the CRC, Ken Holden, had earlier that same year, completed a feasibility study for the airport, in his capacity as leading consultant to Transportation Analysis International. In his *'Memoirs'*, the Monsignor says that in fact he did not have lunch with Haughey that day but met him informally. The Taoiseach laid his hand on Horan's shoulder saying, *"Will you have the red carpet out for me in Knock, when I attend Mass there next Sunday?, I am hopeful that your airport will materialize"*[60]. Those two gentlemen had much in common.

POSTSCRIPTS

1. The funeral of Lady Goulding took place on 1 August 2003, at her parish church in Enniskerry. She was aged 85. It was a gathering of people from many walks of life, who had encountered a great lady at some stage in their lives, and who had been the better for it. Among those who spoke that day was Billy Sugrue, who was the first patient at the clinic and who as a long time employee there, had become the public face of the clinic. On a personal level, it was a reunion with many colleagues who had worked at the CRC. Maureen Byrne, Kathleen Ryan, Treasa MacManus, Tom Galvin, Bey Monnelly, Rita Brown, Terri Garvey, Nora Gallagher, and Liam Heuston. As Jimmy Saville once observed, *"Everyone wants to be on her team"*. She was a Samaritan.

2. On 26 November 2003, many of those who had attended Lady Goulding's funeral gathered again to bury Billy Sugrue. He had been knocked down in his electric wheelchair some weeks previously. All agreed that this event, coupled with Lady Goulding's funeral, represented the end of an era for the CRC. Sir Lingard Goulding, Des Peelo, current Chair of the Board of Directors, Hassia Jameson, Paul Kiely CEO, Patricia McCrossan, Principal Teacher, and many past staff attended. It was gratifying to see Billy's wife, two daughters and grandson attend. The highlight of the morning for me was to be hugged in the middle of the aisle, by a former pupil of mine at the CRC, Oliver Dillon, and to hear of his own and his family's career successes. The meeting brought back happy memories of the fun and camaraderie we had together, as teacher and pupils, thirty years previously.

3. On 13 February 2007, I attended Benedict Kiely's funeral in Donnybrook. Phillip Boxberger, who had been a pupil of mine in the CRC, and who is now involved in writing and arts administration, greeted me. He was kind enough to say that as a teacher all those years ago, I had instilled into him a love of English.

Charles J. Haughey (left) on a visit to the Clinic.
Lady Goulding, commented in 1987 that, "but for Charlie, we'd have no centre today".

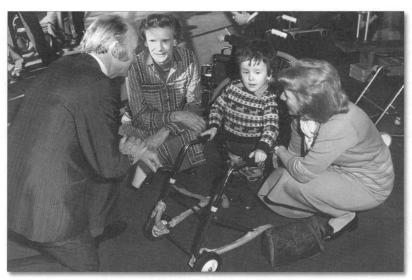

President Hillery, Lady Valerie, and Mrs Hillery
with new young friend on a visit to The Central Remedial Clinic .

CHAPTER 11

MARRIAGE

BIRTH AND DEATHS

Though I only spent a few short years at the CRC, I made many lasting friendships there, male and female. One such was Michael O'Connor, who was in charge of the printing works in the Adult Services section of the Training Center. One afternoon he informed me that he was going to nearby Kilbarrack to inspect a house, which he was purchasing. He was due to be married shortly. He invited me to accompany him. This was to be a rather important journey for myself, creating the momentum for my style of marriage proposal.

A MODEST PROPOSAL

The lady in England, with whom I had been in correspondence for some time, had some months earlier, decided that she would return to Ireland and test the waters in Dublin. She lived on Rathmines Road, just a mile from my own Spartan room in Ranelagh. We saw a lot of each other. My regular routine on a Sunday afternoon was to see Shamrock Rovers play in Glenmalure Park and then attend Mary's flat for dinner. I was quite sure that I could happily spend the rest of my life with her. Unlike many people I had encountered, she knew exactly who she was and what she wanted from life. Her stability, commonsense and reliability never ceased to amaze me. In short, I loved her very much and wanted to wed and bed her. I visited her flat on the evening I had been inspecting houses with Michael O'Connor. *"Guess where I was today?"* I asked. She was very surprised when I later added, *"Maybe we should start looking at houses too"*. *"Is that a proposal?"* she asked mischievously. *"Well it is about time we started to consider buying a house, I think"*, I ventured, adding that I would make a formal proposal, if required. It was required, and I went on one knee and asked the lady if she would marry me. She assented. Though, as I have said previously, I was in the habit of writing my diary 'as Gaeilge', I was determined that no possible ambiguity would occur on that occasion.

Thus, my diary for that day reads: *"13/3/1968. 14 Lower Rathmines Road 20.30. Resolved here tonight that Mary will marry Anthony on August 6th or 20th 1969. Signed: Mary, Anthony"*.

BUYING A HOUSE

Some months later we traveled on the number thirty-two bus to Portmarnock, where new houses had been advertised. It was a wet November day and the shantytown that was then Portmarnock looked most uninviting. We alighted from the bus reluctantly at the seaside terminus and made our way to a caravan on Carrickhill Road, where Frank Dunne was completing ten houses. He was a lovely man and showed us around the site. We were impressed by the space and quality of the workmanship. He told us that he did not have any houses available just then, but that he was negotiating to buy a nearby site, on which he hoped to build up to forty similar houses. To my surprise, he already had planning permission for it and the completed detailed drawings of all the houses. Three days later, I withdrew the one hundred pounds I had saved the previous summer, while laying pipes in Manchester for Joseph Murphy Ltd. I took the bus to Portmarnock, accompanied by a witness, one Brendan Hester from Brickeens. Much to Frank Dunnes' surprise, I paid him the booking deposit in cash, for number seven Woodlands. The annual teaching salary scale for a single man then was £780-£1,1450, and for a married man £975-£1,825. It took twenty-five years to reach the top of the scale. I did not qualify for a mortgage from a Building Society then. I did qualify, however, for a County Council loan at a fixed interest rate. I continually called to their office on Parnell Square to ensure my application was being processed as quickly as possible. My solicitor was a Mr. Boushell from the Arthur Cox Company on Mount Street. When, later, I needed a bridging loan and approached the Ulster Bank in Ranelagh, where I had an account for several years, I received a blank refusal. My lady friend approached the Bank of Ireland in O'Connell St, where neither of us had an account, and received a facility immediately. Afterwards, it transpired that an old colleague of mine, from my Boy Scout days in Mayo, John Kennedy of Swinford worked there.

We agreed to choose an engagement ring on a Saturday in May, during Mary's lunch break. I was playing tennis that morning in Herbert Park Ballsbridge with Michael Holmes, a friend from Ballyhaunis whose family had moved to Dublin. I forgot about my appointment in town until the last moment. Were it not for the fact that Michael had a motorcycle I would not have made it. I well recall the mad dash to Laurence's jewellery shop, then on O'Connell St. We made our choice and Mary put a five-pound deposit on the ring. Some days later I collected it. We went to University Church on St. Stephen's Green, where I slipped the ring on her finger. We repaired to the Shelbourne for a celebratory meal. I needed to make some extra cash and began to give grinds. I charged three pounds an hour. It was hard earned money as the second level pupils I dealt with, were generally very weak and lacked concentration. I applied for and got a job that summer correcting Certificate Examinations – another demanding and very boring task. After that I headed again for England to work for a few weeks, as usual under an assumed name. I was able to stay with my sister Josephine and her husband Martin Connolly in Manchester.

Frank Dunne completed the purchase of his new site and commenced to build. We became frequent visitors to Portmarnock to see the work in progress. If you kept your eyes closed traveling through the village, it was a fairly acceptable location, and the beach, with its views of Ireland's Eye and Lambay Island was delightful. Mary, who was so gifted with her hands, commenced making her own wedding dress. It was stunningly beautiful. We visited the local church in Rathmines and met Fr. Kitt who gave us the date of 12 August for the wedding. Mary was present at 12.30 Mass on 27 April and heard our 'marriage banns' read from the altar. This was a system where the names of people intending to marry, were publicly announced. Thus the community received prior knowledge, lest any member be aware of reasons why such people should be disallowed from entering into marriage. As the house neared completion, Mary ordered the minimum of furniture we would need, a table, two chairs, and a double bed. My mother was to buy us an electric cooker.

WEDDING

Our wedding was a great family reunion occasion. I was awakened that morning by two of my brothers knocking on the window of my ground floor room, near Mount Pleasant Square in Ranelagh. They had just arrived by road from Ballyhaunis. The morning was so wet that the group photographs had to be taken beneath the portals of Rathmines Church. The reception was at the Addison Lodge Hotel, opposite the Botanic Gardens in Glasnevin. That night several of our relatives came out to Portmarnock to view the house. As they did so, I recall being in an upstairs room listening to the radio, about the terrible events unfolding in Derry that day, after the Apprentice Boys March. We were both slept peacefully that first night, in our un-curtained front room upstairs.

The next morning saw us sail to Holyhead from Dunlaoire. We spent our honeymoon in Solihull, a beautiful town outside Birmingham, where my eldest brother, Paddy, had a house. He and his family had remained on in Ireland for a holiday after the wedding. We rested there for a few days before traveling to nearby Stratford-on-Avon, and afterwards to London and Manchester. Then it was back home to discover that the electricity had still not been connected to our house. The neighbours, who were mostly newly-married couples like ourselves, came to the rescue and we survived. Mary returned to work almost immediately. I set about trying to bring order to the front garden, as well as laying a rough path in front of the house at the garden edge. We soon got some carpet laid in our living room. On my return to school, the Principal remarked, 'now you know it all'. The following weekend we visited my mother-in-law. As we went to bed on the Saturday night, a large portrait of Cardinal Conway looked down on us!

The Author (right) and Taoiseach Gareth Fitzgerald TD. at Sandymount School.

The Author (left) and clients fly on an Air Corps helicopter.

DIPLOMA IN SPECIAL EDUCATION

I attended St. Patrick's College in Drumcondra again for most of that academic year, to study for a Diploma in Special Education. One of the requirements for acceptance on the course was to have spent at least one year teaching in a special school. The course was unique in that the Department of Education paid your salary and recouped you for your employment of a substitute teacher. The latter meant that you had to find such a teacher yourself and pay that person. This involved quite an expense in money and time. The best thing about the year from my point of view was that it renewed my direct association with Patrick E. O'Keeffe, who had gone directly into a Special School after graduating from the College. We had remained in contact and I had often stayed in his Sandymount flat when coming to town from my country perambulations. We found the course hard going, particularly on Wednesday afternoons, when we were assigned two hours of occupational therapy. This usually consisted of making wicker baskets or weaving a variety of materials. When the schools rugby season began, many of the matches were played on Wednesday afternoons, so the frustration level increased dramatically, and empty desks became commonplace. The course itself covered the wide spectrum of special education, though it concentrated on the two largest groupings, that of children with mild or moderate learning difficulties. The thirty or so teachers taking the course came from around the country. Most were female, with a high preponderance of nuns. Up to that year the course was regarded as a pleasant year away from teaching, with little pressure involved. But when the College graduation ceremony was held that autumn, it became apparent that one participant had been failed from the previous year. This caused great unease amid our group, as some of the older teachers, said that they would never have applied for the course under such circumstances.

The course Director, the affable but extremely serious Paid McGee, began to introduce several new initiatives into the Course. On the academic side, he began to set topics for study on a weekly basis, and these were examined orally in fine detail. It was like being back in class. Teaching practice was, as always, the most important element of primary teaching. As well as visiting a variety of different special schools during the year, we also spent up to six weeks teaching in different schools. This was invaluable experience. That year the course reverted to demanding detailed preparatory notes, comparable to those we produced during our years as students in the College. This became apparent when the nun, Sr. Gertrude, who inspected our notes, returned them all, as incomplete, and demanded more detailed ones. I recall one of our group, the diplomatic Con Gallogly, raising the matter in a group session with Sr. Gertrude, but being firmly put down by the little nun. The one unnerving experience I recall from the course was a visit we made to St. Loman's in Chapelizod. It was a school for children with autism and as we entered, I noticed the door being locked behind us. The needs of those children were huge and I surmised that most teachers would scarcely survive very long, in such an environment.

One quotation I note in my diary from February of that year is from Bertrand Russell, *"The secret of happiness is to realize that the world is horrible, horrible, horrible, but to go on and do your best"*. The final teaching practice consisted of two weeks in a school, similar to where we taught ourselves. This meant that I could be assigned to St. Brendan's in Sandymount twelve miles away from Portmarnock or the two miles distant, St. Mary's in Baldoyle. I was sent to the former. The contrast between St. Brendan's and the CRC could not be greater. The entire staff there, school and clinic were elderly; the narrow low-ceiling corridors, the small rooms, the whole ethos was from a by-gone age, a backwater that time seemed almost to have forgotten. The Principal, Mrs Langan who lived near the CRC, gave me a lift back to Clontarf every afternoon. The children, who were delightful, were especially interested in me because I came from the glamorous CRC, which they and their parents would have preferred to attend. They were all aware of Lady Goulding and the publicity attaching to the CRC, especially the famous annual Walk and Concert organized by the Disc Jockey, Jimmy Saville. During my stay there, I organized an inter-schools football game with the CRC. Most importantly for the St. Brendan's children, it was held at the CRC, so they got a chance to marvel at our new glass palace. This football fixture was later to become an annual event.

THANK YOU FOR NOT SMOKING

I had my tonsils taken out early in my teaching career, in the old St. Vincent's Hospital on Stephen's Green. I was having difficulties with my throat. Indeed one of the attractions of special education for me was the absence of having to continually address large classes. I also developed trouble with my eyes and was regularly having sebaceous cysts removed from my eyelids. Arising from both these problems, I had an aversion to cigarette smoke and avoided pubs in particular. As these were the venues for most social get-togethers after meeting or conferences, I missed out on much socializing. In truth, alcohol never appealed to me very much, and the practice of going to a pub for a night out dismayed me. I was, however, conscious of the danger that not joining in with the boys or the girls marked you out as somewhat of a loner. I was always very willing to engage in another well-established Irish social occasion, that of attending funerals. I did this for several reasons. I knew from personal experience that it was beneficial for the bereaved. Funerals were also very important social gatherings, where you were likely to meet a wide section of the community, depending on who was dead. But the main reason, I think I attended funerals whenever I could, was that they were a sober reminder of the brutal human condition; that despite your life and activities, you were still going to take this same journey at some indefinite time and circumstances. Sometimes, I felt envious of the deceased, in that he/she had completed the course, had no more worries to contend with, had discovered the great truth or otherwise. I have to say, however, that walking away from the graveyard always gave me a certain fillip, knowing that my time had not yet come. It was in some ways akin to the feeling you get when leaving a hospital, even as a visitor, but more so as a patient. Life indeed could be beautiful!

PREPARING FOR BABY

My mother-in-law got into bad health during the year I was doing the diploma. This put pressure on my wife who had to take her to hospital. Her mother was a very poor patient and though visiting our house after being discharged from hospital, she would not stay with us. She insisted on returning to her own home, where she lived alone. Mary visited her regularly and usually returned in an upset state of mind. She was pregnant at that stage and her own visits to doctors had commenced. She decided to get the best medical assistance and booked one of the consultants operating in the Rotunda Hospital to look after her. An added pressure was the fact that part of my course consisted of medical lectures on the causes of babies being born with disabilities and the shocking consequences. During that year the possibility of Mary's pregnancy going wrong often occurred to me, but we took all the precautions we could, in the matter, including Mary finishing work several months before her baby was due. As the year wore on, Mary began to knit baby clothes. On the 3rd of July we purchased a baby bath, bucket and pot. It was a warm summer and Mary became increasingly uncomfortable, finding it difficult to sleep. In the early hours of the 21st of July, her labour pains commenced.

POST ROTUNDA

After the horror of the Rotunda, Pat Mac Sweeney, one of our neighbors, again drove us back home. There we discovered that she and our next-door neighbor, Carmel Dowling, had prepared a surprise meal for us in our own house, which they soon vacated after our return. The next ten days were very special to me, as Mary depended almost totally on me for most things, as we began to live upstairs. At first she was scarcely able to get out of bed, and I found her crying on occasion, but gradually she regained her strength. We had family visitors and as the bad news spread, friends of ours who had been away on holidays, began to call. This was good and bad for Mary, but mostly good, as she had to respond. The ordinary intercourse of life encourages and facilitates recovery from the worst tragedy. My young nephew, Thomas Jordan, came to stay and his main wish was to be taken into town to attend the forthcoming visit of George Best.

This should have been an obvious task for me, but I began to suggest that it might be an appropriate occasion for Mary to re-engage in a major outing. This she did. When Thomas returned to her from the melee on Henry Street, he was minus his tie, but he only bemoaned the fact that he had caught one of the footballs thrown into the crowd by George Best, only to have it punched out of his enfolding arms. Exactly one month after Mary's early morning entry to the Rotunda, we received a knock on the door at three o'clock in the morning. I knew it was a member of the Garda Síochána by the sound of his motorcycle idling outside the house. I went downstairs quickly, to be told, *"Bad news for your wife, I'm afraid. Her mother is dead"*. We traveled westwards by train in the morning and spent a sad weekend attending the obsequies. It seemed so unfair to Mary that two such deathblows should occur thus.

MICHAEL JOSEPH

52 Bedford Square London WC1B 3EF   Telephone: 01-637 0941 Telegrams: Emjaybuks London

20th September, 1971.

Anthony Jordan, Esq.,
7, Carrickhill Estate,
Portmarnock,
Co. Dublin,
<u>Ireland</u>.

Dear Mr. Jordan,

      I am very sorry to have to tell
you that we cannot make an offer for WAS
IT FOR THIS THE CLAY GREW TALL. I think
the best thing I can do is to give you a
photocopy of part of a report, which includes some fairly direct comments. What
I suggest is that you find somebody who
will help you to edit the book, which does
indeed need a great deal of work. If you
feel like it after this, I would be glad
to reconsider the MS.

      I presume you must really be a woman.
      If so, why use the name Anthony?

      Sorry to have kept you waiting,

      Yours sincerely,

      (Raleigh Trevelyan)

<u>Enclosures</u>
RT/KM.

CHAPTER 12

MY GENDER QUESTIONED OVER A NOVEL

When I started teaching in the CRC in 1968, I used to arrive back to my room at Oxford Road in Ranelagh by three o'clock in the afternoon. I soon realized that I had to do something, which would further occupy the rest of the afternoon and evening and began to write. I decided to attempt a novel, choosing a female as the principal character. Since my eleven-year sojourn boarding in three male environments, I decided to concentrate most of my social intercourse on female company, finding that generally an interesting and rewarding field. I found the writing exercise most exciting, though extremely hard work. Each day as I sat down to write I did not know how the storyline would develop, so that I was as keen as a reader might be to discover what came next. But while my heroine's development ostensibly appeared to depend on me, I discovered that she began to take on an impetus of her own, becoming a real life character for me. I was often unhappy with what she got up to, but that was the way it transpired. It was a long laborious process, written in school copybooks. I had several working titles during the writing. But the one I settled on, eventually, was a line from one of my favorite poems, Wilfred Owens's *'Futility'*, *'Was It For This The Clay Grew Tall'*. When I had finished, I decided to get it typed up. One of the secretaries at the CRC in Clontarf undertook the task for me. She commented one day, *"I was a bit taken aback at first. Its not often you read material like that. The girl has no endearing traits at all, nor has anyone else in it"*. The typing complete, I wondered what to do with it. I was not aware of any Irish publishers at the time, so I choose to send it, at random, to an English publisher, whose name appealed to me, *'Michael Joseph'* in London. Several months passed and I heard nothing. I wrote a reminder letter. I received a short note on 7 September 1971, from a Raleigh Trevelyan the Editorial Director. It read:

"I am sorry to have kept 'Was It For This The Clay Grew Tall' for such a long time. This is just to say that I am getting another report. I do not wish to raise your hopes too high, but the fact that we kept it for so long is a measure of our interest in the book".

At the bottom of the letter I noticed a message in small print, reading:

'A manuscript and other documents submitted to the firm, whither at the request of the firm or otherwise, are submitted entirely on the author's risk; and while every possible care is taken, in the event of loss or damage to manuscripts, etc., the company cannot hold itself in any way responsible'.

Being a native of Ballyhaunis, the thought crossed my mind that the small print might well be the real cause for delay, and that I might never see my manuscript again. I had made no copy. At the same time I had to acknowledge that Raleigh's letter did give me a pleasant surprise. I did Raleigh an injustice for a few weeks later I received another letter from him. It read:

"I am very sorry to have to tell you that we cannot make an offer for 'Was It For This The Clay Grew Tall'. I think the best thing I can do is to give you a photocopy of part of a report, which includes some fairly direct comments. What I suggest is that you find somebody who will help you edit the book, which does indeed need a great deal of work. If you feel like it after this, I would be glad to reconsider the MS".
I presume you must really be a woman. If so, why use the name Anthony?
Sorry to have kept you waiting."

I had tried to be a Samaritan to my female character, but failed.

I have to confess that I got quite a laugh out of his reference to my possible gender. It demonstrated to me that I really must have succeeded in getting into the female character. That was reward enough for me, for my endeavor. It was with some reluctance that I decided I had to read the accompanying report, which I expected would be very critical. It read:

"Anthony Jordan: 'Was It For This The Clay Grew Tall'

"This book is something of a freak. In the first place, I find it incredible that it has (apparently) been written by a man. The assumption of a female person – not to my mind, a particularly attractive one – is totally convincing.

In the second place extreme vividness of observation is allied with some amateurishness of execution. Yet the story does grip.

It might be worthwhile to edit it drastically in collaboration with the author. It needs cutting by a third - there is a lot that is trivial in it; and the recurring sententiousness could with advantage be suppressed. The book is best when the narrator relates flatly what happened to her; it is worst when she tries to draw philosophical or moral conclusions.

That she emerges as a pretty intolerable character does not greatly matter. Her boy friend, her parents and some of the other people of whom she disapproves are far more sympathetic than she seems to realize. The ending suggests that she commits suicide – it is not entirely clear. At all events, it is an abrupt end and unsatisfactory close to the book and the author should be asked to think again about it.

The title is fatuous. A quotation from Owen makes the reader expect a war-novel. Something else must be found".

I was not unhappy at all with the report. It was exquisite to have someone comment, in any way, on my effort. I was quite amused. I did not object to anything in the report. I felt that I had achieved something with my first attempt. The suggestion of me finding someone to help edit the book was interesting, but I was pretty ignorant in that area. I thought about the matter for quite a while. But there was one over-riding aspect to the notion of having the book published which decided my attitude. There was a lot of material in the text, which even now nearly forty years later, would prove controversial, much of it of an explicit sexual nature. I knew that if it was published, my teaching career was at an end. What happened to John McGahern not so very long ago, remained vivid in my mind. I was not so foolish or presumptuous, that I believed that I could ever emulate his subsequent success. In the cold light of the economic facts of life, I knew that I had had my reward, and I could continue the hobby of writing, but that this book could not be published. I was already well into writing another novel, which was autobiographical, and a relatively simple story. In those years, before the advent of the word processor, even getting someone to type up a manuscript, could be difficult. My next efforts at writing would not take place for nearly twenty years, as within a short period, I entered what essentially was a new and very demanding career as a Principal teacher of a school, similar to the CRC. The whereabouts of the manuscript of that first novel remained unclear to me, until one night in 2007 my daughter Judith took me to the Abbey Theatre to see *Julius Caesar*. In conversation she happened to mention that she had the manuscript, but was unclear where exactly it was.

St. Pat's 1966, Author 4th from right front row.

The Central Remedial Clinic, Clontarf, Dublin.

CHAPTER 13

LEAVING THE CRC VIA BALLYMUN AND NEW YORK

One of the ongoing difficulties we had in the CRC, in common with similar schools, was the difficulty in getting access to post primary schools for our pupils, who were ready to enter second level. Regular post-primary schools were most unwilling to enroll students with a physical disability. An inter-departmental committee had been set up in May 1970 to report on the matter. It reported in 1971, detailing the essential additional services which would be required at the designated new Comprehensive Schools at Ballymun. I write Comprehensive schools because they consisted of two co-located single sex schools. The committee had representatives from the Department of Education (T. O'Cuillenáin etc), the National Rehabilitation Board (Dr. Tom Gregg), CIE (Mr. D. Kelly), and the Schools Board of Management (Mother Jordana and Miss B. Foy). During 1972 much detailed planning took place and in March that year the Department of Education informed the relevant feeder schools of the intention to proceed with enrollment, and sought details on prospective candidates. The detailed planning had covered items such as identification and referral of suitable children for September 1972, employment of a specialist teacher, medical, nursing and paramedical services, accommodation and transport. By June the committee reported that it failed to secure a suitably qualified specialist teacher. It decided to seek a teacher from one of the feeder schools. One of the teachers in the CRC, Tom Galvin, was interested, but he had not yet taken the Diploma in Special Education, which was deemed essential. I was asked and agreed to go to Ballymun for the year, while my colleague completed the required diploma.

HOLIDAYS, HOME AND ABROAD

I had planned to spend that summer in Rutherford, New Jersey, on a house exchange scheme, with Mary and our six months old baby Judith, who had been born at the Coombe Hospital under the supervision of a most humane man, Dr. Jamie Clynch. It was to be our first flight. Just two weeks earlier the crash of the Trident aircraft in London with 116 people killed, including many high profile Irish business people, had shocked and frightened everybody. The baby remained awake for the entire journey, peering up from her cardboard box on the floor of the airplane near the emergency exit.

The envelopment of damp hot air when we opened the door to exit from Kennedy Airport, gave us a foretaste of what we were to endure for the entire summer. We survived, just about. We were located only a half hour from Manhattan and after a lone scouting mission there, I reported that it was safe for us all to visit. We used the underground a lot and went on the Dayliner to explore up-State New York as far as West Point where we saw young soldiers preparing for service in Vietnam. Our neighbours in Rutherford were very friendly and Mary joined in regular expeditions to a variety of distant shopping malls, where the bargains were reputed to be. The baby attracted much attention. Groups of teenage girls would call to see her. In New York, particularly in *Maceys* and other stores, she became a creature of some wonderment. While in Rutherford, she became able to turn on her back and reverse again. On one very hot occasion, in the back garden, she collapsed and we had to revive her with water.

For me the highlight of the visit was a series of late night concerts in Central Park by the New York Philharmonic. The conductors included Pierre Boulez, Jean Martinon, and Henry Lewis, with soloists, Misha Dichter, Jorge Bolet, and Gary Graffman. Walking along Broadway to Port Authority after midnight was an interesting experience. The lasting impression I took from my visit was the extent of poverty I saw on the streets of New York City. It seemed totally anomalous in such a rich country.

Our favourite country for holidays was Italy. I began to go there alone in the 1980's, inspired by Joan McNamara's visits. I grew to love it, the cradle of so much of western culture. I came across places and names that had figured prominently in our Latin texts, as well as Christianity. I crossed the *Rubicon*, came across the tomb of the Scipios, walked alone through the streets of Pompeii, visited the *Quo Vadis* church, was chilled to see the hundreds of coffins at Fossa Ardeatina, near the *Catacombe St. Callisto* of those executed by the Nazis, discovered that the plaque in the Irish College saying that Daniel O'Connell's heart was inlaid in the wall was untrue, swam at the Isle of Capri, was in turn humbled and horrified at the Commonwealth, Polish and American war graves, inspired again by the memory of Tomás Ó'Fiaiach at the tombs of the Earls of Tyrone and Tyrconnel in the Spanish church of San Pedro in Montorio on the Palatine. In later years Mary and I traversed many of those same venues, including a visit to a flooded Venice. Our favourite location for holidays in Ireland is at the Lake Hotel in Killarney, which we visit twice each year. I tell friends that I like to go there to listen to the silence and to walk.

When I arrived at Ballymun in September 1972, I was disappointed that much of the planning requirements of the committee had not been implemented. It appears that differences between the Departments of Education and Health on costs had been the problem. Neither wheelchair ramps, nor special toilet facilities or hot meals were available. The seventeen first-year students with disabilities had not been allocated their classes with the rest of the first years, so I completed that exercise immediately on my arrival.

The year was a challenging one for all concerned. In my end of year report I said that, *"The physically handicapped have adapted very well to their new environment. This was no easy change and it was natural to expect some teething problems. Great credit must go to the other pupils who have been very understanding and helpful at all times. The same can be said for the Principals, teachers, office and canteen staffs"*. As the year was coming to an end, I was asked to stay on the permanent staff and offered a promotion. However I was glad to leave Ballymun. I found the environment depressing. The towering flats were full of young mothers with lots of young children. There was no natural infrastructure to humanize the place; no trees, no park bench, no playgrounds. I remember on one occasion at lunchtime walking over to the barricaded shops. Two young mothers walked in front of me while a few of their very young children dawdled behind them playing. One of the mothers turned around and shouted to her children, *"If you don't get up here quick, I'll fucking well kill youse"*.

I had never contemplated leaving the CRC. I had never wished to leave it. During the summer holidays of 1973, however, I read an advertisement for the post of Principal of a similar, though unnamed school. That summer we had bought a caravan and took to the roads of Ireland for about six weeks. We were incommunicado, as my family had only a rough idea of our intended itinerary. One evening a Garda squad car arrived at the caravan park in which we were staying for a few days. There was a message to ring my family in Ballyhaunis. I had been called for interview for the post of Principal. When I heard the name of the school, St. Brendan's in Sandymount, (managed by the National Association Cerebral Palsy Ireland - NACPI) I was very surprised and not in the least interested in going, after my earlier experiences there. St. Brendan's had been fashionable and vibrant in its earlier days, but had since become a backwater. I knew that during the previous year, St. Brendan's had been thrown a life line by the Department of Education, when it was decided that henceforth the free transport service would not cross the river Liffey. Children living on the Southside could only henceforth avail of free transport to St. Brendan's and vice versa for the north side. The Department felt that this tactic would bolster the numbers attending St. Brendan's and reduce the numbers of southsiders crossing the Liffey to the CRC.

I consulted with some senior staff of the CRC and was encouraged to do the interview at least. I interviewed at St. Brendan's on Sandymount Avenue, where I was met by a large woman named Mrs Prince, who when I told her the purpose of my presence there, said, *"but we never had a man here"*. I was interviewed by the Chairman of the Board of Management (BOM), Monsignor Liam Martin and a lay man. It became clear to me that in an era before headhunting, that that term described what was occurring with me. I was offered the post and again spoke with people from the CRC who encouraged me to take it, out of a sense of 'mission' towards those children with disabilities and their families. This is what I did. Afterwards, I resumed our mobile caravan holiday, heading towards the southwest.

It was in Cork that we first experienced Judith's tendency to keep walking without looking back. You had to keep an eye on her or she was gone. We lost her in a Cork suburb and spent some time driving frantically around the area before we located her, still walking ahead. Despite this Mary confessed to me that she could not believe she was getting so much pleasure from her. On another occasion we lost her in the Botanic Gardens, with the river Tolka in full flood. I sprinted the length of the river fearful that she might have fallen in. Our major shocking experience with Fiona was when as a little girl she developed asthma and was prescribed strong medication. One night we discovered that she had opened the bottle of tablets and taken an unknown quantity and scattered the rest. We had no time to piece together the remainder. She had to be rushed to hospital to have her stomach pumped out. Nine of the tablets would have been fatal. As we waited we considered where we would bury her, should she die.

St. Patrick's Teacher Training College, Drumcondra, Dublin.

Board of Management Sandymount School 1978.
From left: Dr. Mary O'Donnell, Patrick Shallow. Monsignor Liam Martin P.P.
Anthony Jordan, Dr. Thomas Gregg.

Sandymount School Staff 1979
with Father Aidan Lohan C.S S.P

St. Brendan's Sandymount Dublin.

CHAPTER 14

NATIONAL ASSOCIATION OF CEREBRAL PALSY

ST BRENDAN'S SCHOOL AND CLINIC, SANDYMOUNT SCHOOL AND CLINIC

THE UNEXPECTED AND UNWELCOME PRINCIPAL

I arrived at my new school early on the first Monday morning in September 1973. I was somewhat apprehensive, as I was directed to the 'teacher's room' along a narrow low-ceiling corridor. I knocked diffidently on the door, not expecting any of the teachers would be present quite so early. I got no response and entered. To my surprise the little room was full of women sitting around a small table. If I was surprised, they were even more so. Eventually, after a momentary embarrassment, I was asked to account for my presence in their school. *"I'm the new Principal"*, I said. I got no verbal response from any of the ladies, but from their pained expressions and shuffling of position, I realized that I had entered a fraught situation. One lady stood up quickly and rushed past me. Three others soon followed. It transpired that they had agreed that only one of their number would apply for the vacant post. She was a lady who had just one year to go to retirement. The Principal's allowance would top her pension allowance considerably. That lady had, moments earlier, opened a letter from the Chairman, informing her that her application had been unsuccessful. The staff was digesting this information just as I arrived. That lady informed me during the week that, *"The teachers wish to have their lunch by themselves, as they have a lot to discuss"*. She never spoke to me again for the entire year.

During the year my salvation came from three recently appointed National Association of Cerebral Palsy (NACP) staff, a superintendent physiotherapist, a social worker and a manager. Each of us was ploughing lone furrows in less than receptive fields. We all agreed that despite what we had been informed about St. Brendan's, prior to arrival, nothing had quite prepared us for the reality. In the school, which operated in total separation from the clinic, the only records on the children were those of daily attendance on the school rolls. The clinic operated in a haphazard way, indicated by a white-coated therapist coming into my classroom one day and saying aloud, *"Now I wonder whom I'll take next?"* It appeared that the school was regarded as an unimportant 'holding center' to facilitate the delivery of clinical services on site.

The social worker and I soon resurrected the 'Parents and Friends Association'. On the occasion of its first general meeting in the school, word came on the grapevine, that the Board of the NACPI was refusing permission for the meeting. I advised the parents to go ahead with their meeting. Some time before Christmas the new manager, Michael Bermingham, who used often join me at lunchtime, said that he would be returning to his previous post within a few months. It had become clear to him that the position he had interviewed for and accepted, did not and would not exist. The social worker, Eibhlín ni Scolláin, had left earlier, and the superintendent physiotherapist, Fionnuala Murphy, some months later. The School Board, speculating that I might also depart, secured a month's placement for me at a course in a rehabilitation center in Wilbad in the Black Forest area of Germany. A group of ten Irish people spent a very enjoyable few weeks there, studying the working operation of the centre. My main recollection of that experience is being met and being welcomed back by my wife and little girl of about eighteen months at Dublin airport. I realized how foolish I had been to stay away from them for so long and resolved never to do again.

In early 1950 a group of 70 parents gathered at the premises of the St. John's Ambulance Brigade and set up a Parents' Association of the as yet unofficial – Irish Association of Cerebral Palsy. It was the first such organization in the field. The first Meeting of the Subscribers and Directors of the National Association for Cerebral Palsy was held on 19 July 1951 at 26 Fitzwilliam Square, the home of Dr. Robert Fitzgerald Collis[60a]. He had been involved in this work at various locations for some time. Collis was an adventurous humanitarian, who had been out and about in Dublin during the 1916 Rising, and had played rugby for Ireland. The site at Sandymount was bought later with funds raised by the Parents and Friends Association. In its early years the Association was a fashionable, vibrant and pioneering body, constantly stimulated by a dynamic parental clientele. But it gradually went into the doldrums, at the very same time as the CRC began to flourish.

CHRISTY BROWN DIAGNOSES

The plight of the Clinic can be garnered from the words of its most famous client, Christy Brown, who in 1956 took the unheard of step of discharging himself. He wrote to his close friend, Dr. Patricia Sheehan, then working at Sandymount:

"Now comes the difficult part of this letter. My exit from the clinical scene and all that. It's not easy to discuss it without being misunderstood. I simply felt that I had reached my pinnacle of progress and could advance no further. Or perhaps I should say – intrepidly - that the clinic had reached its peak of assistance and could benefit me no further. The C.P. treatment at the Clinic, and all over Ireland, had a certain standard, a certain demarcation line of progress, beyond which it was as yet unable to go, not because of technical incompetence, but because the entire system of

treatment here was still in its initial stages... But my physical needs were now greater and more complicated, and a high degree of specialization was required to meet them... But my treatment reached a point where it was all like a circus roundabout, going about and about and yet always at the same place at any given time. It was like a repeating decimal. I understand that a certain amount of repetition is essential, but after six years of going through exactly the same movement and doing exactly the same things, the necessity to implant the movement on the patients memory, to me, is a little over-stressed"[61].

Matters had not been helped when in 1957, Dr. Collis felt constrained by professional and domestic circumstances to emigrate to Nigeria. The Board of NACPI was traditionally composed of well meaning, but mediocre people, who had little empathy with the professional staff. Without Collis it was effectually moribund. But once a Voluntary Body gets accreditation and financial backing from the State for the delivery of services, it appears unheard of for it to lose that status. A Cork branch of NACPI however, the Cork Spastic Clinic, continued to be vibrant in Munster. Cork provided a competent national Chairman for the Association in the early 1970's. He was Augustine Healy, a Fianna Fail T.D. and Lord Mayor of Cork. It was generally felt that a Corkonian's main interest remains in Cork. He brought some new members to the Board however, including one Brian Harrison from Delgany in county Wicklow. It was this Board, which had taken the initiative, which brought in the new staff to Sandymount mentioned above.

1972 REPORT ON ST. BRENDAN'S

Around that time Dr. Robert Collis had returned from his self-imposed exile in Nigeria and assumed a place on the Board. He commissioned a report on Sandymount in 1972 from a leading educational psychologist. I was presented with a copy shortly after my arrival. It made for salutary reading. It advised ...

As St. Brendan's now caters for a variety of conditions perhaps a less anxiety provoking name could be considered without adversely affecting the identity of the institution   It is necessary to provide adequate necessary stimulation for basic development in all the sensor-motor areas for young children... as play is an integral part of socialization ... There is a need for a reappraisal of certain aspects of the educational programme... programmes geared towards leisure pursuits and life, apart from a work situation would be more meaningful sufficient...there is a very great lack of male identification figures... leads to unsatisfactory self-images... Each child should have a suitably constructed file with typed notes to include: a full medical history; a psychological report and a report on the child's position for each year from the school and each other department the child attends... The introduction of conferences and the involvement of staff and parents is a very desirable progression. Would like to see a more lively and positive approach to solving these problems at management level, otherwise the situation will deteriorate into one of immovable pessimism and lethargy".

The Parents Association was naturally very upset to see three of the four new senior staff depart within the year, in 1974. I remained on because the school had a separate and quasi-independent Board of Management, chaired by Monsignor Liam Martin, which gave me every support in introducing sweeping changes into the school. In effect, I was implementing new procedures as identified in the psychologist's report, modeled on my experience in the CRC. However the departure of staff became public when, in October 1975, the *Irish Times* published an extraordinary well-researched and comprehensive story under the headline:

SPATE OF RESIGNATIONS FROM CEREBRAL PALSY ORGANISATION

"The National Association for Cerebral Palsy in Dublin is now operating without a chief executive, a superintendent physiotherapist and a social worker, following a spate of resignations from the professional staff. Replacements are, however, being sought. The association does work similar to the Central Remedial Clinic, which is on the north side of the city and has a day clinic, a school and a tiny workshop at St. Brendan's in Sandymount. In Bray there are residential facilities for up to 30 children. The Cork branch operates more or less independently. Indeed, the expansion there and the success of the CRC have emphasized the lack of growth in Sandymount.

This has been put down to several factors. These include bad communication between the board and the staff, poor liaison among the staff themselves, lack of publicity of the Association's work, a board unreceptive to new ideas, lack of money, and poor admissions policy. Mr. Brian Harrison, a member of the board was inveigled to operate as chief executive. He accepted this position for only some months, however, and at the last annual general meeting of the association in June, he resigned and intimated that he had received little co-operation from the board...

The lack of a chief executive is however, the association's most immediate problem, if the 25 or so children in Bray, and the 100 or so others in the Sandymount clinic, nursery and school and workshop are to get the deal they deserve. A more vociferous parents' association is also vital. Otherwise old rumors about an amalgamation- in effect a takeover- with the CRC will be revived.

ROBERT COLLIS DIES

Many of the above points had a direct bearing on my position. The most positive was Brian Harrison who, unlike any other board member I ever encountered, took a keen and direct interest in the workings of the operation at Sandymount, even before he took up the post as CEO. This was very helpful to all of us. Dr. Collis' frustration with the state of Sandymount was very obvious, and he did not suffer fools gladly. His strategy was to initiate close relations with the CRC and he was instrumental in having Lady Goulding join one of the numerous boards that operated at Sandymount.

This did not appeal to the stalwarts of NACPI, who in their foolishness, talked of NACPI taking over the CRC. In May of 1975 however, when Dr. Collis was killed in a fall from his horse, the calm inertia returned to the boardroom of NACPI. Christy Brown commemorated Collis's death in a marvelous poem called,

Remembering a Friend: Robert Collis.

"You strode rather than stepped through life,
crushing many a demure bloom in your career.
Yet with the blunt sensitivity of one,
trading not with images but imperatives,
you were solicitous of mute mayhem... "[62]

A later Chairman of NACPI, Dr. Bill Roche, based in Wicklow, attended a meeting in the Department of Education held to to award the management of a third school for children with physical disabilities. It was to be based in west county Dublin, which was part of our catchment area. It was felt that in the long run it might render our school unviable. Two competing bodies vied for management, NACPI and the new Spina Bifida Organisation. Though the CEO from NACPI had prepared an elaborate report, seeking the management for NACPI, Dr. Roche agreed that Spina Bifida should get it, on the grounds that his own board had not considered the matter fully. The management of this school has subsequently devolved to the CRC.

CANON JG MCGARRY P.P.

It often occurred to me that I, too, should abandon Sandymount. I did consider it and applied for the vacant post of principal at my old primary school in Ballyhaunis during the 1980's. I was interviewed and subsequently offered the post by the parish priest JG McGarry. But on mature reflection over two days, I decided to remain in Dublin. Among the reasons for my decision was the clear perception that the post would have demanded a very visible role in parish affairs, plus the proviso that I would live within the parish. The one positive aspect that would have been readily available to me in the country was membership of a golf club. The CRC Administrator, Ray McLoughlin, had earlier organized membership of Howth golf club for me. I did not take it up because I decided that time spent with my family would suffer inordinately.

We moved to live in Sandymount in 1977. It was a very congenial seaside location in which to live, with easy access to *loci* of interest to me, libraries, archives, galleries, concert halls, theatres, the Pro-Cathedral for the Sunday Latin sung Mass by the Palestrina Choir, Irishtown Nature Park and especially Croke Park. I also had an early offer of membership of nearby Elm Park golf club. (My attendance at the Pro-Cathedral has lessened somewhat, when in more recent years the local Star of the Sea parish choir, under Deirdre Seaver, soloists Eileen Kavanagh and Sheila Crowley with Liam Carney on the organ, began to perform to a high level at our own Sunday Mass). In Irishtown Nature Park I form a 'club' with other regulars like Carmel, Colman, Charlie, Des, Leo, Paddy, Phil, the Brent Geese in winter and the swallows and tern in summer. Of course, in recent years Sandymount has come under severe pressure from the building boom, with development and traffic changing the quality of life. The location of major sewerage works less than one mile across the strand, with the prospect of an incinerator to follow, makes the contest between local community activists like the admirable Lorna Kelly and Catherine Cavendish and the developers and the planners, almost impossible.

When Monsignor Liam Martin resigned his position as Chairman of the BOM he was, luckily for the school and myself, replaced by Rev.. Aidan Lehane CSSp, then President of nearby St. Michael's College on Ailesbury Road. I say 'luckily' for two reasons. The position was entirely in the gift of NACPI, and Fr. Lehane proved a great friend to the school and to me. He was an astute person and a great educationalist, well respected and deferred to by NACPI. I appreciated the anonymity of the city. One day a teacher friend, Helen Prendergast from Abbeyleix, visited me in school. At lunchtime we walked down to the village, about one hundred yards away. We met a man on the footpath walking towards us. To my surprise Helen spoke in a friendly manner to him. I immediately asked whether she knew him. She said 'no' but that in Abbeyleix it was normal; to speak to people you met on the street. Though I can be quite sociable when it suits me, I think that unfortunately, I am essentially a loner, and not even an observer. I have been known to pass my daughters on the footpath without noticing them.

PROTESTANT ORIGINATION

As can be gleaned from above, NACPI may not have been the most forward or equitable organization to work for. School staffs were in an anomalous situation in that though the Department of Education paid us, we were employees of the BOM, which was under the patronage and control of NACPI. The latter, but particularly its managerial staff, saw school personnel as somewhat semi-detached and they continually sought ways to bring us within their remit. The Association had originated in a Protestant ethos with the school originally named the Orthopedic Hospital Cerebral Palsy School. Dr. Mary O'Donnell pointed out that because most of the children were Catholics, the school should be under Catholic patronage. She was then recognized as Patron, on behalf of the Association, by the Department of Education, with another Catholic, Miss Josie Reed, becoming the school manager. As I pointed out in my biography of Christy Brown, this 'transfer' avoided involving the Archbishop of Dublin, who insisted that all schools serving Catholic children to be under his patronage[62a]. The Association understood 'patronage' as the right to 'manage' the school despite the fact that this was the function of the Board of Management.

In 1977, after the senior pupils told me they were embarrassed to tell their peers that they went to school in St. Brendan's, as it would be assumed they it was the psychiatric institution of the same name, the BOM adopted my proposal to change the name to 'Sandymount School'. My main difficulty as Principal was in ensuring that the school was allowed to operate in as close a fashion as possible to other schools. This resulted in a natural tension within the center, as the clinical personnel saw the children as patients, while we saw them as pupils. Health and educational services traditionally find it difficult to co-exist. As the Principal was in effect the CEO of the school, I was constantly involved in this difficult area. It was relatively straightforward while a Superintendent Physiotherapist managed the clinic. Brenda Green held that post for many years and we learned to co-exist relatively well. She was totally dedicated to the welfare of the children in a hands-on fashion. She later successfully organized the Cerebral Palsy Sports Association, which has made a major contribution to the lives of people with disability. David Kilroy in the Training Workshop brought a new dimension to Sandymount with his work ethic and socially conscious attitude to the trainees. Tony Coffey, as senior in child-care, played a very valued role in the school. All the staff 'on the ground' at Sandymount generally worked very well together. As Principal I was keenly aware of the important roles played by child care, drivers, escorts, secretarial, kitchen, cleaning, maintenance, swimming pool, garden centre, security staffs and volunteers. All played a vital role in the happy running of the school. Among the names that come to mind over the years are Penny Leetch, Brendan Collins, Annette O'Brien, Colette Merriman, Christine Kiernan, David Ryan, Dermot Carr, Seán Murphy. When eventually we got finance for a school secretary, Angela Fearon's common sense and commitment made a qualitative contribution to the life of the school.

One particular volunteer, Jane Bleakley, worked at the school for twenty-nine years. Her presence was particularly valuable as she was prepared to do short term substitute teaching. As she knew the children and they knew her, this avoided the difficulties that can arise with new faces. Among local people who did voluntary work at the school were Marie Corr, Heather Toomey, Mary O'Rourke, Claudia Bevin, Sisters Teresa and Angie Gahan and Mrs Gertie Hollaway. The maintenance men were Jim Healy and Con Butler, both keen historians. The cook was Mary Seaver assisted by Josie Fullam. One of the Association's drivers was the most affable Kit McDonnell. Another person who played a very important role in Sandymount was our long-time Community Garda, Derek Dempsey. He was always available to work with the students or to advise on matters within the wider community, where he still performs an invaluable and well-appreciated service. Among the drivers I recall working with, were Myles Geraghty, Tony Graham, Jimmy White, Dermot Ryan and Eugene Donoghue from Cavan, with whom I used to have intense discussions about our respective counties GAA fortunes. Sandymount was an ideal location for facilities for people with physical disabilities. It was entirely flat and contained all the services that a viable village required.

In the early 1980's, through pressure from Bernie O'Shea of the local community, Elaine Murray one of our Occupational Therapists and myself, Dublin Corporation dished the footpaths making the whole area around the Green and village entirely accessible for wheelchair users.

Dr. Robert Collis.
A great Samaritan.

CHAPTER 15

SPECIAL EDUCATION

THE INTO, NACPI, and PRINCIPAL TEACHERS

Gradually, as the years progressed, the school at Sandymount became recognized as a centre for innovation in many aspects of special education. We were pioneers in the computer age, including their use in communication for those without oral communication; programmes for daily living, leisure time activities, post primary certificate examinations, certification for all, FETAC courses, active links with local schools, including parish sacramental programmes, joint classes and split placements, sports activities including swimming soccer and hurling, individual education programmes, Co-operation North activities, Student Representative Council, music therapy and media studies. For the last we used to plan and record on video, a full 30-minute news programme. Joan McNamara, Colette Merriman, John Boylan and I, personally initiated respite/holiday breaks for pupils/families during the summer holidays at the Association's residential centre in Bray. Dr. Mary O'Donnell solved the financing of this initiative by signing in the pupils under the Health Board. One of our closest relationships was with Ballinteer Community School, which was the designated post-primary school for students with a physical disability in 1975. Many of our students progressed there, where they were well served, particularly by Deirdre Walsh and Principal Austin Corcoran. A large percentage of our pupils moved from our school every year, as we endeavoured to secure 'the least restrictive environment compatible with a suitable education' for them. Some of our new ideas came from my association with Seán Buckley, who was Principal Teacher at Scoil Eoin in Crumlin and a great innovator. During these years special schools often came under criticism, as political correctness often dictated how society should conduct its affairs. I addressed this in a letter to the *Irish Times*:

"Sir, I was somewhat perturbed to read the article in your paper (June 1st 1993), headed "DEALING WITH EDUCATIONAL APARTHEID" and heavily critical of the Irish National Teachers Organization. I can empathize completely with the frustration of parents trying to get the most appropriate educational placement for their disabled children. But I expect a little more detachment, a less closed ideological mind and an absence of emotive language by professionals working in the field. This applies particularly when these professionals are of the non-hands-on variety, whose métier is theoretical.

In the article referred to, Mark O'Reilly, lecturer in psychology in UCD and formerly of the Department of Special Education at the University of Illinois, is quoted as saying, "seclusion of children with learning difficulties in special school is a form of educational apartheid". I ask, what service does such a statement make to anybody? I know of very many people it insults and demeans. Mark O'Reilly rightly says, "The planning has not been done to see what full integration would involve". Yet he is categorical in his belief that all learning disabled children must be integrated in ordinary schools. He adds the illuminating assertion that "research would assert that everybody could learn", as if to suggest that learning does not happen in special schools. He also claims that the "INTO now states that integration must be opposed, regardless of the consequences for pupils and teachers".

In May of 1979 you published the text of an address I gave to the AGM of the National Association of Boards of Management of Special Schools. In this, I noted the various inputs demanded by groups of interested teachers, if the integration of children with disabilities into ordinary schools were to occur in a way that adequate locational, social and functional integration would follow. I pointed out that these inputs would not make integration a cheap alternative to provision in special schools, rather the opposite. I gave it as my opinion then that, for various reasons, the necessary inputs would not occur and that there was a great danger that ad-hoc integration would occur.

The INTO debated the matter for two years and though the draft policy was of the same opinion as my own, the Congress of 1981 decided in a spirit of hope and faith to recommend integration where possible in ordinary schools. The teachers who make up the INTO have worked diligently and selflessly over ten years to operate this policy. But they have now decided that it is time to pause and reflect on what is happening. They are the professional educators and they have put a question mark over whether the present practice is best meeting the needs of children. In doing this so carefully and so conservatively they deserve praise, not condemnation. They have a right if not a duty to act thus. Their recent publication "Accommodating Difference" is the best contribution to the debate to appear in Ireland. It is a comprehensive document, with no simple solutions offered but a lot of pertinent questions asked. I suggest that Mark O'Reilly, and others of like mind, read it, before contributing any further in this matter.

For the record I am Principal of a special school, who is proud of the service we deliver. Our school is co-educational, multi-denominational, caters for pupils with a wide range of physical and intellectual abilities, and has a total social mix. We are not secluded, we do not practice apartheid. We are part of many communities, we have close contacts with many schools and organizations. Over the past twenty years 45% of our pupils have been integrated into ordinary schools. We are an equal-opportunity school and provide a least restrictive educational environment to the pupils and the families we are privileged to serve. We operate in the real world."

Yours, etc. Anthony Jordan Dublin 4

I returned to this subject three years later with another letter to the *Irish Times*:

"A Chara, Your editorial "Disability Blueprint" (January 21st 1996) is welcome as is the Fianna Fail policy document you write about. However I want to take issue with you on the negative way in which you mention special schools. For almost the last 30 years the issue of civil rights has been a dominant theme in the Western world. Integration has been a buzzword and we in Ireland have been inundated with associated tides from Scandinavia, USA, England. Thankfully more and more children with disabilities are being accommodated at their local schools. Teachers in special schools and their colleagues in mainstream schools have been to the fore through the INTO and other representative groups in seeking the least restrictive environment for children's' education, consistent with their special educational needs being met.

However, as with any major change in society you will have people who are entirely ideologically driven and do not know, or wish to know, of the realities of any given situation, Integration for children with disabilities has its full quota of such ideologues. However, most people with a hands-on-experience of the matter, specifically teachers, parents and pupils, realize that there are no black and white answers in this area. As the report on the Special Educational Review Committee 1993 said and the White Paper 1995 has endorsed, "The Review Committee holds no entrenched doctrinaire position regarding the integration into the ordinary school system of pupils with disabilities and/or special needs. We favor, as much integration as is appropriate and feasible, with as little segregation as is necessary. We therefore envisage a system in which there will be a place for both ordinary and special schools".

In this context, I find your attitude to special schools unhelpful to those parents and pupils who are very satisfied with the service provided by dedicated teachers and allied staff therein. Your attitude smacks of the ideologue referred to earlier rather than the measured and realistic tone I expect of the Irish Times editorials. May I add that I agree with you that people with disabilities are not getting a fair deal. Your point that Fianna Fail might have sought measures to ensure that disability organizations themselves fill more of their managerial posts with people with disabilities is well made. I would add that the latter should also be fully represented at Board level within those organizations, and that the State bodies, which put up so much of the taxpayers money to run these services, should insist this upon."

Yours etc. Tony Jordan
Principal Sandymount School & Clinic Sandymount Avenue Dublin 4.

Our school always had a good professional relationship with the Department of Education inspectors. We regarded them as providing a healthy external validation of the vital work we were engaged upon. Seán Hunt was one inspector I was always glad to see arrive. He was a former Mayo county footballer. Seán always bemoaned the fact that NACPI had no drive, no ambition to progress. It had a civil service mentality, he would say, adding that any self- respecting voluntary organization should have a large bank deficit. When the Department of Education did agree to finance a new school in the late 1980s, the Association refused to proceed because it could not get financial approval from the health sector for a new clinic. The school *qua* school was generally a most happy and fruitful place in which to work, and visitors regularly remarked upon its ethos. Many of the clinic staff opted into the school ethos, which was always a boon, but others preferred to operate in a medical model mode, keeping the children and their parents at a safe distance. This was understandable given their training.

A major complicating factor occurred, however, when following Health Board practice, each discipline within the clinic at Sandymount, developed its own independence and got its own Head of Department. This was a culture change, which led to a schedule for departmental administration and departmental meetings. The school was then faced with a multiplicity of clinic heads, in physiotherapy, occupational therapy, speech therapy, social work, psychology, child care, pre-school, adult services, together with new posts of clinic Manager and a Director of Services, all topped by a Chief Executive Officer. This development inevitably led to an element of careerism and a distraction from a hands-on relationship with the children and their parents, which had not been present formerly.

I was responsible to a school BOM which contained some NACPI employees, but which traditionally for most of my tenure had an independent chair. I always maintained excellent relations with the medical directors, who were part-time in Sandymount. Indeed I wrote the *Irish Times* obituary for Dr. Mary O'Donnell, when she died in 1999. She had been Medical Director during many of my years at Sandymount. I also delivered the panegyric at her funeral. Her successor, Dr. Hugh Monaghan, became a close colleague of mine for several years. We both experienced the advent of a management regime, seeking to assume more and more control of the professional educational and health sectors. Indeed, on one occasion I had to alert him as to how his role at Sandymount was possibly in danger of being diluted. He was in position to attend the next NACPI Board meeting in Cork and have his professional role clearly understood and accepted, without demur. Management is a definite skill and generally requires professional training. The most problematical management situations may arise, when sexual relationships, including homosexual and lesbian varieties, became factors in the workplace.

⁕

IRISH NATIONAL TEACHERS ORGANISATION

The Irish National Teachers Organisation (INTO) has played a very important role in Irish education over the years. It is the largest union representing teachers and has represented its members well, improving their status and conditions. Its task has been fairly straightforward inasmuch as the Churches have controlled the schools with the Department of Education as paymaster. The INTO has vast experience in dealing with both quite centralized bodies. Special Schools, however, were often under the patronage of a variety of voluntary bodies. This often created complications for the INTO, as in the case of NACPI. An important insight into NACPI can be seen from its attitude to the Irish National Teachers Organisation (INTO).

At the instigation of our school staff, the General Secretary of the INTO, Gerry Quigley, wrote to NACPI in 1982. He said that the union had concluded agreements with the Catholic Managers Association on terms and conditions of employment of its members. He said that since there were a considerable number of Patrons and Boards of Management, *"I wish to invite you to indicate whether you would be prepared to enter into agreements in similar terms to the attached agreements"*. NACPI did not reply to this letter. In January 1988 the staffs of Sandymount and the Marino School in Bray, (also under the patronage of NACPI), on the advice of the INTO, jointly wrote to NACPI on the matter. In April the INTO received a well crafted, and on the face of it somewhat reasonable, response.

"Your proposal for the adoption by this Association of the INTO Grievance Procedure has been carefully considered by the Board of Directors. There is a tradition of interest in the welfare of each member of staff in this organization. The structure of the schools as part of an organization with educational, medical and social endeavor raises particular problems, which need much special knowledge and understanding. In the event of a matter not being resolved by a school board there can be an appeal to the main board of the Association in its capacity as Patron of the schools. It is clear that any problem arising would be carefully and fairly assessed. The Board did not feel that an additional grievance procedure would be helpful in the particular circumstances of these very special schools".

The staff felt that this matter became crucial some years later, when Fr. Aidan Lehane departed his position as Chairman of the school board, on a year's sabbatical abroad from his own full-time work. NACPI decided that henceforth someone from within its Association would fill that position.

In fact the Patron himself, Dr. Tom Gregg, assumed the chair. It was akin to the local bishop becoming chairman of the local parish school board of management. Dr. Gregg, however, did appreciate the work I had done in the school, and often praised it publicly. He had, however, his own clear view of where the vital relationships within the centre lay. In December 1994, as Chairman of the Association he informed the Chairperson of the Parents Committee at Sandymount Mrs Mary McAnaney, that:

"The centre is primarily a clinic providing therapy for children and, as in any clinic, there is freedom of choice to attend for any parent who wishes for therapy for their child. The school was developed later for children recommended in need of such special facilities by the Medical Director. The important relationship is of the individual parent and child to the Medical and Para-medical staff".

In the early 1990's the staff again met with the INTO to pursue the elusive agreement. This time NACPI introduced another element into negotiations. It asked the INTO, *"to enter into discussions on the acceptance of another agreement covering INTO members and other staff"*. We felt that this was a red herring and despite some pressure from the INTO itself, held that such a type of agreement should be processed by respective unions representing staffs. Eventually, after thirteen years effort, agreement was reached in 1995. NACPI agreed to the INTO's proposal, though with two added qualifications, accepting the special work of NACPI. Despite this long history with NACPI, it later came as a shock to staff, when other difficulties arose, that the INTO did not appear to comprehend how intractable the Association could be. With Dr. Gregg in the chair of the school board of management, and also de facto the Patron, and no Reverend Gentleman to mediate, business at the board could have become rather fraught. In fact, it seldom did. Though he could prove quite frustrating on occasion, as no doubt I could myself, the one great quality he displayed in any important matter was his independence and integrity. This was very important when conflicts arose with NACPI management in its various forms. The later resignation of Dr. Gregg from the Chair of NACPI was an enormous loss in this respect. He had devoted large amounts of time and energy to NACPI and executed his role, with due diligence, and without fear or favor. To my knowledge, he never asked or received any monetary reward whatsoever for all his long years of service. He respected the school sufficiently to ensure that we were always in a healthy financial position and never lacked any necessary resources. His intended successor declined the post and the genial ex-Chairman of the National Farmers' Association, Donie Cashman, accepted the post.

THE INTO AND PRINCIPAL TEACHERS

Another area the INTO has long had difficulty with was the tendency of sections of its members to create special interest groups outside the aegis of the INTO. The educational system had prepared me well for my role as class teacher but I had no specific training for my role as Principal. This was a very different role calling for new skills and new information. There were no established courses available. It appeared to be a question of Principals learning on the job and hoping for the best. I was very conscious of a gap in my education and the urgent need for peer association. After some time as Principal, I discovered by chance, that there was in fact a grouping of Principals from ordinary schools in being. It proved very difficult to make contact with them. I wrote to Gerry Quigley, General Secretary of the INTO on the matter.

He replied to my query, informing me that at the annual congress of the INTO in 1974, the following motion was adopted, *"Congress condemns the formation of a Principals Teachers' Association on the grounds that it would be divisive, and contrary to the professional interests of the Organization".*

That reply came as a great shock. It appeared that the Principals Group I was trying to contact had continued in existence after above condemnation, but operated at a low profile. I eventually made contact with them and became a member. I found their meetings to be of huge professional and personal value to me. It was called *The Association of Principals of National Schools of Ireland* and had its own constitution and executive. In 1978 the INTO had repeated its stance of its official position to all its members.

In November 1981, the Principals' Group had a scheduled meeting at Buswell's Hotel. The Dáil was debating the School Entry Age that same night and many INTO activists were lobbying T.D's in the vicinity. Our meeting was advertised in the foyer of the hotel and several of the activists took note. Subsequently seventeen of the activists named seven of us Principals in a letter to their Branch Chairman. This was communicated to the INTO. Mr. E.G. Quigley placed their letter before the Central Executive Committee on 13th March. We were dubbed by colleagues as *'The Magnificent Seven*. We received correspondence from Mr. Quigley, informing us *"The CEC decided in view of the terms of the letter received, (which he copied to us) it had reason to believe that there was a prime facie case to be investigated by the District Arbitration Committee".* We waited, but never heard anything further and our Association continued to function as normal. Commonsense appeared to have prevailed.

In 1986 our Association organized, with the approval and assistance of the Department of Education, a full day seminar at Carysfort Training College for Saturday 15th March. Among the listed speakers were eminent educationalists, Dr. Sherry, P.P., of Donnybrook, Florence Armstrong, Principal of Dalkey School Project, Fr. Paul Andrews S.J, Director of St. Declan's Child Guidance Center, and Dr. Aine Hyland of the Curriculum and Examination Board and admissions officer of Carysfort College. Prior to that meeting, a letter dated 10th March 1986 from EG Quigley, General Secretary of the INTO, came to each school's INTO Staff Representative and Principal Teacher. It included our conference programme, the draft Constitution of the Association and a list of the Executive committee, which included myself. The letter stated:

"My attention has been drawn to a communication dated 27th February 1986, which has been sent to principal teachers, who are members of a body called "The Association of Principals of National Schools of Ireland". I wish to advise Staff Representatives and all principal teachers, who are members of the INTO, that our 1974 Congress adopted a resolution in the following terms: Congress condemns ...etc Subsequently, the CEC decided that under provision of Rule 116(h) that it would be unworthy conduct which would be injurious to the professional interests of

the Organization for any member to become or remain a member of any association of principal teachers. It is important that each principal teacher should be aware of the Organization's decisions on this important issue. EG Quigley, General Secretary. P.S. A copy for the Principal Teacher in your school is enclosed."

The conference went ahead and was attended by about two hundred and fifty principals. I, in common with all of the principals involved, felt that the INTO should be able to accommodate our group, as our specific needs were not being met within the Organization. Major changes were afoot within primary education and much responsibility for its management rested on principals. Precedents existed for the establishment of special interest groups of teachers. The Irish Association for Teachers in Special Education (IATSE), to which I belonged, had existed for many years. ARTI, an association for remedial teachers also existed. I also attended meetings of Principals of Schools for the Mildly Disabled, hosted by St Francis School in Portlaoise for many years. I found them to be of enormous personal and professional assistance and they achieved much important educational work. Principals of schools for children with physical disabilities would also soon begin to hold regular meetings. The Department of Education saw the need for such groups. In an attempt to highlight the ongoing impasse, I offered to read a paper on the subject at a Drumcondra Educational Conference, organized by District XV of the INTO in Dublin. I believed that the INTO was playing an effective role as a trade union, protecting the welfare and conditions of its members. Many of our own group attended the Drumcondra Conference. My paper outlining our position was subsequently printed in the official proceedings document[63]. Joe O'Toole of the CEC responded to my paper. Among the points he made were: many in the principals' association wished to remain an exclusive grouping outside the Organisation; the existence of our Association took from teachers' unions, the INTO in particular felt that unity was strength; he did not foresee any change in the official position.

The problem was that we were a group of principal teachers and the INTO, understandably, feared how our group might develop. I added that principals groups would continue, and that the INTO should, in the interests of education, and of all its members, find an accommodation. Eventually, and sadly, our group did disband, due to a general air of apathy and disillusion with our role as principals. At our last meeting in the *Submarine* public house in Crumlin we allocated remaining funds to two children's hospitals in Dublin. In later years, however, other younger principals, with a notable Cork dimension, set up another organization called the *Irish Primary Principals Network (IPPN)*. I attended its launch by the newly appointed Minister for Education and Science, Michael Woods, in Dublin Castle. It was ironic to see that the INTO issuing a statement welcoming this development. I was happy to attend several of its prestigious conferences, each of which was hugely over subscribed. In due course, John Carr, the new General Secretary of the INTO, felt able to attend one of my last conferences, and was warmly received. IPPN is now a major player in Irish education, as more and more responsibility devolves on principal teachers.

The antagonism between the two bodies continues to recur, as a motion adopted in private session at the INTO Annual Congress of 2006 indicated, *"Congress condemns the blatant interference in industrial relations issues by the IPPN during the lead up to the ICTU's national day of protest on December 9th last"*[64]. A report in the Irish *Times* of December 2006 said that, *"Old tensions between the INTO and the IPPN resurfaced last week…Tensions have been exacerbated by a recent meeting of the Oireachtas Committee on Education where Senator Joe O'Toole ex-general secretary of the INTO took the wind out of the IPPN sails, as it were"*. Though Senator Joe O'Toole was not a member of the Committee, he substituted for an absent member. He said that it was good to see his old friends from the IPPN, and to see the organization still operating, though he had not dealt with it in some time. He declared that, *"I am stunned by several of these issues"*. He identified one of these as a proposal to have a separate salary structure for principals and teachers. He doubted that the INTO supported such a structure, feeling that it would be bad for education. He thought the IPPN *"was a little disparaging regarding boards of management"*. He realized that *"these ideas are being brought forward with the best of intentions but they are bringing us to the edge of a chasm…I am no longer a person that the witnesses need trouble themselves about… but I am suffering from delayed shock at the moment"*[65]

Jasper Carrot and his wife visit Sandymount School.

Bob Ryan takes to the air before demolition.

Tending Garden at Sandymount School.

CHAPTER 16

CEREBRAL PALSY IRELAND - ENABLE IRELAND
ADVERSE PUBLICITY

In the late 1980's NACPI changed its name to Cerebral Palsy Ireland under the tutelage of a very sophisticated public relations expert, Bob Ryan. He assembled a public relations team at Sandymount, which gradually began to create favorable media coverage for the organization. The important work of this group was under-valued, and it was later disbanded, with unfortunate consequences, as can be seen below. Negative publicity did not seem to cause any concern for the organization. This remained evident on a continuing basis as later under its new name of Enable Ireland, it was found by the Labour Court to have discriminated against an employee who had disabilities. The *Irish Times* reported under the headline:

CEREBRAL PALSY ORGANISATION DISCRIMINATED AGAINST EMPLOYEE WHO HAD DISABILITIES

"The State's largest disability organization discriminated against a disabled employee, who was given tasks she had difficulty in carrying out and was denied the use of a disabled parking space, the Labour Court has found. It has awarded € 9,000 to the woman who claimed that she was constructively dismissed by Enable Ireland (formerly Cerebral Palsy Ireland), in circumstances amounting to discrimination, due to her disability".

This particular episode did not surprise me, as there was never an ethos of positive discrimination towards employing people with disability within the organization. I well remember on an occasion when a vacancy occurred for a receptionist at the center, a parent and myself suggesting that there were several school leavers who could be trained for such a position. At the relevant Board meeting it was stated unequivocally that the policy of the organization was to fill all positions *"with the best available candidates, irrespective of disability"*[66].

ANNOYING AN TAOISEACH

At a later date a decision to cease providing hot meals for the children at Sandymount elicited much adverse publicity as the Parents Association reacted angrily to the proposal. It released a long press release on 19 March 2003 saying:

"After thirty years Enable Ireland Sandymount, are ceasing to provide hot meals to their learners. This decision was made with no consultation with the learners, Parents Association or the School Board of Management... As no satisfaction has been gained from the management of Enable Ireland... the meeting called resulted in the formation of an action committee to take any necessary action to highlight this decision..."

This matter reached Leaders Questions in the Dail when the Labour Leader Pat Rabbitte raised the matter with Taoiseach, Bertie Ahern. An Taoiseach replied on 1 April 2003;

"I understand that Enable Ireland receives annual grants of €16 million under section 65 of the Health Act 2001. The body has a shortfall of €4 million. Enable Ireland has indicated that deficits have arisen for a number of reasons... It always amazes me in cases where organizations have a budget of €16 million or, in some cases €100 million that hot meals to children seem to be cut back before anything else... A detailed review of the activities of voluntary service providers in the physical and sensory disability sector is being carried out jointly by the Department of Health and Children and the health boards to look at staffing deficits with a view to the identification of the exact deficits in those areas. That is the way to deal with them. It is regrettable people do not go through these channels but try to spin issues publicly with a few politicians. That is not the way these issues should be dealt with. Enable Ireland is a good organisation which is trying to do a job and which should do it through the channels available which I am sure it is doing"[67]

However the organisation took Mr. Ahern seriously, for shortly afterwards, it was announced in the *Irish Times* over a headline: "CUTBACKS AT ENABLE IRELAND OVER FUNDS", that three senior management staff have left under a voluntary redundancy package, while four other members of staff have been made redundant. Despite the fact that senior management worked assiduously for the organisation, adopting the particular tradition of the governing ethos at Sandymount, such staff rarely departed happily.

Some time later the Association decided to sell a portion of its valuable Sandymount site. The colour piece in the *Irish Times*, where the land was advertised, suggested a price of €9 million. Some saw this as an exercise in asset stripping, but it was something that had often been mooted in the past and was bound to happen at some stage. My only *caveat* was that the particular piece of land included what had been the children's football pitch for many years. It had been taken over on a temporary basis to facilitate the new building programme. We had been assured that it would be restored for the student usage, but new management decided otherwise.

The Parents and Friends Association at Sandymount hoped that since the site at Sandymount had originally been bought with monies collected by the Parents and Friends, that the windfall should be spent at Sandymount. But by that stage the influence the Sandymount Centre exercised within the Association had lessened as the power basis shifted southwards.

The apparent lack of accountability to anyone outside of itself by Cerebral Palsy Ireland-Enable Ireland cannot be entirely laid at its door. I can recall an occasion when an invitation by the organization to the Eastern Health Board to nominate two people to the Board was rejected. Even as late as 2008 there is no legal obligation on charitable bodies to account publicly on their financial business arrangements. The setting up of an inspectorate to monitor the standards achieved by such organizations has not yet occurred. Yet all the while such groups are recipients of millions of euros of taxpayers' money. It would also appear that the quality of managers in voluntary organisations may not always be of a very high standard.

Despite many internal problems, Enable Ireland continued to give an excellent service to its clients. In particular, on occasions where we had difficulty placing school leavers, the Association always provided same.

RE-BRANDING CEREBRAL PALSY IRELAND

In 1996 the Parents and Friends Committee at Sandymount produced a 109-page study of the center titled, *"MODERN MANAGEMENT TECHNIQUES FOR AN EDUCATION & DEVELOPMENT CENTRE AT CEREBRAL PALSY IRELAND SANDYMOUNT "*[68].

It was a challenging report and demonstrated that the Parents and Friends were very dissatisfied. It stated that: *"Under the present policies and philosophy, the education and development, towards full potential, of the disabled persons committed to their care, will never be realized"*. The Report wanted, *"To ensure that Sandymount is first considered a school incorporating social, recreational and personal development areas, and secondly, considered a therapy area with family support facilities"*. It found that the Board of CPI *"was a closed body without any obligation to divulge any of its procedures except those required by law. It operates with self appointed and self-perpetuating board membership, by invitation only"*[69]

It praised the school and deemed the clinic as based on an acute medical model[70]. This Report eventually led to the setting up of a five-person group to draw up a strategic plan for the Association. I was belatedly appointed to this group, at the insistence of Dr. Gregg. It eventually published a document titled, *Going Forward Together - A Strategy for the Future*, in May 1999. One interesting aspect of being a member of this group for me was to see the generous use of a company credit card on expenses, as we held meetings at various venues. In 1999 the Board, under its Chairman Donie Cashman, had appointed a new chief executive. His background was in the commercial world and he brought an air of dynamism with him. Following on from the published *'Strategic Plan'* and a follow up *'Action Plan'*, he set about restructuring the Association, creating a regional management structure.

He re-branded the Association, renaming it *Enable Ireland*, after a detailed exercise involving all the stakeholders. He, however, did not attain longevity in the Association. In a statement to the *Irish Examiner,* Chairman Cashman referred to serious difficulties within Association management.

The professional staffs within the Association were not privy to any of these matters. A lacuna was created, as the CEO was absent for a long period. Eventually it was announced that he had left the Association on amicable terms.

50th ANNIVERSARY KILMAINHAM

The 50th anniversary of the founding of the organization was celebrated in 1999. President MacAleese agreed to become Patron. Several functions were held to mark the occasion. Among them was a gala dinner on 18 March in the Royal Hospital Kilmainham, presided over by the President. As my biography of Christy Brown had just been published, and contained a history of the Association, I sent a copy of it to Áras an Uachtaráin. The dinner itself was a splendid affair with all the notables from the Association round the country present. I was the sole representative of our school staff invited. President MacAleese referred in her address to Dr. Robert Collis founder of the Association. To my surprise and pleasure she quoted extensively from my book Towards the end of her address, she said,

"I am delighted to have this opportunity to commend all of you. I would like to mention in particular, Tony Jordan, Principal of the Sandymount School and Clinic and, after 26 years, the longest serving member of the Association. I was delighted to receive a copy of his book, "Christy Brown's Women", which charts both the development of the Association and the life and loves of Christy Brown".

I could immediately feel the barely suppressed vibrations of anger and resentment come my way from the top tables.

A NEW SCHOOL AND CLINIC 2000

The Association had long planned to build a new school and clinic at Sandymount. After many years, financial approval became available and a vast logistical and planning exercise was put in train. This demanded a huge extra workload from the staff directly concerned. It involved establishing and moving to and operating in temporary accommodation on our sports field. Great credit for this work belongs to a new Director of Services named Susan Grey. She was from the Midlands of England and had the necessary management and personal skills to carry such an immense programme of work to fruition. Most of the staff, including myself and the parents, hoped that she would become CEO of the Association, as that position became vacant. However, that was not to be, and a most skilled manager with a warm personality was allowed to depart from the Association. It took about eighteen months for the new buildings to be completed and school and clinic operated from very confined space. This meant that the students had to remain within the temporary buildings and could not go out to a playground. This created all kinds of problems with supervision and care and safety for pupils, when they were not confined to their classrooms.

When the Deputy Principal and myself visited the new school building in August 2000, she immediately noticed that the emergency exits from the classrooms were too narrow to allow a wheelchair exit. I informed management that I felt that it would be foolhardy for the school to occupy such a building. This entailed a delay in moving into the school, which was not appreciated by the Association, as the opening was due in a matter of a week. The official opening of the school and clinic, by President McAleese, went ahead in September 2000. The Chairman and CEO officiated at the ceremony, with neither the Medical Director nor the Principal Teacher involved.

INTO RETIREMENT PLANNING SEMINAR

Seminars for teachers contemplating retirement, including their spouses, were held each year by the INTO. Mary and I attended at All Hallows College during December 1999. In 1985 I had suffered a contra-reaction to a general anesthetic at St. Vincent's Hospital, during the first part of a two-tiered operation, and had developed atrial fibrillation. The only unpleasant result for me was being put on permanent medication, and occasionally becoming conscious of the wild irregularity of my pulse. Six months later, when preparing for the second operation, a different anesthetist read my medical notes and offered the opinion that I had been fortunate to survive the first operation. Though Dr. Richard Mulcahy informed me that I should have a normal life span, I was well aware that I was at risk in several serious health areas. As a result of this and other factors, I had been considering retiring in the summer of 2000.

Eighty people attended the two-day seminar, but the only teacher I recognized on the course, was an esteemed colleague from Special Education, Éamon O'Murchú and his wife Nora. The programme was intensive, with detailed presentations on superannuation, an introduction to the Retired Teachers' Association by Denis Desmond, handling lifestyle changes by Patricia Redlich, budgeting, investment, taxation, will and inheritance, social welfare entitlements, and enjoying a healthy retirement. Among the many valuable handouts was a magazine with the title, *Your Heart*. In the event I did not retire in the summer of 2000 but postponed it to 2001, when I would have completed thirty-five years of service and be eligible for a pension.

RADICAL CHANGE TO SCHOOL BOARD OF MANAGEMENT

The new Chairman and Chief Executive of Enable Ireland were effecting major changes within the organization. The new CEO served temporarily as Chairman of the school BOM at Sandymount and was an efficient chair. In 2000 new school Boards of Managements were due to take office and the Association decided to appoint its own Directors of Services, as Chairpersons of the new Boards in Sandymount and at their school in Bray. It was precluded from doing the same at its Cork school, because the local Catholic bishop was Patron and did not agree to a similar arrangement there.

This meant that the Directors of Services, positions previous on a par with the School Principals, now became senior to the School Principals, and in a vital educational management function. The role and status of the school principals were seriously diluted. The hitherto partial independence of the schools was checkmated within the centres, with school board meetings becoming fraught with the realization that, on occasion, the Association was dictating matters. This move had been presaged earlier when a dispute over the constitutionality of the old Board had been raised. The Patron had purported to suspend the Board and appoint the Director of Services as a sole manager. The school staff objected through the INTO and the Department of Education advised the Patron that due process had not been complied with. The Board of Management thus continued to function. In the new situation the Board of Management, in so far as it could, continued to give the school and myself its support.

The teacher representative on the board was Terry Logan. He, Joan McNamara, the Deputy Principal, and Sinead Colvin, the Senior Special Needs Assistant, and others, proved immensely courageous and dedicated in fulfilling their responsibilities to the school community. These changes may have made administrative sense, but on a practical level, for anyone who was familiar with the situation, it was a recipe for added difficulties, placing both the Directors of Services and the School Principals in ongoing confrontational situations. The traditional tensions between educational and clinical roles became even more contentious, and with the Association 'controlling' the Boards of Managements, life became very fraught and volatile. The reported suicide of a member of the clinic staff around that time only added to the tensions. I inadvertently upset a plan by some of her friends to attend the burial together, when I gave an instruction that the school party at the funeral mass, would as usual, not attend the burial. I later learned that this may have led to a situation, which had to be formally dealt with by the Board of Management.

Another attempt to change the ground rules within the Association came with a resurrection of the proposal to have one grievance procedure cover staffs of both the schools and the clinics. The INTO were surprised by the total vehemence with which the schools staffs, objected to any such move. Luckily, the staffs in the schools were very united, though, as always, some individuals played every matter for their own personal advantage. The entire staffs held some meetings with the INTO on this and other matters. On one such occasion we were stunned to hear that the Association had earlier been informed of our meeting with the union. It is not unusual for union members to sometimes feel that on occasion their union appears to understand management stances better than their own members. After this particular meeting we felt that we would certainly not be exposing ourselves to such an experience again. The new management at Enable Ireland was very skilled at dealing with union personnel and establishing good personal rapport with them. The INTO were used to dealing with a clerical management which was interested in education, and the teaching of religion. It could, therefore, do business with them on a *quid pro quo* basis, within an established understanding and structure. It proved difficult for the INTO, however, to realize that *Enable Ireland* were not fundamentally interested in managing schools, and saw them as something it reluctantly had to be involved in, yet insisting in doing so on its own terms.

Another example of the dramatic change in the balance of power structure at Sandymount was a series of unprecedented and gratuitous criticisms of school staff by a very small section of clinic staff, concerning our management of pupils within the school. This made the school staff quite defensive as they had responsibility for the care, safety and discipline of the pupils *in loco parentis*. This created a particular difficulty in the new school playground, which was overlooked from the clinic. A poisonous atmosphere was created for a time. The Department of Education and Science inspectors, Brendan Murphy and Liam Walsh, were very supportive of the school, but their role was very restricted. As so often in Ireland, ownership of property is of fundamental importance and confers great rights, and *Enable Ireland* owned the school.

In fairness to *Enable Ireland*, it later recognized the error of its way and reversed the policy of appointing Directors of Services to chair Boards of Managements in its two schools, when new school boards were formed in 2004. (In 2008 when new Boards again took office, the Association returned to the original position of having independent Chairs). During these difficult years, I sought to maintain good personal relations with the Chairman of the School Board, even though we were often pitted against each other. On occasion, when we were observed in apparently friendly conversation, one particular member of the school staff would subsequently and jocosely whisper in my ear "traitor". On previous occasions the Chairman of the Association, in his capacity as Patron of the school, was available to mediate in differences between association management and myself, but during this period the attention of the new Chairman was concentrated on the major difficulties, which had arisen between senior Association management staff. Donal Cashman, with whom I always had a good relationship, explained his position to me in a subsequent letter.

As the situation at Sandymount got problematical and vicious during the school year of 2000-2001, I took sick leave prior to the summer holidays. My doctor, Damian Rutledge, advised me to retire as planned that summer. I was disposed to do just that. At the last meeting of the School Board of Management, which I did not attend, the members of the Board expressed the hope that I would return refreshed in September. During the summer it gradually became clear to me that the Association did not favour my return. I discovered that a senior administrative official of the Department of Education, without my knowledge or permission, had earlier informed the Association that I would be eligible to retire on pension that summer, having completed 35 years service. Some school staff, and others, urged me to postpone my scheduled retirement for the sake of the integrity of the whole school community.

As no meeting of the Board of Management was held during that summer, where I knew I would receive comprehensive backing, I felt that I had to demonstrate that the school and its Principal could not be steamrollered by forces external to the Board of Management. I belatedly contacted the INTO, which entered into dialogue with the Association on my behalf. As no agreement was forthcoming, the INTO advised me that if I agreed, it would seek an immediate injunction in the High Court. I agreed to this. When the Association was informed of its intention by the INTO on a Friday afternoon, I was invited to return to work on the Monday. While I have had some criticisms with my union over the years, I have to acknowledge and salute its decisiveness in vindicating my rights. Unions may not be perfect institutions but without them employees' rights could easily be trampled upon.

On the following Monday morning I returned to school, where I received a hearty welcome from the staff. I then met with the Chairman of the School Board of Management and proposed that we should institute a weekly meeting at which we could discuss any upcoming issues, which might have the potential to cause conflict between school and clinic. We carried out this exercise as scheduled and it proved quite successful in defusing potential problems. In the event, I remained on in the school for another eighteen months, until matters had settled down sufficiently. I eventually retired in November of 2002. It has been a matter of great sadness to me that so many excellent teaching staff have left the school, within a few short years of my own departure. These included, Hilary Campbell, the last appointment made to the teaching staff during my time there. She is a highly principled Northern Presbyterian who used to describe herself to me as, 'your last appointment'.

Claire Pringle with the Author on her confirmation day,
photo taken by her father Pat.

Our Xmas magazine was produced early in December and began with a letter.
This was my last offering.

XMAS NEWSLETTER FROM THE PRINCIPAL

This year my return to school was delayed to the 24th September. The Deputy Principal, Joan McNamara, had to take my role from the first few weeks of term, at very short notice. At such a time of the year this involved a multitude of tasks. On my own behalf and on the whole school community I want to express my gratitude to Joan on a job well done. This term, on the 27th November saw us mark our first anniversary in the new school. To mark the occasion a framed photograph of the opening occasion hangs in the Post Primary corridor.

Mary Hannifin T.D. Minister for Health and Children, visited the school and presented the F.E.T.A.C. Awards to those students who successfully completed their courses during the year.

Marie Heaney unveiled our new mosaic of the Children of Lir. It is situated at the school entrance. The artist Michelle McQuinn based it on drawings and conversations with the students.

Mrs Rosemary Murphy resigned from the teaching staff and has been replaced by Mr. Damien McGrath.

I would like to clarify the role ofthe Special Needs Assistants in the school. They are sometimes referred to as "helpers". I don't think that most people realise that for the most part, they have third level qualifications in the discipline of childcare. They are now paid directly by the Deparanent of Education. They are a valuable and essential group of staff for the proper functioning of the school.

It is with great sadness that I recount the deaths of two of our students, Hannan Axmed and Stephen Mulrennan, May they both rest in peace. A Bereavement Meeting will take place at 14.00 on Tuesday 12th. Mass will be celebrated at 13.45 on Friday 14th.

Two new initiatives this term concern music, Anna-Maire Higgins teaches one day per week and the Drake Project attend on Wednesday mornings. They both will combine for a Christmas concert on Wednesday 19th December.

As you know our school policy is that as many students as possible should receive Certification for their study here. The Junior Certificate and the F.E.T.A.C. Awards are gradually opening up this possibility for the majority of students. These can provide a basis for ongoing study when students leave school.

The multiplicity of business here can well be gauged by this calendar for the last few weeks of term. (See overleaf). There are six in-service days for teaching staff on the new curriculum due this school year

I wish everyone a safe and a happy Christmas.
School re-opens on Monday 7th January 2001.
Tony Jordan.

A SURPRISE CELEBRATION

During April of 2002, on the occasion of my 60th birthday my wife and I had the pleasure of being totally surprised by our two daughters. On the subterfuge of having dinner in a Ballsbridge hotel before going to the National Concert Hall, most of my siblings and their spouses from Ireland and Britain, suddenly appeared in the lobby to join our nuclear Dublin family. When we got home later that evening, and I was still recovering from the shock and pleasure of it all in my study, I detected the arrival of a stream of people at the house. On investigation, I discovered that the celebration was to continue, as we were being joined by up to forty or so of my closest friends from around the country. It was a night to remember[71.]

RETIREMENT PRESENTATIONS

I returned to the school some weeks after my retirement in November 2002 for an elaborate presentation ceremony, in which the Board of Management, the Staff, the Parents and Friends Association, the school children, the past pupils and individuals, made presentations. A concert took place in the gymnasium, and several displays in the assembly area, covered my interests in art, poetry, Mayo, and Manchester City F.C. My 'magic moments' at Sandymount had occurred daily, when I relieved the 'teacher on the bell' to take lunch. I thus spent a session in a different class each day, reading/reciting poetry, telling stories, discussing football and generally having such fun with the children. Principal Teachers from the local National Schools in Sandymount, Ringsend and Donnybrook attended, as did Fr. Peter Briscoe, parish priest of Sandymount. Staffs from throughout the centre were present. Joan McNamara presided, with Dr. Hugh Monaghan representing the BOM, speaking very graciously. As I spoke, quite emotionally, I had arranged to have beside me, a large framed photo-montage of children who had died during my thirty years at Sandymount. Tracy (Sorahan) Carr, Yvonne Kidd and I had assembled it during the previous year. Each face had such a story to tell. It was part of a bargain, as I had promised the parents that their children would be remembered. The function ended with a beautiful lunch provided by the Parent's Association, through their Chairman, Noel Farrell.

Some few weeks later I was invited to join with the Principal Teachers Group of Schools for Children with Physical Disabilities, who were meeting at Jury's Hotel in Ballsbridge. This in fact turned out to be a special lunch in my honour at which they made a presentation to me. We had made some major achievements in our field over the years in negotiations with the Department of Education officials, none more so than a major reduction in our pupil ratio from 14:1, down to 8:1. It is a very satisfying feeling to be acknowledged and thanked by ones peers. It was a particular pleasure that Joan McNamara was present, as she was acting up as Principal in my place. This was a role she was to play for nearly a year, as it took the Board of Management a long time to find my successor.

Neither Joan, nor any of the other staff in the school, was interested in applying for the post, having witnessed the slings and arrows that could come the way of that role at Sandymount. Despite that sad fact, it was a pleasure and a privilege for me to have worked with the children and their parents. The parents generally responded in exceptional fashion to their cruel fate and overcame it, to make their children a positive source in their own and society's lives. It has been a great consolation and joy for me to realize that such people have included me in the love and care of their beautiful children.

"AT THE GOING DOWN OF THE SUN AND IN THE MORNING, WE WILL REMEMBER THEM"

One aspect of life, which did not become easier by its frequency, was the fact of children dying. We had to develop a structure, a protocol, and a rubric in the school to allow the entire school community to survive such ordeals. The final rubric, the final patch on the quilt of memory, was the 'Month's Mind' Mass in the school, in which the family and friends of the deceased child, joined the school community in a celebration of a life. On one occasion it was a Muslim girl we were commemorating. The Imam had forgotten his skullcap and used his white handkerchief instead. As it looked so comical, I thought some of the children might laugh. But no; Mary Heneghan and Yvonne Kidd had put such work into the ceremony that everyone retained his or her full composure. I have written and spoken in some detail about such deaths in a piece about the last child to die during my time in Sandymount, Conor Farrelly[72]. One of the routines I recall was that of traveling with Joan McNamara to so many different churches around Dublin. Some memories are etched clearly on my mind. Every time I hear the hymn *Be Not Afraid,* I think of Keith Ryan's funeral in Ballybrack.

I think of another funeral attended by five people only: another where the distraught parents discovered their treasure too late: another; of Shane Green, whose final plea was not to be left alone overnight in the church: another whose treatment brought early death: another who knew he was dying, but whose parents could not communicate with him. On the last occasion of a death, at Christmas in 2001, as we gathered in Knocklyon for Conor Farrelly's funeral, we were joined by several 'past' parents and ex-staff. Among them were Jean Boylan and Ursula Scanlon. We laughed and we cried when we remembered other children who had died.

We spoke of the unique Angela Boylan. I referred to the letter on the following page, and got permission from Mrs Boylan to include it in my later writings. Despite much of the management difficulties I have referred to above, the central salient fact about Sandymount was that the staff who knew and worked with the children and their parents, combined to create a school, a centre, of the type described in the letter below. Thank you all.

1993

Dear Mr. Jordan,

"Just a short note to express our deeply felt thanks and gratitude to you and all your staff for the care, attention, and love you showered on Angela during her time attending the school. I remember my first visit to the school very well. I didn't know what to expect, as despite Angela's disability I had never been to a 'special' school before. The best compliment I can pay you is that I know, as did Angela, that she was going to be okay in your care. From her first day with you she enjoyed every minute. All the staff from the kitchen staff, nurses, physios, helpers and teachers, all the way up to yourself are gifted people. Donal always said that the ten minutes or so he spent there every morning did him good because it always put life into perspective for him.

It was the same for all my family, we all felt the better of visiting Sandymount, not because we felt sorry for the children, but because it was such a happy place and more like an extended family and we felt honored to be part of it. Angela benefited very much I feel from her time with you. Not just academically but in an all round sense. Her appreciation of life, art, and reading and all the things that go into a happy life were nurtured so much in Sandymount that I feel she was very lucky to attend your 'special' school. I hope she did not cause too much trouble because I know to my cost how outspoken she could be, and I'm afraid that was one thing that she couldn't be taught, either at home or at school, and that was to keep her opinions to herself. I'll tell you an incident Mr. Jordan that I always felt summed up the great attitude to her disability and that of the other children in Sandymount, taught to her in the school. My niece, aged ten or eleven, visited the school with her one day and on the way home in the car wanted to know what was wrong with ----.

Angela became quite concerned and wanted to know if he was crying or upset. It took a few minutes of toing and froing in the conversation before the penny dropped, and Angela quite exasperated said, "Ah he's just in a wheelchair; that doesn't mean there's anything wrong with him!" It tells its own story. By their attitude and kindness the staff in Sandymount always made Angela feel 'right' and not 'wrong'. For this gift we will always be grateful.

Please convey our best wishes and thanks to all in Sandymount, we will always remember ye all with a smile for the happy days Angela had with you. Remember her too with a smile."

Yours sincerely

Jean & Donal Boylan

Angela Boylan (right) with Trophy.

Susan Grey and a young friend.

A selection of Anthony Jordan's book cover designs

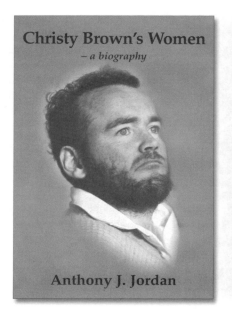

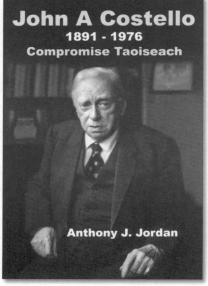

CHAPTER 17

WRITING BIOGRAPHIES

JOHN AND SEÁN MACBRIDE, AND CONOR CRUISE O'BRIEN

The acquisition of the Christy Brown letters and my attempts to turn them into a book proved a ready introduction to the business of writing a biography. At first I thought that the letters alone might form the material for a book and wrote a draft in that form. But I soon discovered that the letters proved only the basis for a beginning. They were to come midway in the pyramid of the story. I had to conduct background research on the period and the main players and organizations involved. I interviewed many people. Some spoke readily, others had to be persuaded, while some, including Mary Brown herself, refused. She said that the whole business was still too painful for her. Others I was unable to contact at all, remaining unsure whether there were alive or dead. I was lucky enough to attract more letters from a variety of people who had known Christy, including Peter Sheridan. I began to sound out publishers who might be interested in the work and began to realize that publishing was just a business like any other. It traded in books and the ethos of the market place, not unnaturally, held sway. One man who, fortunately, was very keen to publish the book was Seán Feehan of *Mercier Press*, with whom I had several meetings along the way. He was also a participant in the story and provided me with valuable material. But then quite suddenly, in early 1990, I was diverted entirely from my work on Christy Brown and remained so for nearly ten years. Christy Brown, though, had resurrected my earlier writing career and provided me with another life, another existence which gradually became more

MAUD GONNE

My daughter Judith had given me a biography of Maud Gonne by Margaret Ward, called, *Maud Gonne, Ireland's Joan of Arc,* as a Christmas present. I found it a fascinating read. It explored the lives of people whose names I was very familiar with, but about whom I knew little detail. It was a work of scholarship with copious references, notes and bibliography. The longevity of Maud Gonne's life had enabled her, an English born woman who converted to Irish nationalism and Catholicism, to span the era stretching from the aftermath of the Fenians, localized famines in Mayo and Donegal, land agitation with Davitt and Parnell, the foundation of Sinn Féin, the literary renaissance of the Celtic Revival with WB Yeats, Home Rule, First World War, 1916 Rising, the foundation of the Irish Free State with W.T. Cosgrave, the rule of DeVelera, Second World War, to Clann na Poblachta and the first Coalition Government, 1948-1951, where her son Seán MacBride was Minister for External Affairs.

The only matter that caused me some unease in the book was the treatment of Major John MacBride. He was a fellow Mayo man, of whom we in Mayo were proud, admittedly in a rather unexplained subdued way, because of his role in the 1916 Rising and subsequent execution and burial in Arbor Hill, with the rest of the executed leaders. Even his military title was something of a mystery. As a student in St. Jarlath's College, I was quite familiar with WB Yeats' famous poem, *Easter 1916*, though the unpleasant references therein to MacBride were never explained. For the first time I read of his disastrous marriage to Maud Gonne, and the shocking allegations brought against him in their bitter divorce case in Paris in 1905. The close involvement of WB Yeats, of whose poetry I was an ardent admirer, and his condemnation of MacBride during the battle with Maud Gonne, only served to cause me further concern.

I then read Maud Gonne's own autobiography, *A Servant of the Queen,* and was further perplexed to find no word against her husband there, rather a positive and loving account of him. She wrote about his Irish Brigade in the Boer War, "*I felt that little band of Irishmen in the Brigade had done more for Ireland's honor than all of us at home, for it is action that counts*"[73]. Significantly, she makes it very clear that her daughter, Iseult, hated MacBride. She wrote about how so many of their friends and relatives advised them not to marry. She ends her story before their marriage, writing; "*we both sat silent; then I got up and laughed. John those whom the gods love die young; a short and merry one. Let us go to dinner. We must hurry or we will be too late for the love of gods or for dinner. I am thirty six, you are thirty five and it is ten o'clock. Next morning we were married in the church of St. Honore d'Eylau and started our honeymoon from which, we both thought, there was a great chance we would never return*"[74].

I read the 1979 biography of Maud Gonne by Nancy Cardozo, entitled, *Maud Gonne: Lucky Eyes and a High Heart*. I found that book far more condemnatory of MacBride than Ward's. It appeared to have access to letters written by Maud to Yeats during the 1905 divorce case. I discovered that several other authors who had written on Maud Gonne and WB Yeats, had all, more or less, accepted that the charges made against MacBride were factual. The only text I came across which cast any possible doubt was a 1979 article, published in *Éire-Ireland* by Conrad Balliet entitled, *The Lives - and Lies – of Maud Gonne*. Balliet had been preparing for several years to write a biography of Maud Gonne, but was frustrated by the unavailability of material he knew was extant and made available to other writers.

Of the charges against MacBride he wrote: *"Most details about it however, come from undocumented sources, primarily the accusations of the unreliable Maud filtered through Willie, an often-inaccurate gossip. My own belief is that the incident may have been less serious than Maud's charge; the court did not find MacBride guilty of that account. He evidently was, on occasion drunk; whether he was a 'vainglorious lout' remains to be proved, and the truth awaits further research"*[75].

NOTHING ON JOHN MACBRIDE!

I then decided that it was past time for me to read directly about MacBride himself. I looked for a biography and found there was none. In fact, there appeared to be nothing written specifically about the man himself. In desperation, I rang the local library in Westport Co. Mayo, where MacBride was born, to be told that they had nothing on him. I obtained a Reader's Ticket for the National Library of Ireland, where I felt sure I would find material on the man. There were lots of references to Maud Gonne but nothing specific on MacBride. I then began to write about Maud in a fictional way, which gave me the freedom to explore what I thought her character might have been. Her early life, leading up to her majority and financial independence, and her meeting and falling in love with Lucien Millevoye in Royal, was a fascinating story. Then I came across a reference to a book entitled, *Devoy's Postbag Vol 11, 1880-1928,* by W. O'Brien and E. Ryan, published by CJ Fallon in 1953. There were references to MacBride in it. I repaired to the National Library again, this time with a definite reference. The book consisted of letters written by Irish nationalist leaders to the famous leader of Irish America, John Devoy. Several of them were from John MacBride himself. I had found my starting point, which proved the key to more material. I discovered almost immediately that MacBride had been an important figure in Irish Nationalism over many years and a respected colleague of its leaders.

Of most immediate excitement to me, was the information that he had founded and co-led the Irish Brigade in South Africa, which fought alongside the Boers in their war against Great Britain. This placed him in a long historical tradition of Irish Brigades fighting abroad. His military title came from President Kruger himself, who commissioned him as a Major in the South African Army. This led me to the first writings of the man himself in the *Freeman's Journal,* wherein he had written a series of thirteen articles about the Irish Brigade's activities. Later, I also discovered that the local historical journal in Westport, *Cathair na Mart,* had published articles about MacBride, which were very illuminating. Unfortunately, these did not deal at all with his disastrous marriage to Maud Gonne. I was left to rely on the contemporary newspaper accounts, which had gleefully reported the divorce case, eager to damage MacBride and Maud Gonne and Irish nationalism, as much as possible. These papers listed the allegations made against him by Maud Gonne. MacBride successfully sued the *Irish Independent* for its reporting of the case.

One surprising fact for me was the close association between Arthur Griffith and MacBride who appeared to be such different personalities. Griffith had joined MacBride in South Africa at MacBride's suggestion. They both fell in love with Maud Gonne. MacBride later became the conduit for American money to support Griffith's *United Irishman*. In one fascinating personal letter to MacBride, Griffith pours out his soul at his involvement in, and hopes for, the Irish nation. The events of MacBride's actual preparation for his execution in Kilmainham were readily available from articles written by the priest who ministered to him on 5 May in 1916. But there appeared to be nothing to rebut the allegations made against him in 1905, except the fact they were not substantiated in court, as no divorce was granted and MacBride retained some rights over his baby son, Seán. As the case was *in camera*, the reporting was restricted, though the published allegations did great damage to MacBride. Nothing of his defence appeared to be extant. As I could not uncover any new material, I had to rely on the contemporary account in my work. The title for the book was relatively easy, *Major John MacBride 1968-1916*. I felt that I had to include in the sub title, Yeats's refrain, which still echoed in my ears from its recitation by Fr. PV O'Brien in St. Jarlath's College; '*MacDonagh and MacBride and Connolly and Pearse*'.

WESTPORT HISTORICAL SOCIETY

Writing the book was a difficult enough exercise. But when I had it completed and approached publishers, none were in the least interested. The message was that MacBride was a minor figure, in whom there was little interest, and therefore of no commercial potential. Eventually a friend of mine, who had earlier ministered in Westport, told me that the *Westport Historical Society* published books. He felt sure they would be interested in my manuscript. The Chairman of the Society was Jarlath Duffy, who had been two years ahead of me as a student in St. Jarlath's College. He was then Principal of the local Vocational School. He read the manuscript and decided with his committee that they would publish it, as their contribution to the celebration of the seventy- fifth anniversary of the 1916 Easter Rising. The editing process taught me many lessons, as Jarlath sought several references to material in the text, for which I had not given references. Unfortunately, I had not been diligent enough with my reference keeping, and had to revisit the National Library for many laborious sessions. Proof reading was a tedious exercise, as I spent several weekends indoors at Caraholly in Westport, amid the beautiful surrounding scenery. My youngest daughter, Fiona, who had just become a teenager, undertook the compilation of a 'person's only' index. This led to an amusing moment when I discovered that she had listed 'Ben Bulben' after 'Buller General'. I enjoyed going on location to take suitable photographs. Fiona and I had some laughs as we trespassed in the front garden of a house in Glenageary, where MacBride had lived, and from which he left on Easter Monday morning, 1916, to meet his brother in Dublin. Instead, he met Thomas MacDonagh in St. Stephen's Green, and ended up in Jacob's Factory, and in Kilmainham Jail.

Jarlath Duffy asked me to try and generate some publicity in Dublin for the book. This proved a very interesting and educational exercise. The highlights for me were a very long RTE interview with Pat Kenny on Good Friday morning 1991. It was interesting to become aware of all the background work done by producers and researchers before the interview itself takes place. The concentration required during a live interview was intense. The twenty-five minutes it lasted passed quickly. I found Pat Kenny intelligent and a gentleman to work with. The other publicity I most enjoyed getting was a full *Irishman's Diary* in the *Irish Times* of 18/4/91. It was written by Uinsionn MacDubhghaill and suggested that the text would be very suitable as a film script, moving from Dublin to Johannesburg, to Paris, to New York, to London and back to Dublin again. As Pat Kenny was ending his interview, he asked me what was the price of the book. I did not know and guessed at a figure. One problem with all the publicity I got was that the book itself did not appear until June, some few months later. Up to then, I was working with proofs.

PAUL O'DWYER

In the preparation of the book, I had collected a lot of material on the Major. As part of my publicity drive, I decided to exhibit it in Dublin. I invited Maud's grand daughter, and Seán MacBride's daughter, Anna MacBride White, to open the exhibition. Her brother Tiernan MacBride also attended, bringing with him, one of the Major's decorated walking sticks from the Boer War. They both expressed their intention to attend the launch of the book in Westport. I had sent a copy of the proofs to some members of the MacBride family. I learned at the launch that they were taken aback that the allegations against the Major were stated without being proved or rebutted. I later explained that I hoped to revisit the story, when, as I felt sure, further evidence on the matter became available. I later presented a copy of the book to Anna MacBride White, who was not able to attend the launch, though Tiernan did. Anna had lived with Maud for much of her life. A biographer enters into the history of any family at his peril.

Paul O'Dwyer of Bohola, Cheshire Home and New York fame, launched the book. He told me how he and Conor Cruise O'Brien had been close allies in New York during the protests against the Vietnam War. O'Dwyer was then a Commissioner at the New York Commission for the United Nations and Consular Corps. He told me that he understood that there were two biographies of Seán MacBride then "in the making". When I got my first copy of the book, I commented to my wife that writing a book was a bit like having a baby. Wise person that she is, she commented, "You must be joking; having a baby is a simple exercise compared to producing a book". Who was I to argue? One thing I did know was that the dedication on a book gives the author an opportunity to make a very personal statement. In this book it read: *"For Antonia, who never saw Mayo, and like the Major, lies in a mass grave in Dublin"*.

Jarlath Duffy had another surprise for me. He phoned one day to say he was sending a few boxes of books to Dublin, with a named friend. He wanted me to collect them at Heuston Station. When I asked him what he wanted me to do with them, he replied in his persuasive Mayo fashion, *"You can throw them across the wall into the Liffey, if you like, but what I would like you to do, is to approach some of the big bookshops in Dublin, Eason's for instance, and ask them to stock the book. You'll have no trouble after all the publicity, and the way you'll handle them"*. *"But Jarlath"* I started to say, *"I've never done this before. I wouldn't know how to do it"*. *"There coming in on the six o'clock train. Make sure you're there. They're quite heavy"*, he said. As I began to protest again, he said, *"You'll have no problem. I put a delivery receipt book in and filled a sample form for Eason's. I have to go now. Good luck, a mhaicín"*. I hated the thought of going into shops and asking them to stock my book, but Jarlath had left me with no alternative. I did not have the sophistication of making preliminary phone calls, but rather carrying a large bag of books, began my odyssey of visiting all the city centre bookshops The surprise for me, was how pleasant and courteous the book-buyers in the business proved to be. Thus I came to learn the various aspects of publishing, promoting, distributing and selling books, courtesy of my good friend, Jarlath Duffy of Westport.

SEÁN MACBRIDE

At one level the story of John MacBride and Maud Gonne appeared to be from the distant past. But the fact that their son was the famous Seán MacBride gave it a modern flavor. He had been a national figure for most of his life and an international figure since the 1960s. I had attended his last public function, chairing a meeting in Liberty Hall, Dublin, prior to Christmas in 1983, concerning the imprisonment of the *'Guildford Four'*. He had fought in the War of Independence and the Civil War. He had become Chief of Staff of the IRA in 1936, yet was Minister for External Affairs in the First Inter-Party Government of 1948, which ended sixteen continuous years of Fianna Fáil government. As an international statesman working for the United Nations, he was awarded the Nobel Peace Prize in 1974, the Lenin Peace Prize in 1977 and the American Medal for Justice in 1978. He was a natural subject for my next book, and I had begun collecting references and materials while finishing the book on his father in 1990. This time I was in a position to speak to people who had known and worked with my subject.

INTERVIEWS

One of my main sources, particular about MacBride the man, was a lady who had known and lived in Maud Gonne MacBride's family home in Roebuck House for many years, Louie Coghlan O'Brien. She had also been his private secretary at the time he became Minister for External Affairs[76]. She gave me certain private information, which my publisher was anxious I include in the book. An article appeared in *The Phoenix* about the matter. I decided against using it, as I detected a possible conflict of interest. I decided, however, to include one sentence which would indicate that I was privy to certain information but was not including it[77]. Another woman I interviewed was Muireann McHugh O'Briain. Her father Roger McHugh, had edited Maud Gonne's *'A Servant of the Queen'* and been on the executive of MacBride's party *Clann na Poblachta*. Muireann was a lawyer and had worked for Seán during his international career[78]. Jonathan Williams[79] edited the text for Glendale Publishing[80]. When I met Jonathan to receive the result of his work, I saw that there was an enormous further workload ahead of me. He had indicated passages, which he suggested needed working on; terms which required elaboration, points of fact, queried excisions etc. It first appeared to me that the whole text needed revision, as I saw nothing but green stickers with neatly written messages in every paragraph on every page. But the choices were mine to make, the decisions to rework the text mine. Jonathan said he was giving me his opinion. He is an exceptionally affable man, and I discovered as I studied his work, an excellent editor. A date for publication was nominated but at the last moment Glendale decided to cease operations.

Another completing factor was that an American company named 'Media Xchange' was interested in the book with a view for developing a film on Seán's life. They had been in discussion with Glendale on my behalf, and I was given their correspondence. I was naturally very disappointed with the new situation, but felt that I had a marketable product which would interest other publishers. This proved to be the case, as within a few weeks four publishers were reading the text and sounding very positive. One of them, John O'Connor of *Blackwater*[81] *Press* invited me to meet him at the Berkeley Court Hotel. I accepted his offer to publish the book. I later received a better offer, but I felt bound to proceed as already agreed. I informed Media Xchange in New York that Folens were now to publish the book. Folens suggested that it might be beneficial if they were to be the copyright holder of the book for the purpose of negotiating with any third party. I agreed with this. The dedication on the book read:

"This work is dedicated to three people whose courage and perseverance I have admired. Ciaran Barry, Enda MacDonagh, Conor Cruise O'Brien".

The book was published shortly before Christmas in 1993. Tiernan MacBride launched it at Staunton's on St. Stephen's Green, before a great gathering of my family and friends and admirers of Seán MacBride. Tiernan accepted my invitation to do the launch even before he read the text. On reading it he commented that, unfortunately, what I had written about the family life in Roebuck was accurate. Tiernan told me that he intended to speak about his family's unhappiness that their father had not left his papers to them. In the event Seán's secretary, Caitriona Lawlor, who was given custody of the papers, and her sister Mary, both attended the launch.

They took up a prominent position in front of the podium as Tiernan spoke and he did not refer at all to his father's papers. The book was widely reviewed and somewhat to my surprise and probably naivety, was reckoned to paint quite a negative picture of its subject. Some reviewers tended to select passages in the book, which were critical of MacBride. The *Sunday Tribune* in particular gave T. Ryle Dwyer large space, as he wrote, "Notwithstanding the author's sympathy, the Seán MacBride that emerges from this fascinating book was a mean, arrogant and hypocritical individual"[82]. I was further shocked when the following Sunday's *Tribune* gave extended coverage to people's critical reactions to the review and the book. Among these were Dr. Noel Browne, Martin Mansergh, Dermot Keogh, and Ruairí O Brádaigh. The latter was reported as being, *"very angry at the image painted of MacBride by both Ryle Dwyer and Anthony Jordan"*[83].

TEA WITH PRESIDENT ROBINSON

Early in 1994, I read that President Robinson was to address the Council of Europe in Strasburg at the end of June. Since Seán MacBride had such a close link to that body, I thought the President might be interested in that section of the book. I wrote to her, offering to present her with a copy. I got a reply saying that she would indeed be happy to do so on 14 June, at Áras an Uachtaráin, "provided that State business does not intervene". On inquiry, I was assured that my wife and two daughters would be very welcome also. This was indeed an exciting event for us and we prepared diligently. We arrived in the Phoenix Park with plenty of time to spare so we parked outside the Zoo for some minutes. As we approached the security hut on the road leading to the Áras, at the appointed time, I had my official invitation ready to show to the Garda. Before I could do so, or introduce myself, he said in such a friendly voice, *"Ah you must be Mr. Jordan. I was expecting you"*. He then directed me towards the parking area. I had assumed from the start that we would be part of a larger visiting group on the day, but to our surprise, there were few cars in the parking area. As we reached the entrance, a female army officer met us. She brought us into a large room where the portraits of past presidents hung. I learned from her that we would be meeting the President alone.

At that point I became quite nervous, as I had never envisaged such a situation. I discussed some details with the officer, particularly as to how long would the meeting last and how would it be ended. She told me that when she would reappear in the room that would be the sign. She also told me that we would be served tea with the President. This was becoming more complicated. 'What are we going to talk about, for twenty minutes or half an hour?' I asked my wife. The two girls were quite cool, enjoying the excitement. Within a few minutes Mrs Robinson entered the large room and approached us. I introduced the family and myself. She told me that there were a few photographers present from the newspapers and that perhaps we should complete the formalities of that business first.

We went out on the lawn and three or four cameramen took their shots of the book presentation. Mrs Robinson spoke about the Áras and its architectural features. I commented approvingly on the candle lighting at an upstairs window. We then re-entered the large room, where tea was served, though she took water. To my surprise and pleasure, she was perfectly at ease, without any of the stiffness she sometimes presented at official functions. She was very happy to have a 'Mayo family' visit. She inquired about our personal details. We discussed places in Mayo, Ballina, Ballyhaunis, and in Sligo, the seaside resort of Enniscrone, where many Mayo people used to spend their summer holidays. After that, to keep the conversation going, I mentioned some current events in which she was involved. Again to my surprise, she discussed them, giving her own point of view without any inhibition. She was gracious, open and keen to listen, particularly to the two girls. It was a most enjoyable visit to a hugely impressive and warm President.

CONOR CRUISE O'BRIEN

Some people had assumed from my two previous subjects that I was an avid republican. I decided to write about Dr. O'Brien in order to remove that perception. I already had correspondence with him concerning Major MacBride about whom he had been most helpful. I had sent him a copy of that book and informed him that I was beginning to write about him. He replied, on 11/09/91, thanking me for the book and adding, *"Naturally I am also looking forward to seeing whatever you may write about me. Please keep in touch"*. He was also somebody whom I greatly admired and about whom there was plenty of material available on the public record. John O'Connor offered to publish this book also on the condition of *"bringing O'Brien on board"*. I eventually sent the manuscript to Dr. O'Brien. He replied in February of 1993, with an accompanying letter. This six page closely typed letter, contained his commentary on certain points, which he felt needed elucidating and elaborating upon, from his point of view. He declared that, *"I think you have approached what you rightly called 'my varied career' in a spirit of fair inquiry and given a good account of it. I wouldn't of course agree with everything you say, but then it wouldn't be healthy ever for a biographer and his subject to be in entire agreement about everything"*. Among other matters, I had been critical of his role in the resignation of President Cearbhaill O'Dálaigh. Dr. O'Brien wrote a long paragraph defending the role of the Government, and Minister of Defence, Paddy Donegan. He made it clear that he had little sympathy for the President's action. I was very pleased with this letter, as was John O'Connor.

I particularly enjoyed interviewing Christine Hetherington, Conor's first wife. I discovered quite late that though I had known her well in the *Samaritans*, I had not realized that she had once been married to my subject. I had a few very enjoyable sessions with Christine and her husband George. When I eventually asked her what was the breaking point for her in the marriage, she thought for quite a while before replying, *"After a certain amount of time, you find it a shade difficult to live with...God"*.

During March of 1993, I heard, accidentally I believed, that Dr. O'Brien might have had my manuscript copied and sent to a Professor Donal Akenson of Magill Queen's University in Kingston Ontario. Dr. Akenson, I was told, was writing the authorized biography of Dr. O'Brien. I mentioned this to my publisher, who encouraged me to write to Akenson. This I finally did one year later in March 1994, saying, *"you have I am given to understand, acquired a copy of my manuscript on Dr. Conor Cruise O'Brien. If this is indeed so, could you confirm same. I would also like to know what your intention to my manuscript is?"*

I did not receive any reply. As that year progressed I became uneasy that my book was not appearing and there appeared to be little urgency in the matter. I feared that the authorized biography would appear and submerge my work. This is what occurred. It attracted great publicity, though Dr. O'Brien was conspicuous by his absence from the launch in Dublin. I then became very frustrated and wondered whether my book would emerge at all. I heard an announcement that Dr. Akenson and Tim Pat Coogan were to appear on the *Pat Kenny Radio Show.*

I phoned RTE and succeeded in getting an invitation to join them, on the strength of my forthcoming book. When leaving RTE I mentioned to Akenson that I had been told that Dr. O'Brien had photocopied my manuscript and sent it to him. I misunderstood his reply and thought he had indicated that he was aware that the manuscript had indeed been copied, but that he never got it. The agreed title was, after discussing about a dozen possibilities, *"To Laugh or to Weep"*. This was meant to be a phrase of endearment that Conor's friends might use on occasion, as he sallied forth to attack or defend some controversial topic.

I had favored a quote from Christina's interview in which she described Conor as "never a careful man". She had used this phrase in a most positive sense, indicating that he was always courageous in speaking his mind. When I called her to discuss the title, she demurred, feeling that such a title might be misinterpreted as a criticism of him. The dedication read: *"In Memory of the late lamented, Cardinal Tomás Ó'Fiaich, who remembered my song".*

'CONFRONTING' DR. O'BRIEN AT HOWTH

Shortly after the book appeared, I arranged to present a copy to Dr. O'Brien at his home in Howth. The publisher insisted that I raise the matter of the manuscript with him. A photographer accompanied me on the trip. The thought of having to confront such a formidable man in his own home and in such circumstances was not appealing. We were received graciously and completed the presentation of the book and the accompanying photographs. I then asked the photographer to be left alone with Dr. O'Brien. I told him of what I had heard. To my surprise, he informed me that the story was true and gave reasons for his action. A short time later I wrote to Dr. Akenson in Canada informing him of what Dr. O'Brien had confirmed.

I also wrote to Dr. O'Brien, saying: *"I want to thank you for receiving me so graciously at your home on 12/11//94 and accepting a copy of my book. I hope it finds favour with you and your family. I want to thank you most sincerely for all the assistance you gave me in connection with the book. However I have to admit that I was very taken aback when you confirmed that you had indeed photocopied my manuscript and sent it to Professor Harman (sic) in 1992. I did not feel it was appropriate to pursue the matter while I was a guest in your home. I feel I must though, look for an explanation for your actions, which I still find almost incredible. As I am sure you can appreciate, no writer could contemplate handing on the fruits of his/her labor, particularly to a rival author"*.

Professor Akenson replied on the 1st December saying: *"I am afraid that you misunderstood me; I did not say that I knew your manuscript had been copied, but only that if it had been, I had not received a copy"*.

The manuscript had obviously gone missing in the post. He added that he was ordering my book from Blackwell's and graciously wished me *"every success with it"*

Dr. O'Brien replied in a long letter, early in 1995. There was, as usual, a clear logic in what he wrote. He stated that as Professor Akenson was his authorized biographer, he felt that the materials/elucidations/positions he had sent to me should also go to Professor Akenson.

"In sending him the corrections and manuscript, without notifying you, I acted precipitatively, and I owe you, and hereby tender, an expression of regret with regard to this aspect... I do hope that on consideration you will accept my expression of regret for failing to keep you adequately informed of what I was doing ...".

John O'Connor was quite happy to fund a launch and Dr. O'Brien had already indicated his willingness to do the honours. However, Christmas was nearly upon us and I did not feel like organizing a guest list. I was very disappointed that my book had come out so late. I did not wish to have a launch at that time as I had another book on the stocks and I felt that I might have to pursue a fresh departure with it. I was constantly tempted to return to my first experience of writing fiction, but one biographical figure presented after another. These had generally not been written about previously and I felt that they merited a book. By that stage also, I came to think that possibly such work was more important than fiction, which though I thoroughly enjoyed it, appeared like so much self-indulgence.

*Conor Cruise O'Brien receives his biography from Author Anthony Jordan
at his home in Howth 1994.*

CHAPTER 18

PUBLISHING WINSTON CHURCHILL

William Manchester, who wrote the famous book on the assassination of John F. Kennedy, had earlier written a two volume biography of Winston Churchill called *"The Young Lion"*. In this well researched book, I was very surprised to see Churchill described as *"The Founder of Ireland"*. This led me to begin a study of Churchill's life, as he encountered Ireland. I was surprised to find that Churchill's earliest experiences were of living in the Phoenix Park as a young boy. His grandfather was the Viceroy and Winston's father had acted as his secretary. Churchill was an imperialist and regarded Dublin as the second city of Empire. He could not understand why Irish people were not proud of that fact. Irishmen often formed the heart of the British army. He was a soldier, a journalist, politician, who was constantly encountering the Irish. Over the period of the Anglo-Irish War and the Civil War, he played a pivotal part in the emergence and stabilization of the Irish Free State, due to his positions as Secretary for War and Secretary for the Colonies.

I had my book on Churchill finished in mid-1994 and wanted it published to mark the 50th anniversary of the ending of World War Two in April 1995. I was aware that Prince Charles was interested in visiting Ireland if a suitable opportunity arose. I wrote to him at the start of 1994, informing him of my project on Churchill and the hope to have it published in the lead-in to the 50th anniversary of V.E. Day in 1995. I suggested that he might consider launching such a book as an appropriate occasion for an Irish visit. I received a gracious reply expressing interest in the project but saying that currently there were no plans for an Irish visit by the Prince.

SECURITY AT THE BRITISH EMBASSY

It was important that the book be a reasonable and fair interpretation of Churchill's relationship with Ireland. I concluded that William Manchester's title for Churchill as *"the founder of modern Ireland"* was not tenable, but that it was not entirely off the mark either. I had encountered the British Ambassador in a social context and told him of my work. He had expressed interest and agreed to read the manuscript. I wrote a formal letter and addressed it to, "Mr. Bladderwick". His secretary phoned me to say that before she passed on the letter to him, I might like to re-address it, as the correct spelling of his name was 'Blatherwick".

I live quite near the embassy and am a regular cyclist. I put the manuscript on the back carrier and cycled to the Embassy on the Merrion Road. As I got to the entrance, a car was exiting through the security barrier. I cycled in past it and stopped at the main door of the embassy. As I did so, I heard a man shouting from the area of the security barrier, which was then closed. Just then two burly men appeared round either corner of the embassy near me. I could ascertain they were armed detectives. One asked me my business. I said I was delivering a parcel to the ambassador. *"What's in it?"* the English voice asked coolly. I told him, adding that the Ambassador was expecting it. *"Would you remove it carefully from the back of the bicycle?"* he asked/ordered. I did so and he peered carefully at it. *"Would you like me to deliver it for you"*, he asked. *"No thanks, I'd like to do that myself, if you don't mind"*, I replied. *"Ring the bell then"*, he said. This I did and a lady opened the door and I gave her the parcel. The two detectives returned round their respective corners and I made for the exit/entrance. I noticed that there were ramps there, which came up from the ground to allow vehicles to enter/exit. I then realized what had happened. The security man was concentrating on the exiting car and did not see me enter. He then felt obliged to activate an emergency button, to alert the detectives that an unauthorized person was on site. Given the recent history of British Embassy buildings in Dublin, and the current expectation on the possibility of an IRA ceasefire, his concern and that of the detectives was understandable. Indeed, I was foolhardy in cycling past the security barrier without clearance. I should have known better, especially after my earlier experiences at British embassies.

1981 BATTLE OF BALLSBRIDGE

In early 1972 I had been among the vast crowd, which had marched on the British Embassy in Merrion Square in the aftermath of the shooting dead of twelve people in Derry City. When I saw petrol bombs being fired through the windows, I left and went home. In 1981 during the Hunger Strikes another huge march took place on the new British Embassy. This time events in the North had deteriorated drastically and anything seemed possible, including the overthrow of our own southern state. In order to observe the march from a safe distance, I, along with a neighbour Michael McAuliffe, had taken up position on top of a garden wall at the intersection of Sandymount Avenue and the Merrion Road and Simmonscourt Road. Michael had also been at the scene of the 1972 confrontation at the British Embassy in Merrion Square. This was the strategic junction where the Gardaí Síochána had planned to prevent the marchers, who included thousands of angry Northerners, from approaching the embassy. There was an eerie silence between the Gardai and the few spectators as we awaited the arrival of the march. Then, in most dramatic fashion, the sounds of the approaching throng became audible as they reached the RDS. As they came into our view, they appeared to present an unstoppable tide, chanting and banging on metal, banners and flags flying.

A large force of Gardaí stood within the intersection ringed by crash barriers. As usual the Gardaí acted coolly and appeared to ask for a leader to come forward as the marchers paused close to the barriers. A delegation was allowed through the cordon, presumably to deliver a letter to the embassy, a hundred yards further up the road. That done, a tall woman wielding a long pole emerged from the crowd and began flailing at the Gardaí inside the cordon. This led to the crowd to push onto the barriers, seek to lift them and throw them on the Gardaí. The latter responded with their batons and a close quarters, vicious fight, ensued. Flagpoles became weapons as the crowd surged from the rear on to the barriers. Those at the front bore the brunt of the flailing batons, with the tall woman who had instigated it, receiving many blows but still erect, armed and fighting furiously. Garda reinforcements, with plastic shields and helmets, reinforced their colleagues in the vanguard, as rocks pulled from garden walls began to fly. After about ten minutes, fighting, I noticed from my perch-top that many of the marchers had broken through nearby back gardens and were approaching the cordon from behind me and to the right flank of the Gardaí. They were heavily armed with rocks. The Gardaí realized that they were outflanked, as they were attacked from the side.

Several Gardaí collapsed to the ground having been hit by rocks. It was sickening in sight and sound to witness the spectacle of those guardians of the peace being viciously assaulted. The main body of marchers realized what was happening and they intensified their headlong attack. Very quickly the Gardaí realized that unless they could take effective counter measures immediately, they would be cut to ribbons. Within minutes they organized an attacking party, which scaled their own barriers cordoning off Sandymount Avenue, and prepared to charge headlong to thwart those attacking them from that flank. At that stage I realized that we might be in their path and they would not be in a frame of mind to take prisoners or distinguish between friend and foe. So I decamped and ran headlong down Sandymount Avenue in front of the onrushing Gardaí. I did not look back until I reached the safety of our own house off the bottom of Sandymount Avenue.

This episode became known later as the *Battle of Ballsbridge*. The Gardaí held their line and dispersed the marchers, saving the country from we know not what. I learned later that the army was in position at the Embassy and under orders to shoot anybody who tried to attack them[83a]

Mr. Blatherwick later replied: " *You kindly sent me your manuscript on Winston Churchill and asked me whether I might be interested in launching it in 1995. I am sorry not to have replied earlier, but I wanted time to look at it properly. I return it herewith. It is a most interesting work, but I fear a bit too political for me to become involved with. However, I look forward to seeing it in print and hope it has the success it deserves*".

I decided that because of the approaching deadline of April 1995, I would attempt to persuade my *alter ego* Mike Walshe from Westport, to publish the book. We chose Brunswick Press as the printers. They operated from the same road as I lived on, so that was very convenient for us both. I felt that the experience with Jarlath Duffy of Westport Historical Society had given us the basic understanding about book publishing. Jarlath offered to act as nursemaid, if we requested specific advice. We then had to set about all the paraphernalia concerning publishing; ISBN numbers, choice of and permissions to use materials, printers, barcodes, editing, layout, proof-reading, deadlines, distribution, costs, print runs, publicity. We decided to name the publisher as *"Westport Books"*, due to the link with Jarlath and Westport Historical Society. Unlike with my last book, I decided this time to have a launch, for purely commercial reasons. We priced the book at £6.95, and ordered a print run, which would give us the possibility of recovering our outlay. We were definitely not in the business to make a profit.

The current Minister for Finance was a long time acquaintance of mine, and a TD for the constituency of Dublin South East. He was a very sophisticated man, who would attract many people to the launch. Ruairí Quinn accepted my invitation and on the day, arrived in casual dress and on foot, to do the honours. The launch was very successful from a commercial point of view, though for the author/publisher a rather frantic experience. Without the assistance of my wife and daughters, it would not have been possible. It was frustrating to have such a large gathering of friends present and yet to be able to devote so little time to each of them. Yet business was business and that was what the day primarily involved.

The title I settled on for the book was: *"Churchill, A Founder of Modern Ireland"*. The dedication read:

"This book is dedicated to Lance-Corporal Thomas Kedian, 10th Battalion Lancashire Fusiliers (step-brother to my mother Delia Jordan), who died at the Somme, aged twenty six, on 7 July 1916, and whose grave is unknown, but is commemorated on the Thiepval memorial in France. and
The pupils of Sandymount School-Clinic, with whom parts of this story were enjoyed".

The book was well-reviewed, with some reviewers questioning of the accuracy of the title and thereby displaying ignorance of the period under review, or else not reading the book. I particularly enjoyed a review in the *Irish News* by Andrew Boyd who wrote, *"Anthony J. Jordan, a county Mayo man who lives in Dublin writes about 'Winston' (Winston Churchill) as though he were a dear family friend or a long-lost brother. And he claims Churchill to be 'a founder of modern Ireland".*

SIR PATRICK MAYHEW

I had often been struck by the Churchillian tones adopted, on occasion, by Sir Patrick Mayhew as Secretary of State for Northern Ireland. I thought he might be interested to read the book and offered to present him with a copy. He accepted my invitation and an appointment were made for the nearby British Embassy on a Friday afternoon at 17.30. As I drive up Sandymount Ave with my daughter, Judith, the traffic was very heavy and the clock was rapidly approaching 17.30. A helicopter passed overhead flying towards the Merrion Road. I said, *"that could well be Mayhew heading for the Embassy"*. I knew he had been at a conference out in county Meath that afternoon. The traffic had come to a standstill, so there was nothing for it but to abandon the car on the footpath and run the remaining few hundred yards. We entered the Embassy grounds and could hear the noise of the helicopter. We reached the front door where the ambassador, Mrs Veronica Sutherland waited anxiously. Almost immediately Sir Patrick walked round the corner, full of bonhomie and handshakes. As we entered the Embassy, Mrs Sutherland asked him if he would like coffee. He said he would but added, *"what I really need just now is a chance to pee, if you don't mind"*. She directed him to a toilet. Then she instructed her staff to open up the way to her own office and have coffee delivered there. As we proceeded to her office, I could see that several security tunnels had to be reopened en route, before we emerged to a large bright airy room with a good view out over the back of the RDS. Sir Patrick, a very tall man, joined us shortly. He took charge of the conversation paying great attention to both his guests. He could see in broad outline a parallel between what Churchill was engaged on with Ireland and himself. Judith took a photograph of the presentation. The clampers had not arrived in Dublin in 1996 and our car remained safely on a, by then, traffic-free Sandymount Ave. I later received a letter from Sir Patrick at Stormont Castle, stating:

"It was a great pleasure to meet you and your daughter Judith in the Embassy in Dublin on Friday and also to receive a copy of your book about Sir Winston Churchill. I can quite understand from our short conversation the passion with which you have approached the subject. It is indeed an intriguing thesis and I will read it with great interest. Thank you once again and good luck with your future projects".

The only person I encountered, who immediately understood the accuracy of the title of that book was Martin Mansergh, when, several years later, I had occasion to engage him in conversation on Irish/British history. But that came as no surprise.

EXHIBITION AT RATRA HOUSE

One very exciting offshoot from that book was another exhibition I mounted on my subject. This took place in the house in the Phoenix Park where Sir Winston had lived for several years as a boy. It is now called Ratra House, after President Douglas Hyde used it as a retirement residence. Ratra is the name of a location in county Roscommon associated with Douglas Hyde. It was then used by Civil Defence.

The most important materials I displayed came from Sammy Leslie of Castle Leslie in Monaghan. These included the christening dress worn by Churchill, rare photographs and items of armour he had used as a child. These were kindly lent to me by the Leslie family and were priceless. I therefore had to take them home with me nightly. The exhibition attracted a lot of interested visitors and the *Sunday Times* did a long feature on it. Among my guests at the opening were two distinguished Mayo men, Jim Higgins, Minister of State at Department of An Taoiseach and at Department of Defence and Seán Dublin Day Loftus, Lord Mayor of Dublin.

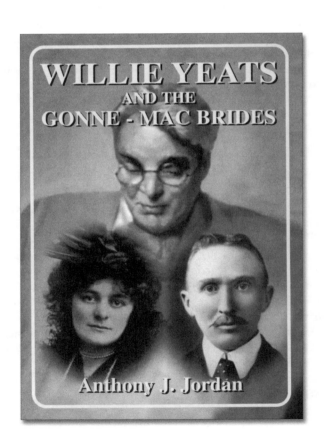

CHAPTER 19

WILLIE YEATS AND THE GONNE-MACBRIDES (1997)

I had been eagerly anticipating the 1992 publication of *The Gonne-Yeats Letters 1893-1939*. Anna MacBride White and A. Norman Jeffares edited it, and wrote Introductions. As its title states it is a compilation of letters exchanged between Maud Gonne and WB Yeats. Thirty of the letters are from Yeats and three hundred and seventy two are from Gonne. The Introduction and extensive notes gave an invaluable background to the letters. Introducing the years 1905-1907, they write of the divorce case between Gonne and John MacBride, "As such situations are, it was a nasty bitter game, but on the whole Maud Gonne's letters give a reasonable account, allowing for a certain obvious one-sidedness"[84]. The letters outlined in great detail Maud's marriage and separation from John MacBride and WB Yeats's close involvement. After a very close study of the book, I felt that the promise I had made some years earlier to Mary MacBride of Westport, that I would follow up on the story if new sources became available, could now be attempted. Anna MacBride White graciously gave me *carte blanche* to draw on the Letters.

My new book was called, *Willie Yeats and the Gonne-MacBrides*. Some Yeatsians felt it demeaning to refer to the great poet as "Willie". But that was what his contemporaries called him and how he was addressed in the letters. The book argued that Willie Yeats emerged from a dysfunctional family to become fixated on strong women, one of whom was his muse, Maud Gonne. Despite repeated rejections, a double betrayal when she became a Catholic and married Major John MacBride, constant hectoring on political and theatrical matters, Willie persevered, wishing to be "Father of the Family". Even after his own happy marriage, he continued to write beautiful poetry about Maud. My book traced their intertwined lives, putting the love poems into context. It also vindicated the good names of John MacBride and Eileen Wilson MacBride, Maud's own half sister, and sister-in-law of her husband. Using the letters, I was able to state that the serious allegations against her husband, made by Maud concerning Iseult, prior to the divorce case in Paris, were in fact only raised in court at the insistence of her husband, and were not substantiated. In pursuing this action, he had taken a huge legal risk to clear his name. After her husband's execution in 1916, she wrote to Yeats that she could then pray to him.

'SECOND SANDYMOUNT MAN WINS NOBEL PRIZE'

The book was dedicated to Tiernan MacBride, who had so impressed me on the launch of the book on his father, and who had died suddenly two years earlier. I considered having a launch in Dublin, if I could get a personage who would attract an audience. I aimed at the top and wrote to Séamus Heaney, who lived locally in Sandymount. In my letter I referred to my reaction to the announcement of his own nomination for the Nobel Prize for literature. I had put up a notice on a school bulletin board I had control of, with the headline, "*Second Sandymount Man Wins Nobel Prize*". Heaney replied, in a lovely letter, saying that he had recently declined a request to launch the authorized biography of WB Yeats by Roy Foster. He declared himself, "*more or less in flight from engagements like this*". He ended his letter jocosely, by saying, "*Although, in my capacity* as *the second Sandymount man in line, I was tempted for* a *moment*". In the event *Westport Historical Society* organized the launch for 5 May, which was the anniversary date of John MacBride's execution.

That book elicited a lot of correspondence. One letter came a Dr. GB Malone Lee of London, a distant cousin of the MacBrides, who recalled some vivid memories of the Major, whom he met while holidaying with Molly Gill outside Westport. John had played with my correspondent and his sister Doreen. He recalled, "*That must have been about 1911 – 86 to 87 years ago! – There was something very nice about a man like that, light hearted and good natured*". One very pleasant thing about that book was that it renewed my direct contact with the Central Remedial Clinic. My good friend Michael O'Connor was in charge of their ultra modern Adult Desktop Publishing Training Unit and Printing Works, where the book was designed and produced. Though many publishers have in recent times begun to print their books in cheaper economies, we never contemplated doing this. I regard the CRC as more like a partner in our publishing endeavours. It is reassuring in this age of the 'bottom line' to deal with people of the calibre of David Lowe, whose interest in the various books matches my own.

This book sold out quickly but we resisted the temptation to order a reprint. Our aim was to convey a message rather than make a profit, though it was important to break even. We were never quite sure whether we ever achieved that basic aim, as the only expenses we kept a record of was that of printing. One ongoing difficulty for business was bad debts. We already had experienced this in our brief publishing career. I recall driving through a suburb of Dublin and seeing a sign on a shop that had received a number of our '*Churchill*' books, reading 'Closed Down'. We never traced the owners. It was our experience that there was a greater risk of incurring bad debts from smaller outlets than large ones. One incident that amused me greatly with this book was when we received a letter from the Joint Receivers of a company called TC Farries & Co Limited. It had ordered and received some books but we had not received any payment. The company was continuing to trade while the receivers examined its affairs. It invited creditors to contact them. The last sentence in their letter read: "*If you are interested in purchasing the business or assets of the company please contact me under separate cover*". We declined both invitations.

JESUS CHRIST

During the summer of 1998 I was looking for a new subject, when the notion of writing a biography of Jesus Christ occurred to me. The resource material was readily available, as were the fruits of many other writers. I read several of these latter books, some modern, some ancient. Then I decided that I would attempt the work by relying almost exclusively on the works of the New Testament. There were a few other texts, which could be seen as relevant historical documents. It was an extraordinary experience to study closely the four gospels in particular, and, to discover what different documents they each were and how little detailed information most of them contained about Jesus. One problem I had to overcome quite early on was to ensure that I approached the sources, as if I was writing about any other individual. This was most evident in a passage from St Mark's gospel, chapter one, verse 18-24, which reads:

"This is how Jesus Christ came to be born. His mother Mary was betrothed to Joseph; but before they came together she was found to be with child through the Holy Spirit. Her husband Joseph, being a man of honour and wanting to spare her publicity, decided to divorce her informally. He had made up his mind to do this when the angel of the Lord appeared to him in a dream, and said 'Joseph son of David, do not be afraid to take Mary home as your wife, because she has conceived what is in her by the Holy Spirit'.

I tried to plot the available facts in as concise a manner as possible before seeking to widen my base. In the end I completed about one hundred pages but felt that there was too little material available to complete a secular work, which would be of interest. This intellectual experience is not to be recommended as a necessarily healthy exercise in faith formation. The historical human person of Jesus Christ, though, is of itself a most attractive one, with his life and teachings providing a template for devotion and fervent hope.

PAUL DURCAN

It may be pertinent to mention here of an experience I had around this time concerning religion and the writer. I attended a public interview with the poet Paul Durcan in the Writer's Center in Parnell Square in Dublin. The interviewer asked Durcan, somewhat condescendingly, why in this modern age there were so many references to matters religious in his work. Paul replied that, whether we like it or not, religion and the Catholic religion in particular was part of what we are. It was a huge part of our culture, and it was inescapable for him to avoid writing about it, even if he so wished, which he did not. Some days later I met Paul in Sandymount and we discussed the kind of thinking which lay behind that question. Paul laughed in anticipation of reactions, as he told me that he had just come from RTE, where he had recorded a programme in the series 'A Giant At My Shoulder'. His choice of person, whom he most admired, was Pope John XXIII.

My own view of religion was that, at a minimum, it was a very valuable social instrument, in which everyone should be encouraged to participate. Faith was a gift, though it had to be worked at, and hope was an essential part of human existence. The practice of the Catholic religion is as much a part of me as the air I breathe. I love the ritual of the Mass. I enjoy visiting Rome for its beautiful churches, and the realization that I am part of a two thousand year old world-wide tradition of endeavouring to follow the bare-footed Nazarene. The Church often offers one of the few readily available 'local communities' in the modern city.

THE YEATS GONNE MACBRIDE TRIANGLE (2000)

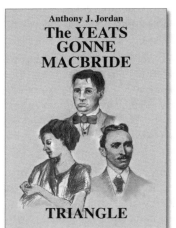

Anthony J. Jordan
The YEATS GONNE MACBRIDE
TRIANGLE

Two major developments occurred almost simultaneously in 1997 around the time of the publication of my book. The first was my discovery that Major John MacBride's papers existed and had been made available to the National Library of Ireland, under the title of, *"The Fred Allan Papers"*. MacBride had been friendly with Fred Allan and his wife Clara for many years. He had been living with them for several years prior to the Easter Rising. That family retained MacBride's papers for six decades, until Dr. Patrick Henchy of the National Library consulted them [86]. It was in a state of great excitement that I first perused these extensive manuscripts. The second development was the publication of the first volume of the authorized biography of WB Yeats by Roy Foster. I had been looking forward to this for some time. Foster is Carroll Professor of Irish History at Oxford. I knew that Denis Donoghue had earlier worked on the biography but had ceased to do so. I felt that as an acclaimed historian, Foster would deal with the involvement of John MacBride particularly well. As soon as the book was available, I looked at the index and read what he had written about the Major concerning the divorce case with Maud Gonne. I was disappointed and shocked by what I read: He wrote that Yeats,

*"had for long been hearing rumors about the marriage - some true, some not. But the **truth** was spectacularly shocking. On 9 January, having had an interview with May Bertie-Clay, WBY wrote to Gregory. He was still reeling at the catalogue of MacBride's **crimes**; violence, sexual abuse, threats to children. Two days later he wrote in even greater shock, having heard details of MacBride's seduction of the seventeen year-old Eileen Wilson (Gonne's half-sister) and his molestation of the eleven year-old Iseult, the blackest thing you can imagine"[87].*

Professor Roy Foster is a darling of the Irish literary media and receives massive deferential coverage from RTE and the *Irish Times* for his books. He is regarded in England as the authoritative interpreter of Irish history. Once again John MacBride had the odds stacked against him. It transpired that Foster knew of the existence of the *Fred Allen Papers*, for he wrote in a footnote, *"MacBride's version is preserved in a testimonial he wrote for Fred Allan"*[88]. Foster appeared to assume that because the papers were so titled, that the manuscript he refers to was written for Fred Allen.

This possibly indicates a lack of familiarity and understanding of the complexity and totality of MacBride's Papers in the National Library. MacBride's so-called 'version' was not in any way written *"for Fred Allan"* and it is but one file of a very large collection of papers on the divorce case[89]. Nor does Foster even advert to the fact that the charges against MacBride were not substantiated in the divorce court, and that MacBride's side raised the most serious charge, the molestation of Iseult, to have it dealt with, and his good name vindicated. In another illuminating footnote Foster writing of 1905-06 says that Eileen Wilson was, *"Subsequently married off to MacBride's brother Joseph, summoned from Westport for the purpose"*[90]. In fact Eileen had been married in August 1904 in London[91]. She and Joseph had been engaged as far back as the Easter of 1904 when they both attended the baptism of Seán MacBride in Dublin and Maud had presented Eileen with a trousseau[92]. I was later to pen the following letter to the *Irish Times*.

DEANE ON FOSTER ON YEATS

"Madam, - Seamus Deane's celebratory review of RF Foster's second volume of WB Yeats's biography (Books, September 27th, 2003) makes compelling reading. Of course, Foster as the authorized biographer was carefully chosen and has well rewarded that choice, with two volumes of staggering detail about his subject. Most readers will not have the breadth of knowledge to assess all of the detail accurately. Much of it has to be taken on faith. Individuals may well be able to make judgments on particular areas of the work. But who would even dare tread such a course, with a man so well regarded, and at a time Deane describes as 'a moment of cultural re-articulation in Ireland'?

Deane adverts to the 'alarming rate of industrial production in Yeats studies', and hopes that this work might 'give pause to the prolific'. I doubt it, for Yeats has become such an icon for so many adulators, and raw material for so many academics, that the industry might well grow geometrically. Deane, to his credit, is quite content to list Yeats' negative attributes: anti-Catholic, racist, a cultural snob, a panic-stricken member of the sectarian elite described by Deane as "a vile ascendancy", a dabbler with fascism in the face of democracy. Deane asks pertinently if there can be some ideal form of detachment from the subject in the biographer. Whether or not the author is ideally detached from his subject, he treats many negative aspects of Yeats in a non-judgmental way, such as betrayals of Lady Gregory, his shocking treatment of Lollie Yeats, his Machiavellian actions at the Abbey theatre. Foster's sympathies seem to this reader to be with WBY all the way. As Deane notes, "Foster has great fun with the Catholic Bulletin, but too little with Yeats".

The reviewer writes of "a routine understanding of a poem such as 'Easter 1916'", concerning the image of the stone being understood as a representation of a republican fanaticism, but finds this work "reveals a more complex situation". That is indeed so.

Foster's interpretation of Yeats' inclusion of the name of his bitter enemy, John MacBride, in the same poem, together with MacDonagh, Connolly and Pearse, is, for me, untenable. Foster reads it as Yeats taking "penance". Hardly not! As Deane has noted, "Yeats never wholly abandoned any previously held position", and he certainly did not assign penance for himself. Rather is "Easter 1916" another opportunity for Yeats to express his undying hatred of MacBride for his temerity in capturing his muse and for her conversion to Catholicism. As Deane notes, Yeats always had an eye on the future, and was setting MacBride up for unfair ridicule by posterity. Maud Gonne understood what Yeats was at, and though unspoken, it may have been her main reason for detesting this canonical poem. She had mellowed towards her husband and had a son to think of. Yeats wrote, "My glory was that I had such friends". Seamus Deane adds, his glory and luck in having such a biographer. Roy Foster too, can be congratulated in the glory and luck of his friends and admirers. – Yours etc."

Tony Jordan, Gilford Road, Sandymount, Dublin 4.

I spent much time studying the voluminous MacBride Papers in the National Library. Here, at last, was John MacBride's version of his marriage and the events concerning the divorce case. The details of the London negotiations intended to avoid going to the Divorce Court, as well as Maud's deposition and John's rebuttal to the court are there. It was a sorry story, with erstwhile friends and family members taking sides, swearing affidavits and appearing as witnesses. One shocking aspect of it was that Maud had accused her husband of adultery with her own half - sister, Eileen Wilson. That lady traveled from Westport to refute the charge. Using this material together with the *Gonne Yeats Letters*, it became clear to me that John MacBride was greatly maligned by Maud, particularly in her letters to her mentor, Willie Yeats. He was naturally disposed to believe the worst about MacBride, anticipating the possibility of recapturing his muse again. This is the version Roy Foster accepted, after Yeats, and published in his biography. I felt that Foster should be challenged. This was not easy, as his pre-eminent reputation militates against it. I wrote a long essay and sent it to, *The Irish Literary Supplement, A Review of Irish Books*, which was published by Boston College, Massachusetts, bi-annually.

Many months later, I received a letter from Paul Durcan, congratulating me on the essay, which was published under the title, *"John MacBride's Good Name"*. Durcan had given an interview to the *Irish Literary Supplement* on the same subject in 1991.

Paul was intimately involved in the story, being a blood relative of Maud Gonne and John MacBride. Eileen Wilson was his grandmother. He regarded my essay as the definitive word on the subject. In it, I challenged Roy Foster to respond, but to date he has not done so, though he has had many opportunities. In his 2007 collection of poetry titled, *The Laughter of Mothers,* Paul Durcan includes a poem called *The MacBride Dynasty,* where he writes of the affection and pride in which the Major was held in his mother's family.

The book which resulted from my study of the MacBride Papers was titled, *The Yeats Gonne MacBride Triangle* and appeared in the summer of 2000. I sought to lay down the two sides of the story because there are always at least two sides to every story. My purpose was to put all the available material on the record since no one else had chosen to do so. The book received wide publicity on radio and in the newspapers. The headline in *The Sunday Tribune* in a review by Stephen Collins *"Vainglorious Lout Recovers his Reputation"*[93], appealed to me, as did one in the *Irish Times* on an interview with me by Katie Donovan, *"The Good Soldier*[94]*"*. The dedication on that book reads: *"This book is dedicated to my wife Maire"*. We spent an enjoyable holiday in Paris during the writing of that book. I did not tell her, until we got there, that my ulterior motive for visiting Paris at that time was to 'go on location' to take photographs for the publication.

WB YEATS: VAIN, GLORIOUS, LOUT
A MAKER OF MODERN IRELAND (2003)

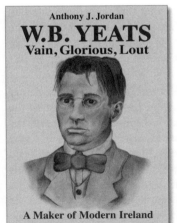

I decided that I would attempt a biography of Willie Yeats himself. I well realized that there were huge pitfalls in such a massive project. He was such an icon to so many people. The field was well trodden. So many academics and scholars spent much of their lives studying, teaching and writing about him and his works. I would have to be very selective. I had negative and positive attitudes towards him. Though I felt that he was most unfair to John MacBride, I absolutely loved his poetry. One of the constant pleasures of my life was to read his *Collected Works,* or better still get my wife to read aloud from it. I began by reading several of the standard biographies, beginning with that of Joseph Hone. Then I read his *Autobiographies,* and his *Memoirs,* edited by Denis Donoghue. I was luck enough to acquire the four volume *WB Yeats Critical Assessments* edited by David Pierce and published by Helm. These contained contemporary reviews and assessments from 1887 to 2000.

For further aspects of his life and career I used the excellent *Yeats Collection*, in the library of St. Patrick's College, Drumcondra. I found Elizabeth Cullingford's books on Yeats particularly useful. Armed with all this reading, I had to decide what areas of his life I was going to tackle. The canvas was so extensive that I had to be very selective. There were certain areas that I knew I would not be competent or interested in tackling. I was not interested in writing about his marriage or his later philandering. I had already written in a detailed chronological order of his love poetry in my 1997 book. I then outlined a series of areas I would like to write of and made notes and thought about them. Then the evil day for a writer arrived, when I had to put pen to paper. I always wrote a first draft in longhand.

I had come to the conclusion that many important aspects, mostly negative, of WB Yeats's life had been avoided or glossed over by most writers. I became aware that despite the record available, the fraught relationship between Willie and Lady Gregory had been greatly minimized, if alluded to at, all by some writers. This occurred, I believed, due to her willingness to generally defer to him on matters literary and cultural, and her willingness to act as a cipher for the great man. His action in refusing to defend her against the barbs of Edmund Gosse in 1910 over his State Pension, added to his mealy mouthed attempts to rationalize this in his *Journals,* were especially base. His adherence to the philosophy of Nietzsche and his adoption of the role of 'superman' in his authoritarian relations with all, except selected female friends and JM Synge, had also been avoided. The complete fecklessness of his father JB Yeats , and the shocking family life to which he reduced his wife and children to, were only hinted at. The long-term repercussions for each of the family were traumatic. On a positive side, I concluded that his genuine and all embracing patriotism and nationalism had been underplayed. I was full of admiration for his early and later work on behalf of his country. He stood up to be counted for Ireland on very many important occasions He truly deserved to be called, "*A Maker of Modern Ireland*".

The title of the book caused controversy among some academics and literary minded people, as they felt it demeaning for such an icon. But I could not resist the temptation of playing with the words Willie had used on John MacBride, believing that those words were far more appropriate to Yeats than MacBride. Those critics who hated the book, however, ignored the play on the words. In my research, I had been irritated at his treatment of most of the women in his life, especially his mother, his sister Lollie, Lady Gregory, and later his wife. While arguing that Willie acted the lout in his personal relations, I gladly acknowledged that he also well deserved the epithet '*glorious*', for his contribution to poetry and national and cultural life. The dedication gave me great pleasure as it afforded me an opportunity to thank those who had looked after me in difficult times. It read:

"This book is dedicated to: Mary (Jordan), Joan (McNamara), Pat (O'Keefe), Terry (Logan), Sinead (Colvin), and Mr. Michael Murphy, whom I love, despite or may be because of, his affinity with Robert Browning's Last Duchess, which so annoyed the Duke".

MURPHY

Murphy is the name of our beloved dog, whose arrival in our family circle added a dimension of incalculable proportion, the like of which can only be appreciated by those lucky enough to love a dog. I speak at length with him, particularly in times of difficulty. He listens carefully, giving me his undivided attention, unless and until the possibility of acquiring food intervenes. On one occasion he had to spend the night in the nearby Vet College, recovering from an operation to his jaw. When he emerged in the reception room the next morning, he jumped into my arms and would not move until we reached the car outside. On another occasion, when he got fishing hook enmeshed in his jaw our genial vet. Dick Lavelle of the Sandymount Pet Hospital, asked me if I would be able to hold his mouth open, while he sought to remove it. I said *"no way; he would bite the hands off me"*. Murphy is his own man and a dog has to do what a dog has to do. I love him very much and believe that his presence in life is as least as significant as mine. When my wife comments on how Murphy gulps his food, I say that he might, like me, be a past pupil of St. Jarlath's College.

Once again *Westport Historical Society* organized a launch. This was done in conjunction with the restoration of a plaque on *The Helm,* the house on the quays in Westport where John MacBride was born. Minister Éamon O'Cuív did the honours. He spoke at length and well, saying that the founders of modern Ireland, who included Yeats and John MacBride, and his own grandfather Eamon DeVelera, would be proud of how far we have come. In my reply, I agreed wholeheartedly that WB Yeats deserved to be included in such an Irish pantheon. The most pleasing aspect of the reaction to the book occurred when two poets praised it highly. One wrote: "I'm afraid the sub-title struck me as a bit of an uppercut, but as I cast my eyes over the text, I realized it was more vehement than the substance of the book you have actually written. A lot of work there". The best review came in *History Ireland*, where the reviewer, Derek Hand of St. Patrick's College, was astute and brave enough to write, *"Yeats's real crime, though, and indeed, a crime perpetuated, as Jordan sees it, by all subsequent Yeatsian scholars, is his treatment of John MacBride as an abuser of Maud Gonne and her children. Here Jordan is absolutely correct. So many readers of Yeats accept without question much of what he has written or said. They become overwhelmed by the force of his rhetoric and his authoritative tone, forgetting that Yeats is not only the 'arch-poet' but the arch-self-publicist as well"*[96].

I was somewhat surprised when no review of the book appeared in my favourite newspaper, the *Irish Times*. I encountered the Literary Editor in the Hugh Lane Gallery on the occasion of the launch by Michael Yeats/Seamus Heaney of Roy Foster's second volume of his authorized biography of WB Yeats.

I spoke to her and she told me that it was not her plan to review my book. I subsequently wrote to the Editor. I received a reply on 20 February 2004, saying, *"I have talked to the Literary Editor and she will consider your book for the purposes of a review again"*. A highly critical review appeared shortly after. None of my subsequent books has ever been reviewed in the literary pages of the *Irish Times*. That newspaper is one of the most important institutions in Irish society. It is a broad church and all my subsequent books have received good coverage in other sections of the paper.

RTE CENSORSHIP?

The *Today* programme on RTE phoned my home in July concerning appearing on their show, but at the time I was engaged on jury service. It later agreed to cover the book provided I would appear with a Yeatsian scholar. I readily agreed and provided the three extra copies of the book they required. This plan was later cancelled, without explanation and at short notice. I had a similar experience with *Tonight with Vincent Browne* programme in November. A date was agreed for an interview together with a Yeatsian scholar, but cancelled at a late stage. At Easter in 2004 *Morning Ireland* contacted me for an interview, again on my agreement to appear with the same Yeatsian scholar as the previous show had nominated. I told the producer of my earlier experiences. She assured me that her proposed interview would proceed within a matter of days. It did not. I felt that the national broadcaster had been at least complicit in censoring my work. This contrasted greatly with *News Talk* where George Hook conducted a lengthy and perceptive interview with me, without any preconditions.

Minister Éamon O'Cuív, Jarlath Duffy, and Tony Jordan.

Chapter 20

BOER WAR TO EASTER RISING

WRITINGS OF JOHN MACBRIDE (2006)

The idea of such a book had often occurred to me, but I had felt that there probably was not enough material to justify it. But as time went on and I began to discover the extent of MacBride's letter writing, and particularly his public speaking career, I came to a different view. The extent of his public speaking around Ireland and Britain, came as a surprise to me. It demonstrated how highly regarded he was by his contemporaries. But more particularly his lengthy speeches indicated what an erudite and clear thinking man he was. However, it was his letters which I found especially fascinating. These give the personality of the man and indicate how central he was to the national movement. The correspondence that he received, which does not form part of this volume, is even more illuminating in this regard, as he received letters from most of the main protagonists of the period. The bulk of the work involved was collecting from the sources and locations I knew of. But the most laborious work involved trawling through contemporary newspapers and journals for articles and particularly letters.

Much of this work took place in the friendly atmosphere of the *Gilbert Library* on Pearse St. I also wrote a short letter to newspapers seeking material and this evinced some interesting results. This book carried a forward by Mary MacBride-Walsh of Westport, a granddaughter of the Major. One person I became very interested in during the writing of the book was the poet Ethna Carbery. She had written letters to John during the Boer War. One of them contained shamrock. When I located the letter in the National Library, I was staggered to find that the shamrock was still there after one hundred years, wrapped carefully in a special sheet of paper. She appears to me as an exceptionally attractive personality, who loved John, and died prematurely aged thirty-six. I would love to write a book about her. The book received good coverage in the *Irish Times,* principally in an article penned by Joe Humphries from Pretoria, where there is still great interest in the exploits of *MacBride's Irish Transvaal Brigade*. I had finished the book in 2005 but decided to postpone publication to 2006, which was the 90th anniversary of the Easter Rising, when I knew there would be greater interest in the exploits of John MacBride. I dedicated the book to my friend and ally, Jarlath Duffy, who had died prematurely that same year. Due to his death the usual launch in Westport did not occur.

W.T. COSGRAVE 1880-1965
FOUNDER OF MODERN IRELAND (2006)

I discovered, to my surprise, that there had been no biography written of W.T. Cosgrave. In fact, there was hardly anything at all written about him. He had been the President of the Executive Council of the Free State for ten critical years 1922-1932. The only book of significance was *The Cosgrave Legacy* by Stephen Collins. It concerned itself, however, much more with ex-Taoiseach Liam Cosgrave than his illustrious father. During the course of writing this book I attended a three-day seminar marking the 30th anniversary of the death of Eamon DeVelera, in October 2005. One of the lecturers mentioned that there had been at least fifteen biographies alone written about DeVelera. The conference was attended by several Fianna Fail notables and sponsored by Fianna Fáil. During that month the *Irish Times* carried a substantial article marking the anniversary. The following month saw the 40th anniversary of Cosgrave's death and, as I guessed, it passed without any public notice. That conference was very useful to me as it afforded me an opportunity to speak with Garret Fitzgerald, Risteard Mulcahy, and several historians including John Regan, who had written the definitive book on Cumann na nGaedheal. W.T. Cosgrave had been a Sinn Fein Councilour from 1909. He was on the platform party that founded the Volunteers. He was in Howth with his men to receive guns from the *Asgard*. He fought alongside Eamon Ceannt and Cathal Brugha in the South Dublin Union in 1916. Sentenced to death, he awaited execution with John MacBride in Kilmainham. He was reprieved and interned in England. He was the first member of Sinn Féin to be elected an MP. Due to his expertise, in Dublin Corporation, he became Minister of Local Government. He faced down DeVelera on the Treaty. On the deaths of Griffith and Collins he became head of Government. He defeated DeVelera and the IRA in the Civil War.

When I had the text completed, I felt duty bound to offer Mr. Liam Cosgrave the opportunity of reading it. I was contemplating this early in 2006. At that time I had been invited to lecture at the *Military History Society* at Griffith College on Major John MacBride. I was very pleased to see Mr. Liam Cosgrave among the audience. I had met him some years earlier, and had some resulting correspondence with him on the relationships between his father, John MacBride, and WB Yeats. I decided that I should take the opportunity offered and sat with him for a few minutes before proceedings begun. I told him about the book and how I would be writing to him shortly about it. We had a very amicable talk before I delivered the lecture, which included several references to his father and John MacBride being together in Richmond Barracks and Kilmainham Gaol awaiting execution in 1916. I subsequently wrote to Mr. Cosgrave and he replied graciously, thanking me for my kind references to his father. He had decided not to take up my offer of reading the manuscript. In the course of my research I had been told that there had been one 'reconciliation' meeting between W.T. Cosgrave and Eamon DeVelera, while the latter was President. It appears that W.T. Cosgrave attended a dinner at Áras an Uachtaráin in 1961, given by President DeVelera for the retiring Apostolic Nuncio, Dr. Liberi. Cosgrave and DeVelera were seen to speak together briefly.

I consistently found an enormous ignorance about W.T. Cosgrave, even among generally well-informed people. This did not surprise me, as it was clear from my study that Cosgrave himself had not been interested in preserving his name and work for posterity. He was a modest man who did his duty as he found it. He had no time for recourse to the cult of personality, the writing of memoirs, the preservation of voluminous papers or even being interviewed. Yet, for ten years he kept the ship of State afloat in desperate and dangerous times, and handed it over to his greatest enemy in a peaceful democratic manner. Though he was a slight and unremarkable figure, he surely belongs to those covered by the epithet *errant gigantes in diebus illis*. When the book came out I sent a copy to Liam Cosgrave. I later received a gracious letter expressing his commendation after an early perusal of the contents. The book received good publicity in the *Irish Times, Sunday Independent* and *Sunday Business Post, Books Ireland, and News Four.* I was again interviewed on Newstalk's '*The Right Hook*' programme. Enda Kenny TD, Leader of Fine Gael, launched the book in Sandymount, where he made a very impressive speech about the role and character of W.T. Cosgrave.

The dedication read;

"FOR THOSE WHO DID AND DARED
THOSE WHO DIED AND THOSE WHO LIVED".

One of the particular joys of producing books has been the practice of my wife in reading them carefully in bed at night. When I arrived upstairs, she would usually be full of pertinent questions and comments, indicating clearly that she had got to the heart of each book.

Early in 2007 the Director of the National Museum, Dr. Pat Wallace, invited me to give a series of lectures on W.T. Cosgrave at Collins' Barracks. These attracted full houses on each occasion and were graced by the presence of ex-Taoiseac Mr. Liam Cosgrave and members of his family. On the last night Mr. Cosgrave spoke and said how pleased he and the family were with my book and the lectures series. They were particularly glad that I had been able to establish that the street named Burke Place at Ceannt Fort in Rialto, commemorated, Frank Goban Burke, who was killed while fighting alongside his step-brother W.T. Cosgrave in the South Dublin Union during Easter Week 1916. A particularly enjoyable aspect of these lectures was that my wife was in attendance. I was also invited by the Military History Society to give a lecture at Griffith College on *"W.T. Cosgrave: From Sinn Fein Councilor to the execution cell in Kilmainham"* in 2008, when the vote of thanks was proposed by Liam Cosgrave and seconded by Ristard Mulcahy.

JOHN A COSTELLO 1891-1976
COMPROMISE TAOISEACH (2007)

When I was interviewed by George Hook on his programme, *The Right Hook* on Newstalk, about the Cosgrave book, he asked me why there were so many books on DeVelera and none on W.T. Cosgrave until my own? I responded by saying that in part at least, the reason lay in the reality that the victors usually wrote history. Fianna Fáil has been in almost permanent government in this country since 1932, and exercises a patronage that permeates every facet of society. Books about its founder are therefore politically correct and more likely to be well received in various quarters. It came as little surprise to me when I discovered that John A Costello of Fine Gael, who had been Taoiseach twice, from 1948-1951 and 1954-1957, had never had a book written about him, since his death more than thirty years earlier. He was an obvious subject for me as he had been W.T. Cosgrave's Attorney General from 1926-1932. After the defeat of Cosgrave in 1932, Costello became a Fine Gael TD and developed a very successful practice at the Bar. When Fianna Fáil lost the 1948 general election, and the opposition parties came together in an unlikely coalition, they prevailed upon a most reluctant Costello to become Taoiseach. The current Fine Gael leader, Richard Mulcahy, was unacceptable to some due to his record in the civil war, and graciously stepped aside for Costello.

The new Taoiseach stunned the country when he 'stole Fianna Fáils republican clothes' and declared a Republic. DeVelera was annoyed that he had not taken that step and refused to attend the ceremonial occasion on Easter Sunday in 1949. Costello completed the Cenotaph on Leinster Lawn originally erected by WT Cosgrave to commemorate their Party's heroes Griffith, Collins and Kevin O'Higgins. Seán MacBride of Clann na Poblachta was one of the leading figures of the Coalition Government as Minister of External Affairs. A party colleague of his, Noel Browne, has entered folk history for his abortive role in the *Mother and Child Scheme* of 1950-51. Though Noel Browne emerged as a folk hero from that debacle, with MacBride and to a lesser extent Costello being seen as the villians, the truth is not so clear-cut. Browne was an almost impossible man to deal with, as his subsequent career amply demonstrated. If he had been otherwise, no crisis would have taken place. Costello showed his mettle with the Catholic Hierarchy in his second government. On the formation of the Agricultural Institute, he castigated the bishops for their sectarian intervention on the matter and defended the rights of Trinity College and the Protestants of the whole country. Unfortunately, this particular episode is almost totally unknown.

I found it difficult to generate much enthusiasm for this book or its subject. Though he was a good man, he lacked any charisma and appeared to treat his high office as almost another legal brief. Still, he has earned his place in history for the Declaration of the Republic, and his demonstration that coalition government can work. His life revolved around his family, his legal practice and his golf, with politics a hobby that overtook his life on occasion.

Professor John A . Murphy reviewed the book well in the *Sunday Independent,* with the *Irish Times* running a long article on Costello's confrontation with the Catholic Hierarchy during his second period as Taoiseach. Enda Kenny TD and leader of Fine Gael, received a copy of the book at the historic though largely forgotten Cenotaph on Leinster Lawn. The *Irish Times* carried an *Irishman's Diary* from me on the 40th anniversary of Costello becoming Taoiseach on 18 February 2008.

MARY HANNIFIN, AIRE OIDEACHAIS

The Royal Irish Academy published a book entitled *Judging Dev* by Diarmaid Ferriter in late 2007. The Minister of Education and Science, Mary Hannifin announced that her Department would distribute two copies of the book to every post-primary school in the State. This met with political criticism that Fianna Fáil was seeking to further propagate its own version of Irish history. The Minister denied this suggestion in RTE interviews with Seán O'Rourke in 2007 and with Ryan Tubridy in 2008, adding that if there was a suitable book from the 'other political side', she would consider doing the same with it. I knew the Minister over many years as a fellow teacher and had recently met her at a function in her own constituency. I wrote to her on the 29th November 2007, suggesting that my book on W.T. Cosgrave be considered as a suitable book for distribution to the schools looking at Irish history from 'the other side'. As with Diarmaid Ferriter's book, it contains the first publication of much original material from the period. I later received a letter from the Minister's office saying it had been decided *"at present it would not be a proper use of resources to distribute it (W.T. Cosgrave book) to second level schools"*. She later answered a parliamentary question from Brian Hayes TD, saying that the *"original material was not made available independently of the text, making it unsuitable for use by students"*.

The Author with the Hogan Cup.

St. Jarlath's past pupils reunion.

CHAPTER 21

ON CIRCUIT

After my early retirement in November 2002, I decided that I would confine myself to writing for a couple of years. Arising from the INTO Retirement Seminar I had attended in 1999, I immediately joined the Retired Teacher's Association. Denis Desmond, an ex-colleague of mine from Special Education, ran the group in a dynamic fashion. It provided an excellent forum for renewing contacts with old friends and ensuring that the interests of retired teachers were looked after. My daily routine was unchanged as in the morning I would depart into my 'office' and remain there writing until lunchtime. Afterwards I would usually visit libraries, archives, lectures, or afternoon concerts. I have been a member of the RDS for many years and it provided a congenial facility for all of the latter activities, as well as a most comfortable venue for meeting people socially or for business. In this way I did not impose myself on my wife unduly, and she was able to pursue her normal routine in almost the same fashion as when I had been at school. Of course the sweetest aspect of being 'retired' was the freedom it afforded to spend time as you wished, to do or not to do. This was especially so on Monday mornings.

I soon discovered that there was great scope for me to get involved in a variety of lectures on subjects relating to my books. The first outside activity I got involved in was brought about by the centenary of Seán MacBride's birth in Paris in January 1904. Because I had written the sole biography, to date, I felt under an obligation to see that his centenary was marked in some suitable way. I notified several institutions of the impending anniversary, suggesting that they might mark it. I also contacted Brian Cowan, Minister of Foreign Affairs, and the Irish College in Paris, which had been under the aegis of the Irish Catholic bishops, but is now called *Centre Culturel Irlandais* promoting Irish-French affairs. This led to the Irish College organizing a major international conference on Human Rights in conjunction with NUI Galway and the University of Paris. The conference was in honour of Seán MacBride and one full day was devoted to lectures on him. I was one of the invited speakers and spent a most enjoyable week staying at the Irish College. Among the speakers from Ireland were Maurice Manning, Evelyn Conlon, Carol Coulter, Colm Ó'Cuanachain, Kevin Boyle, Pádraig MacKiernan, Tom O'Malley, Ignaid Muircheartaigh, John Rowan, James Sharkey and William Schabas. During the week, I paid a visit to nearby Chartres amid a snow clad terrain and attended Strauss' *"The Bats"* at the Opera in the Bastille.

Guided by Nora Meydad, I visited the grave of Samuel Beckett and his wife, and that of Captain Dreyfuss in Montparnasse. I received numerous invitations to lecture on Seán MacBride. While at one of these in Letterkenny, I attended a series of BBC recorded piano recitals in Christ Church in Derry city by John O'Connor, Barry Douglas, Finghin Collins and Hugh Tinney. The venue was a Protestant church, which had been burned to the ground during the Troubles, but restored with generous assistance from the local Catholic community. Christ Church was almost across the road from the Catholic cathedral where the bishop was Seamus Hegarty. He had been one year ahead of me in Maynooth. Prior to one of the concerts, I called on him and we spent an enjoyable hour taking tea in his parlour and reminiscing about old times. I returned to Derry the following year as a speaker at a conference on African Studies, where I spoke about the experiences of John and Seán MacBride relating to South Africa. During this visit, I witnessed the annual Lundy march by Apprentice Boys around the streets of the city. I was fond of marches and have participated in many. But I was shocked by the threatening nature of this march. It was evident that the message from those marching and their hangers-on was that they saw themselves as a master race. I spoke at the Humanities Institute at UCD on John MacBride. The Institute understood, due to my email address ending with '.uk' that I was based in the UK. It offered to pay for my flight and overnight stay, at the adjacent Montrose Hotel. However, no money exchanged hands! I was also very pleased to be invited to mark the anniversary of the 1916 Rising by lecturing on John MacBride at the historic City Hall in Dublin.

"AN IMPERTINENT PUP"

I also gave some lectures on WB Yeats. The fall-out from one of these, at a most impressive library in Tubbercurry Co. Sligo, was most amusing and instructive. During research for my book on Yeats, I visited the Museum in Sligo where there was a detailed display of contemporary material concerning the poet's exhumation in France and reburial at Drumcliffe in 1948. It reported that there was genuine concern that the exhumation had resulted in the very strong likelihood that the wrong remains had been recovered. I mentioned this in the book but did not dwell on it. I decided to explore the matter in a lecture based on the contemporary reporting that was displayed in the Museum in Sligo. The following days *Irish Independent* made it their lead article on the front page. The report appeared as fresh news based on my own investigation on Yeats. At least two English papers, the *Guardian* and *Daily Telegraph* took up the story. A local Sligo paper carried an indignant report calling for Sligo people to defend the authenticity of the Drumcliffe burial site. An old boyhood friend from Ballyhaunis, Tony Greene, read about it in an American newspaper and said he knew it must be me stirring the pot, when he read the name of 'Anthony Jordan'. The following Sunday I received a call from relatives in Ballyhaunis saying that I was severally criticized in that days *Sunday Independent*. The article, tongue-in-cheek, reported that I could destroy the tourist industry in Sligo, referring to me as *"an impertinent pup"*.

JURY SERVICE

When the Circuit Criminal Court Jury Summons arrived, it seemed an acceptable demand on my civic duty. Failure to attend without reasonable excuse would entail a fine of 63.49 euro. I presented myself at Court No. 25, Chancery Place, Dublin at ten o'clock on a Monday morning. The courtroom was already tightly packed with about 200 people, standing room only. After about ten minutes a court official read a long list of numbers and names. He invited a response from those present. As he re-read all the names of the absentees, five more people indicated their presence. We went downstairs to a waiting room. Surprise was later expressed that at no time did any panel/ jury member have to establish identity. This appeared to us to leave the way open to a possible manipulation of a jury. This contrasted markedly with much of the security we experienced. The extensive categories of ineligible and excusable persons make a jury truly representative of society difficult. Our room had a vending machine, a water dispenser and several television monitors. There was little conversation, rather a tense air of uncertainty, as the atmosphere became increasingly sticky. Shortly before eleven o'clock the T. V. monitors focussed closely on a judge in a courtroom. He began to address us below, asking us to pay close attention as the first jury was about to be empanelled. His instructions were clear and precise. We learned the details of the charges to be tried and the identity of the accused. Twenty names were drawn from a drum in the courtroom and those went up to the courtroom.

The defence was entitled to object to any seven of those without cause. Jurors could seek to be excused service by the judge, with his decision made public. Three juries were empanelled that morning, before the rest of us were released with the instruction to appear again the following morning. The next morning saw a repeat process with two juries being empanelled. The remaining panel members were again released. It was only then that most people began to realise that this process could continue for the entire two weeks of our service. We were in the hands of the Court. The third morning saw some fraternisation among the panel as we waited, watching the monitors, until the judge addressed us. As the names came from the drum, the panel members left for the courtroom. At number seventeen I heard my name called. The courtroom was full of people, barristers, lawyers, prison officers, Gardaí, and court officials. The new jury was then charged by the Judge and instructed on our important and onerous function. He read the charges, as we looked across the room at the accused. He said that he was taking the case himself and would be commencing shortly. A Garda was then sworn in as jury minder and we were escorted upstairs to the interlinked jury room. This contained a large table flanked by twelve chairs, a microwave oven, water dispenser, and tea and coffee making facilities. It overlooked Chancery Place, where builders were busy reconstructing an entrance to the Four Courts complex. Our first duty was to elect a foreman from the ten men and two women. We spent about ten minutes discussing the matter and as nobody was willing to act, I volunteered. Relief all round!

ELIZABETH GASKELL

Manchester University organized a conference on local novelist Elizabeth Gaskell in July 2005. I spoke there on the theme of Irish emigration to Lancashire during the latter half of the 19th century. I used the story of Michael Davitt's family as my template. I was interviewed on local BBC radio concerning the lecture. On one of the nights during the conference I repeated my lecture at the Irish World Heritage Centre in Chatham Hill. An overflow audience attended it to my surprise. Many had traveled from the town of Haslingden, where the Davitts had lived, and which had an active Davitt Society preparing for centenary of Michael Davitt's death in May 2006. My main source for material on Davitt was Theo Moody's partial biography, which had been given to me by Monsignor Eoin Sweeney. On the last day of the conference we went on a tour of 'Elizabeth Gaskell's Manchester'. She was born in nearby Plymouth Grove, where her house was preserved. That same afternoon, as I traveled southwards by bus, I heard a news report on bombings in London. At first I thought it was referring to the earlier bombings, but soon realized that this was a fresh report of more bombings that morning in London. I, in company with many others I am sure, began to look with some trepidation around the bus, hoping that there was no suicide bomber in our midst. I was relieved to reach my destination at Solihull. There, that night, my recently widowed sister-in-law, 'Mena, read some letters written to her fifty years earlier by my beloved brother Paddy. She described them as "the most valuable things I have". They had been written from Plymouth Grove in Manchester! I had first heard about the Omagh bombing from my dear sister Josephine late one summer's evening, as I arrived at her home in Manchester after traveling from Birmingham. The lectures in Manchester led directly to me being invited to speak at a major conference celebrating Davitt's centenary at St. Patrick's College in Drumcondra in the summer of 2006. This conference was organized by Dr. Carla King, who is the recognized expert on Davitt, and was very interested in my research concerning the interaction between Davitt and John MacBride in South Africa. I was also invited to contribute to the series of lectures organized by Mayo County Council, which co-coordinated the Davitt commemoration. After my lecture in Ballina, I was presented with a specially commissioned portrait of Davitt. The next day afforded an opportunity to renew acquaintance with Joan McNamara, then teaching in Mayo.

ETHNA CARBERY

During the Anglo-Boer War, John MacBride received some letters from Belfast written by the poet Ethna Carbery. Volunteers, whom she had organized to join MacBride's Irish Transvaal Brigade, which was fighting for the Boers against the British delivered the letters by hand. I located the actual letters in the National Library, and was exhilarated to find that one hundred years later, the shamrock she had sent was still wrapped carefully in a separate sheet of paper. The letters themselves demonstrated to me that she was very fond of MacBride and looked forward to his safe homecoming. I spent a few months researching Ethna Carbery's life as she became more and more attractive to me. One of the tragic aspects of her life was its brevity compared to most of her contemporaries, who lived to ripe old ages. I read a paper on her at a Women's Studies Association conference at the University of Limerick, where I was the sole male participant. However I was also attracted to Limerick by the realization that it would offer me the opportunity to spend some quality time with a man, I still regard as a very dear friend, Michael Holmes of Ballina, Ballyhaunis, Kilmacud and Limerick. During the summer of 2006 I shared my passion for Ethna Carbery by penning a widely-read *Irishman's Dairy* in the *Irish Times* on my interpretation of her letters to John MacBride. I like to believe she was a Good Samaritan.

RETURN TO MAYNOOTH

I read a notice in the papers announcing that a new Governing Authority was in the process of coming into office at the National University Maynooth. On this occasion, two graduates of the university were to be appointed to the Authority. Graduates of the old university at St. Patrick's College Maynooth were eligible for appointment. It did not take me very long to decide that I would apply. I secured a proposal from Patrick Wall, a long time friend of mine and current lecturer at Trinity College Dublin. My younger daughter Fiona, also a graduate of NUIM, seconded my proposal. In due course and much to my great pleasure, I received a letter from the President informing me that I was appointed to the Authority. This has meant that I attend meetings of the Governing Authority about five times annually under the chair of the affable Dan Flinter. It is a particular pleasure for me to witness how seamlessly the University works with St. Patrick's College in a spirit of mutual respect. The President of NUIM, Professor John Hughes deserves great credit for this. But most important for me has been the opportunity to frequent the old College on many occasions. This has been of intense spiritual, social and cultural significance for me.

As I walk through the beautiful St. Joseph's Square, I can see, high up on the edge of the College chapel, the window of the room where I spent my last year of 1964-5. Looking east I see the room which Paddy Waters and I shared during our degree year of 1963-4. All around, especially at night, I entertain *shades* of the past walking along the various paths between the elegantly laid out parkland. It is a return journey for me into a past that is passed, but which evokes good company, fun, great seriousness and a youthful idealism to serve one's own Christian people. On each occasion I move through the corridors of St. Mary's, guarded by the portraits of mostly long dead bishops and priests, or sit in Pugin Hall or pray in the College Chapel, even if I am amid a throng, I am on pilgrimage with my own private thoughts and memories. I am with the spirit of those boys and men of the 1960's, who are mostly scattered around the globe, alive or dead. In the summer of 2006, the University awarded honorary Degrees to Paul McGinley and Pádraig Harrington. It provided me with the opportunity to invite my brother Tommy, a keen golfer, to join us from Ballyhaunis for the magnificent occasion.

It was thrilling to see him get so much pleasure in speaking to both gracious men and having his photograph taken with them. Another honorary degree ceremony took place in the summer of 2007. This time I was accompanied by my daughter Fiona, returning to her *alma mater* like me. A friend of hers, who then worked at NUIM, told her that the name tag on the lunch diagram listed her as Mrs Fiona Jordan. On the 12th of March 2007, my wife and I attended a performance of Beethoven's *Mass in C* and Hayden's *Nelson Mass* by the Maynooth University Music Society in the College Chapel. There was a reception afterwards in the Pugin's refectory. Mary spotted the current Archbishop of Tuam, Michael Neary among the gathering. He had been two or three years behind me in St. Jarlath's College. When we met, he identified me as the, *"right-half forward on the Hogan Cup winning team of 1960"*.

MENTAL HEALTH COMMISSION

In later years I have become a member of the Mental Heath Commission Tribunals, which hear appeals from people who find themselves involuntarily committed to Mental Hospitals. This has been an interesting exercise for me. I had to make formal application, provide references and Garda clearance and be interviewed. Then there were intensive training days to prepare us for the very important work ahead. The Tribunals were provided for in the 2001 Mental Health Act, and became operational on the 1st of November 2006. It has proved very challenging work.

ROMANTIC IRELAND AND JOHN O'LEARY

John O'Leary had featured in several of my books. I alerted the Tipperary Historical Association that their countyman's centenary was approaching. I detected no public sign that it would be commemorated. In some desperation I penned a short letter to the *Irish Times* on the14th March 2007. It read,

"I write to you least the centenary of a great patriotic Irishman should pass unnoticed. This Friday, March 16th, is the 100th anniversary of the death of John O'Leary. His portrait by John Butler Yeats hangs in the National Gallery. Perhaps his greatest service to his country was his 'capture' of the young poet Willie Yeats for Ireland. He was buried from St. Andrew's church in Westland Row to the republican plot in Glasnevin. He is immortalized in two poems by WB Yeats, 'September 1913' and ' Beautiful Lofty Things'. These will be read at his graveside at 3 P.M. on Friday".

Among the small group who gathered there was John Maher, who had taught with me in Sandymountt many years earlier. He told me that when he was in St. Patrick's Drumcondra with Patrick McCabe, one of their favorite haunts was Glasnevin. John's latest literary work *'The Silver Bullet'* had just come out.

CHAPTER 22

OCCASIONAL POEMS

MARY

A Christmas dance
Became our chance;
Your voice and full bust
Drew me at Tooreen
To note your Pennine route.

You say I recited poetry
In your kitchen
When I came to stay,
Announced though uninvited.

I was building houses
Back to front for Wimpy,
With Martin Bones,
Who wore wide bottomed blue trousers.

Letters passed; you infiltrated me
Across the Irish Sea;
Returned, burned your boats
And came to live in Anna Villa.

"I was looking at houses today"
Was my way of proposing
In a flat on Rathmines Road
In nineteen sixty eight.

Unlike you, I did not believe in fate,
An optimist or realist, maybe.
Suffer you did, alone at first,
Like me, but then together.

Time heals, time healed, did it
Really or was it an adjustment?
Tempus fugit and dies irae
Become a nightmare or a dream.

No one is rock solid
A beacon amidst a storm
A book of confidence.
You are to me, to me, forever.

JUDITH

How you cried in that
Box room, at the top
Of the stairs, for those
First six months
In nineteen seventy two.

Oh you were a pearl
Among the clouds, boxed in,
Travelling to Battery Park and
Ferrying to Staten Island.

Put you down, and you went,
Not like Lot's wife,
Straight ahead, out of sight,
Among the flats at Togher.

The heart chased as we
Circled, dashing to the
River bank, back to the
Front gate, searching
Among the potted plants.

Never again would I leave
For so long, not to see
Wilbad, for such a welcome
In a flowery dress.

You were not the first born
Yet you must plough the furrow
Explore the ground
Be blown by the wind.

You do not go so fast now,
You pause and hesitate,
Finding a way
To tread the millstones around.

ERRIT LAKE

I sit on an upright block
On the shore of Lough Errit,
On the border of
Roscommon and Mayo.

In the summer of eighty -nine,
We swam here,
Bernie Freyne and I.
Today is New Year's Day nineteen ninety,
Almost as beautiful.

The long snake of water
Stretches towards
The distant hill
Of Fr. Horan's airport.

Across the lake,
A tractor splutters momentarily, cuts out,
Returning the silence to myself
And some playful birds.

The water surface is moved
by a gentle breeze.
The wooden jetty
And the new stone pier, jut out alone.

The sinking sun,
Low over Harrington's House,
Still lights up the lake,
And I am reluctant to leave.

A robin hovers from the water,
As if encouraging me to depart.
"But I belong here too" I say,
"Just as much as you".

The tractor starts up again;
Harrington's House has trapped the sun.
It is cold and I must retrace my steps,
From whence I came.

FINAL YEAR RECITAL

The pianist paused at the piano,
The audience clapped courteously;
She did not sit and compose herself,
But remained standing.

Her father said she intended to speak
Though he questioned the execution;
Her mother was certain she would,
Knowing her determination.

The piece, by Sergei Prokofiev,
Sonata number eight, opus eighty four,
Had a war theme, appropriate,
Played andante, dolce, sforznado, vivace.

The small but select audience hushed,
It was most unusual, so pressurized,
In the old Parliament building
On Dublin's College Green.

A clear crisp and egalitarian message;
A symphony in my mind,
A grieving father, mother, sisters,
A whole people on the street.

"I would like to dedicate the next piece
To the memory of my classmate,
Private Billy Kedian from Ballyhaunis,
A peacemaker,
Killed in the Lebanon last week".

XMAS 1987

The stars shine brightly
On this cool Christmas night.
A red candle flames
From our window.

I wave to my wife and daughter
As they pass to midnight Mass.
A white stocking hangs limply,
A young girl sleeps expectantly.

Happiness wells within me
Unwished for, unwanted.
So soon, by thought of you,
My first born, my cross, my joy,
The swell is overtaken.

Thrice I saw you,
Yet you are
The measure
Of all I am.

The eyes fill.
The tears fall
On my cheeks.
It is a sacrament I receive from you
My girl in the incubator,
Who was not there,
When last I called.
But removed, transferred,
To a cold loose wet clay
In a wooden shoebox
Beneath a tree
Beside a stony path,
In nineteen seventy.

FIONA

Your damp black hair glistened
In the large white towel
When the nurse
Presented you to us.

The workman cradled you to me
Across the gate,
Hair matted by your flowing blood.

The phone rang late
But no one answered,
I called the hospitals
One by one until...

If twelve could kill
Ponder the missing thirty-six.
The stomach pump churned;
We considered a funeral.

I crept beneath the bed in hope
It was our only chance for you;
The same for us,
There on the floor.

I counted the white pearls
Reformed the particles;
All the time subtracting
Forcing it down, to nine.

I felt like singing.
I was a bird
Whose young should not die
Whose nest could survive.

ANTONIA

Twenty winters have passed
Since I lay alongside you
Our first- born daughter,
Encased within my wife.

My hand pressed firmly
On your mother's bulge
To feel your life
Deep within the womb.

I was not there
When they cut you out
Of flesh of my flesh.
A belated affair.

The cot was empty
A red bow, tied,
To say, to say,
Mother, but no child.

Wife without words
Tummy now clamped.
Offspring visible
Within a glass box.

For forty-one hours
Antonia lived.
Thrice I witnessed her
In that incubator.

Cleaners consoled (me)
Nurses embarrassed
Doctors patronized
Matron billed.

Wooden shoe-boxes
Exposed in gaping hole
Received you rudely
Bereft of obsequies.

IN MEMORY OF MARY DUFFY 1980

Slow moving anti-cyclone
Awaited from May to mid-August
Arrived but briefly
As time petered out.

Mounted on my 'fifties' Raleigh,
Which ignorant Easterners
Thought antique,
I journeyed through my country
Of Sheefrey, Maamturk, Beanna Beola.

The land and sky-scape
Barren and beautiful
A people not prosperous
but proud and at their ease.

I entered the valley at Recess
And pedaled towards the lake
The turf garner spoke of tenant farmers
But could not name the peaks.
We looked at my detailed map
And saw Bencorr and Derryclare
Hold the west while Maamturk
Completed the Inagh valley.

"Its three years next month" he said,
"Down there in the Boat House
And over beyond opposite the Big House
Is where they found her".

Suddenly the sun did not warm me
My mind froze at the two poles
I wished Maamturk and its partners
to coalesce
Pouring the evil out or entomb it forever.

A beautiful white body
With flowing black hair
Manacled with a twelve inch
Cavity concrete block
Anchored.

Two men in a basement cell.
The mountains did not obey
They turf man spoke away
I jumped on my bicycle
And sped through the flies
Eyeless
Out of that valley.

Bibliography

Books

Major John MacBride. Westport Historical Society 1991.
Seán – A Biography of Seán MacBride. Blackwater Press 1993.
To Laugh or to Weep – A Biography of Conor Cruise O'Brien. Blackwater Press 1994.
Churchill – A Founder of Modern Ireland. Westport Books 1995.
Willie Yeats & the Gonne-MacBrides. Westport Books 1997.
Christy Brown's Women – Biography. Westport Books 1998.
The Yeats Gonne MacBride Triangle. Westport Books 2000.
WB Yeats: Vain, Glorious, Lout. A Maker of Modern Ireland. Westport Books 2003.
Boer War to Easter Rising – Writings of John MacBride. Westport Books 2006.
WT Cosgrave 1880-1965, Founder of Modern Ireland. Westport Books 2006.
John A Costello 1891-1976, Compromise Taoiseach. Westport Books 2007.

Selected Articles

The Silhouette, Maynooth 1964: *"How Ireland was expelled from the Olympics"*.
Quiet Corner, Anthology of New Irish Writing, Xmas 1987: Edited by Eoin Brady.
Cathair Na Mart Journal of Westport Historical Society:
1997: *The Case of John MacBride versus Maud Gonne: A Primary Document*.
1998: *The Major John MacBride Manuscripts*.
1999: *The Boer War Centenary*.
2001: *How Major John MacBride became involved in the Easter Rising*.
2004-5: *Centenary of Birth of Seán MacBride*.
2006-7: *John MacBride's Account of the Irish Transvaal Brigade*.
Western People 28/6/'89: *Impressions of Leningrad and Moscow*.
The Irish Literary Supplement Fall 1997: *John MacBride's Good Name*.
Studies Summer 2005: *Yeats and the Abbey Theatre*.
Parent-Teacher Magazine Vol 9 No.7: *A Fulfilling Life Conor Farrelly* 1986-2001.
Sunday Tribune: *An American Literary Heroine – Betty Moore*.
Irish Times 1981: *National Association Boards of Management of Special Schools*.
Books Ireland: Book Review Articles 1996-2001.
Reach articles on various aspects of special education.
Irish Times: *In defence of a national hero* 1/5/1997.
Irish Times: An Irishman's Diary; *Ethna Carbery*.
Irish Times: *Leader of Free State stood firm against church pressure; 23/10/2006*.
Irish Times: An Irishman's Diary, *John A Costello becomes Taoiseach. 18/02/08*.

Footnotes

1. Irish Times.
2. Dublin Archdiocesan Archives, Drumcondra.
2a. Cooney John, John Charles McQuaid, O'Brien 1999. p. 394.
3. Fitzgerald Garret, All in A Life, Macmillan. 1991. pp. 83-4.
4. Archives.
4a. In interview with Patricia Hastings-Hardy
4b. McDowell RB & Webb DA, Trinity College Dublin 1592-1992, Red Press 2004. p. 475.
5. Irish Times & Irish Press. 4/3/1971.
6. Twenty Five Years of Listening; The Story of the Samaritans in Dublin, 1970 1995.
6b. In interview with Mrs Phil Bates.
7. Irish Times. 30th April 1971
8. Varah Chad, The Samaritans in the 70's, Constable 1973 p. 45 passim
9. ibid p. 43.
10. In correspondence with author.
11. ibid
12. Varah Chad, Before I Die, Constable, p. 238
13. ibid p. 315
14. Sunday Times Magazine, 15 February 2004. p. 48.
15. Twenty- Five Years of Listening, op. cit .p. 25.
16. Jordan Anthony, Major John MacBride, Westport Historical Society 1991.
17. Jenkins Gary, Daniel Day-Lewis, Pan 1995 p. 55-7.
18. Christy Brown Collected Poems, Minerva 1982. p. 63
19. Collis Robert, To Be A Pilgrim, Secker 1975.
20. Irish Times Magazine, 18 February 2003.
21. The dedication reads, "FOR BETH; who with such gentle ferocity, finally whipped me into finishing this book"
22. Jordan Anthony, Christy Brown's Women – A Biography. Westport Books 1998 p. 63.
23. ibid p.
24. To Be A Pilgrim op. cit.
25. Christy Brown's Women op. cit.
26. ibid.
27. ibid.
28. Douglas Hyde.
29. Western People, 18th June 2002.
30. Lee Joe, Ireland, 1912-1985, Politics and Society, Cambridge 1989 p. 374.
31. Commission on Emigration Dublin 1954 + The Lost Decade in the 1950s, Dermot Keogh, Finbar O'Shea, Carmel Quinlan, Mercier Press. 2004, pp. 87-104.
32. Murphy John A, Ireland in the Twentieth Century. IPA 1985 pp. 123-4.
32a. Atherton Mike, My Autobiography, Hodder 2002 p. 229. (With thanks to Camilla O'Brien of Sandymount, whose two sons, Niall and Kevin, helped the Irish cricket team to beat Pakistan in the World Cup in the West Indies in 2007)
33. Michael Waldron's papers are available in the National Library of Ireland.

33a. Irish Times, Eye On the 20th Century, 30th December 1999.
34. Geoffrey Prendergast's role in the controversy on the appointment of a librarian in Mayo in 1931 can be read about in JJ Lee's Ireland, and in the Connacht Telegraph, circa January 1931.
35. Cunningham John, St. Jarlath's College, 1800-2000 SJC 2000 p. 197.
36. ibid.
36a. I recounted this story to Leon Ó'Moracháin at the Maynooth Reunion in 2007.
37. Iarlaith, St. Jarlath's College Tuam Past Pupils Union Magazine 1961. p. 112.
38. MacGreil Michael, ED. Monsignor James Horan Memories 1911-1986 Brandon 1992 p 34.
39. St. Jarlath's College op. cit. p. 201.
40. ibid. p. 10.
41. ibid. p. 3.
42. ibid. p. 6.
43. ibid. p. 6.
44. Kalendarium Collegii Sti Patritii Apud Maynooth in Exuentem Annum MCMLX
45. Corish Patrick, Irish Catholic Experience, Gill & MacMillan 1983 p. 16.
46. Jordan Anthony, Boer War to Easter Rising - Writings of John MacBride, Westport Books 2006.
47. Dialann Antoine Ó Siúradáin.
48. Kiberd Declan, Inventing Ireland, Vintage 1996. p. 582.
49. RTE Television Interview, One to One 2007.
50. Jordan Anthony, Seán, A Biography of Seán MacBride. Blackwater 1993, pp. 125-139.
51. Cooney John, John Charles McQuaid, O'Brien Press 1999. p. 381.
51a. Corish Patrick, Maynooth College 1795-1995 Gill & Macmillan 1795 p. 375.
51b. The term 'chub' indicated a first year student.
52. Irish Times, 21 May 2002.
53. ibid.
54. John Charles McQuaid op. cit. p, 370.
55. Power Vince, Send 'em Home Sweatin' The Showbands' Story, Kildanore, 1990 p. 114
56. Monsignor James Horan, Memories op. cit.
57. Irish Times, 22nd April 2002.
58. Hayden Jacqueline, Lady G. Town House 1994, p. 110.
59. ibid. p. 110
60. Monsignor James Horan, op. cit. p. 203.
61. Christy Brown's Women, op. cit. p. 53.
62. Christy Brown Collected Poems, op. cit. p. 173.
62a. Christy Brown's Women, op. cit pp. 31-2.
63. Proceedings of the Fourth Annual Drumcondra Education Conference District XV INTO March 1987.
64. In Touch May 2006.
65. Oireachtas Reports.
66. Irish Times. .
67. Irish Times, 31 March & 2 April 2001.
68. Modern Management Techniques for an Educational and Developmental Centre at Cerebral Palsy Ireland.
69. ibid p. 12.

70. ibid.

71. Annagh, Ballyhaunis, 2003.

72. Parent & Teacher Magazine, 2000.

73. United Irishman.

74. Gonne Maud, A Servant of the Queen, Gollancz, 1938.

75. Balliet Conrad, Eire - Ireland 14. The Lives and Lies of Maud Gonne p. 16.

76. Seán A Biography op. cit. p. 107.

77. Elizabeth Keane, who wrote the second biography of Seán MacBride in 2007, identified and quoted this sentence when speculating on Seán'a family life. Her biography, written fourteen years after mine is naturally a fuller book. She gives a comprehensive account of the divorce between Major John MacBride and Maud Gonne. She does herself less than justice, however, when she writes, *"The Boers disbanded the Irish Brigade on 25 September 1900. At a loose end, Major MacBride traveled to Portuguese East Africa, following the example of O'Leary and other displaced Fenians"*. Some 'loose end'!

78. Seán, op. cit. p.165.

79. Jonathan Williams is now the leading literary agent in the country.

80. Glendale was an excellent publishing house, managed by Tom Turley.

81. Blackwater Press was the imprint used by the well-known Folens Publishing Company.

82. Sunday Tribune, 27th February 1993.

83. ibid.

83a. Dr. Garret Fitzgerald stated this at a seminar in Trinity College on 27th April 2005. Coincidentally the occasion was a lecture by the academic John Regan, from Aberdeen University, on the divergence of Southern nationalists from their Northern compatriots. My different reactions in 1972 and 1981, as outlined in the text, may indeed illustrate his thesis.

84. MacBride Anna & Jeffares, A Norman, Eds. The Gonne-Yeats Letters, 1893-1938 Pimlico 1993 p. 184.

86. Manuscript 26769, NLI.

87. Foster Roy, WB Yeats A Life, Oxford 1998 p. 330 -1.

88. ibid. note 16 p, 592.

89. For an elucidation of this matter Cf. Yeats Gonne MacBride Triangle, Anthony Jordan, Westport Books 2000.

90. WB Yeats A Life, op. cit. note 3. p. 592.

91. ibid. p. 181.

92. Jordan Anthony, The Yeats Gonne MacBride Triangle, Westport Books 2000 p. 86.

93. Sunday Tribune.

94. Irish Times.

96. History Ireland, Summer 2004. p. 56-58.

INDEX